Studies of the Wild Turkey in Florida

Bulletin of the Florida Game and
Fresh Water Fish Commission

Tommie Peoples

Lovett E. Williams, Jr.
and David H. Austin

Studies of the Wild Turkey in Florida

Technical Bulletin No. 10

Published in cooperation with
The Florida Game
and Fresh Water Fish Commission
Division of Wildlife

Partially funded by the
Federal Aid in Wildlife
Restoration Program
(Pittman-Robertson Act)

UNIVERSITY PRESSES OF FLORIDA
University of Florida Press/Gainesville

Library of Congress Cataloging in Publication Data

Williams, Lovett E.
　The wild turkey in Florida.

　(Bulletin of the Florida Game and Fresh Water Fish Commission)
　Bibliography: p.
　Includes index.
　1. Wild Turkeys—Florida 2. Birds—Florida.
I. Austin, David. II. Title. III. Series.
QL696.G254W56　　　1988　　　598'.619　　　87-14730
ISBN 0-8130-2430-7

UNIVERSITY PRESSES OF FLORIDA is the central agency for scholarly publishing of the State of Florida's university system, producing books selected for publication by the faculty editorial committees of Florida's nine public universities: Florida A&M University (Tallahassee), Florida Atlantic University (Boca Raton), Florida International University (Miami), Florida State University (Tallahassee), University of Central Florida (Orlando), University of Florida (Gainesville), University of North Florida (Jacksonville), University of South Florida (Tampa), University of West Florida (Pensacola).

ORDERS for books published by all member presses should be addressed to University Presses of Florida, 15 NW 15th Street, Gainesville, FL 32603.

Printed in the U.S.A. on acid-free paper.

Copyright 1988 by the Board of Regents of the State of Florida.

Contents

List of Figures ix
List of Tables xv
Preface xix

Chapter 1 **Study Areas and General Methods 1**

Study areas:
 Fisheating Creek 1, Lochloosa 6
Capture methods:
 Procedures Common to Most Capture Methods 10, Establishing a Bait Site 10, Observation Blinds 11, Handling Live Turkeys 12, Confining Live Turkeys 14, Shipping 20, Releasing Live Turkeys 20, Using Cannon Nets 20, Prebaiting 21, Setting the Net 22, Firing the Net 23, Care of Equipment 23, Cannon Net Materials 26, Using Oral Tranquilizers 27, Bait Sites for Oral Drugs 30, Preparing and Presenting Baits 31, Narcosis 32, Pickup and Handling 33, Side Effects of Drugs 36, Response to Drugs by Age and Sex 36, Weather Conditions 38, Capturing Flightless Poults 38, Capturing Hens on Their Nests 40, Banding and Other Marking 40

Chapter 2 **Physical Characteristics** 50

Molts and Plumages:
> Age Determination Methods 52, General Plumage and Molts 53, Plumage at the Time of Hatching 53, Postnatal Molt and Acquisition of Juvenal Plumage 55, Postjuvenal Molt and Acquisition of First Winter Plumage 57, First Winter Plumage 64, Annual Molt 68, Molting Differences Among Populations 76

Indicators of Age and Sex other than Plumage:
> Droppings 77, Beard and Spur Length 78, Color of the Beard Tip 78, Head and Neck Coloring and Feathering 79

Color of the Tarsometatarsus:
> Age, Sex, and Subspecies of Material Used 81, Color Changes After Death 82, Color Changes With Age of the Bird 83, Color Variation of the Tarsus Caused by Other Factors 84, Anomalies in Tarsus Color 84, Spur and Nail Color 84, Summary of Tarsus and Foot Coloration 85

Anomalous Physical Characteristics:
> Plumage Coloration 85, Hens with Spurs and Beards 88, Multiple Spurs on Gobblers 89, Multiple Beards 91, Absence of Beard and Spurs in Males 91, Male-type Plumage in Females 92

Chapter 3 **Reproductive Behavior and Performance of the Hen** 93

> Egg Covering and Nest Construction 96, Laying Posture 99, Multiple Nesting 99, Egg Dropping 100, Nest Attendance During the Laying Period 100, Clutch Size 103, Renesting 105, Nest Disturbance by Man 105, Incubating Behavior 105, Nest Attendance During the Incubation Period 107, The Incubation Period 111, Hatching Behavior 112, Egg Hatchability 114, The Imprinting Period 114, Time of Nest Departure by Broods 116, Hatching Synchrony 116, Attendance of Infertile Eggs 117, Nesting Habitat 117, Nesting Seasonality 121, Nesting Success and Predation 123, Defensive Behavior 126

Chapter 4 **Life History and Other Observations** 129

Roosting of Young Broods:
> Preflight Roosts 130, Roosts in Trees 131, Movement Between Roosts 133, Early Morning Behavior on the Roost 135

Flight Attainment 136
Foods 137
Summer Movement of Hens with Broods 145
Defensive Behavior of Young Broods:
> Huddling 148, Freezing Posture of the Poults 149, Regrouping 149

Poult Losses During the Ground Roosting Period 151
Wariness and Fear of Man 154
Hazards of Rain and High Water 157
Homing Tendency 158
Maximum Longevity Observed 160
Maximum Movement Observed 160
Imprinting Studies:
  Dispersal 162, Nesting 162, Precocious Strutting 163, Other Observations on Human-imprinted Turkeys 164
Movement in Relation to Habitat Quality 165
Utilization of Forest Openings 167

Chapter 5 **Harvest Management 168**

Harvest Patterns on a Heavily Hunted Area:
  Overall Harvest 171, Harvest Rates of Relocated Turkeys 172, Harvest Rate by Age Class 172, Harvest Rate by Sex 173, Test of Hunting Skills 175, The "Caution Effect" 177, Crippling Losses 179, Escape and Dispersal Behavior 179, Further Discussion on Hunting Pressure 184
Limited Quota Spring Gobbler Hunting Season:
  Setting the Harvest Goal 189, Finding Criteria for Hunter Density 189, Determining Hunting Effects on Turkeys 190, Measuring Hunter Satisfaction 190, Timing of the Open Season 190, Quota Permit Procedures 191, Summary of Hunting Regulations 191, Weekend Versus Weekday Hunting Success 192, Effect of Hunter Density 192, Gobbling Activity During the Hunts 192, Interviews With Successful Hunters 194, Experienced Hunter Survey 194, Hunter Satisfaction With the Hunts 196, No-show Hunter Survey 198, Disturbance of Hens 198
Spring Harvest Rates:
  Illegal Hen Kill 199, Gobbler Harvest 201
Standard Kill Index:
  Index Based on Days Open to Hunting 201, Index Based on Man-days of Hunting 202
Recommendations for Spring Hunting on WMAs 203

Chapter 6 **Synopsis of Research and Management Needs 207**

Gobbler-only Fall Hunting 207
Tagging System 208
Legal Shot Sizes and Gauges 209
Hunting Closure in West Florida 209
Ingredients of Satisfying Hunting 209
Habitat Improvement 210
Timing of the Spring Gobbler Season 210
Population Model 210
Poult Survival 211

Census Method 211
Harvest Estimates 211
Law Enforcement Needs 212
Other Needs 213
A Management and Research Philosophy 214

Appendix 215
Experimental Regulations at Lykes Fisheating Creek
  Wildlife Management Area 215
Dates of Hunts 216
Open Season 217

Literature Cited & Publications of the Turkey Project 219

Index 230

Figures

Frontispiece Tommie Peoples
P.1 The range of the wild turkey in early America. xx
P.2 The range of the Florida turkey and the zone where it intergrades with the eastern subspecies. xxi
P.3 The distribution of the turkey in Florida at the time of the most recent survey in 1973. xxii
1.1 The approximate locations of the Lochloosa and Fisheating Creek study areas. 2
1.2 Lykes Fisheating Creek study area, Glades County, Florida. 2
1.3 Cypress woods (Fisheating Creek). 3
1.4 An open live oak hammock (Fisheating Creek). 4
1.5 A grazed glade (Fisheating Creek). 5
1.6 Oak scrub (Fisheating Creek). 6
1.7 Aerial view of a typical cross section of the Fisheating Creek study area showing saw palmetto prairie, ecotone between prairie and grazed glade, grazed glade, and cypress woods. 7
1.8 Lochloosa study area, Alachua County, Florida. 8
1.9 Pine woods (Lochloosa study area). 9
1.10 A drop-door trap—the first trap to be used successfully in the Florida turkey restoration program. 10

1.11	Turkeys around an observation blind at a bait site.	12
1.12	A tower blind, especially useful in semipermanent situations.	13
1.13	The cubical sections of the tower blind can be used separately to make large, roomy blinds but are more difficult to transport than the umbrella type.	14
1.14	The best way to hold a turkey is snugly against your body or under one arm, grasping the intertarsal joints of both legs with the other hand.	15
1.15	An alternate way to hold a turkey is to grasp it by both humeri. One hand should hold both legs at the intertarsal joints.	16
1.16	The paraffin-treated cardboard turkey transport box, in use in Florida since 1964.	17
1.17	One way to close the end of a turkey box is with a piece of elastic cord strung between a rivet on each flap.	18
1.18	A light trailer designed for hauling turkeys in cardboard boxes.	18
1.19	Turkeys can be held temporarily in feed sacks.	19
1.20	Diagram of a cannon net set up.	22
1.21	A flock of turkeys approaching the trap site.	24
1.22	Turkeys on the bait line.	24
1.23	The cannon net is fired.	25
1.24	Turkeys flounce in the net while the trappers run to them.	25
1.25	A netted turkey is secured by lifting it with a fold of net and twisting the net to bag the bird, after which the bird is placed back on the ground.	26
1.26	Narcotic stages of turkeys on alpha-chloralose.	
1.26A	Stage I. After about 40 minutes, narcotized turkeys begin to stumble backwards.	33
1.26B	Stage II. After about one hour, little dispersal occurs.	34
1.26C	Stage III. After about one and one-half hours, most turkeys are down.	35
1.26D	Stage IV. After about three hours, general anesthesia.	35
1.27	A dip net is used to catch a lightly narcotized turkey. (**1.27A, 1.27B, & 1.27C**).	37–38
1.28	A darkened, cloth box (in background) is used to temporarily hold hand-caught, flightless poults in the field.	39
1.29	Riveted leg bands have proven to be satisfactory. Different sizes are used for hens and gobblers. Bands are delivered flattened.	41

1.30   After 11 years on a wild turkey, this band had begun to show wear.   42
1.31   Patagial wing markers permit identification of turkeys at a distance.   42
1.32   A miniature transmitter with batteries and rubber tubing is ready to install on a turkey.   43
1.33   A portable telemetry receiver.   44
1.34   A direction-finding antenna pointed toward the strongest radio signal source.
1.34A Double-element hand antennas are used when on foot or at close range.   44
1.34B Multi-element antennas are highly directional and necessary for distant signals.   45
1.35   To affix a transmitter to a turkey, the bird is held firmly at the intertarsal joints by a helper and laid breast down on a flat surface.
1.35A The transmitter is positioned in the midback area.   46
1.35B The ends of rubber tubing are tied in a square knot under each wing.   46
1.35C The harness fit is tested before the knots are firmly tied—it should be unstretched even with a wing partly extended.   47
1.35D Excess tubing is cut away.   47
1.36   The hen on the right is wearing a transmitter.   48
2.1   Diagram of the molt of the Florida turkey, showing old and new terminology.   52
2.2   The egg tooth remains on the tip of the upper mandible of the poult for two or three days after hatching.   54
2.3   Wing of a four-day-old turkey poult.   55
2.4   An eight-week-old poult with two pairs of juvenal outer rectrices.   59
2.5   Extended central tail feathers of a young gobbler in first winter plumage.   60
2.6   Sexual differences in the feathering of the head and upper neck of turkey poults are evident by 12 weeks of age and become more pronounced for about a year. The hen (upper) and gobbler (lower) are the same age, in midsummer.   62
2.7   A female poult in midsummer showing mixed juvenal and postjuvenal plumage. The post juvenal plumage will be mostly replaced in the next molt which occurs in late summer and early fall.   63
2.8A   Wing of a juvenile male in first winter plumage, showing two distal juvenal primaries and the typical

	configuration of the juvenal greater upper secondary wing coverts. 67
2.8B	Adult (foreground) and juvenile hens. Arrows point to the greater upper secondary covert patch which is broader and shinier in the adult. 68
2.9	Tail molting patterns.
2.9A	The typical juvenal pattern. The molt begins with the middle pair (number 1) in the fourth week. 73
2.9B	The typical juvenal pattern of molting the central rectrices during the prealternate molt. 73
2.9C	The most common annual molting pattern seen in adults begins with the shedding of rectrices eight, seven, and six, followed by nine, four, and five, and finally three, two, and one, in that order. 73
2.10	The characteristic shapes of hen and gobbler droppings. The nearly straight "j-shaped" dropping is the gobbler's. 78
2.11	Head feathering and coloration differences by sex.
2.11A	Adult gobbler 80
2.11B	Adult hen 81
2.12	Female smoke-gray color mutants from Baker County, Florida, about four months old. 86
2.13	A tarsometatarsus of an adult gobbler that had two spurs on each leg. 90
3.1	Unattended nests are partially covered with leaves by the hen before she departs after laying. 97
3.2	Unattended nests during incubation are not covered with leaves. 98
3.3	The pattern of egg laying by Florida turkey hens. 101
3.4	Time spent on the nest with the laying of each egg. The lines are separate least square linear regression curves for eggs one through 5 and 5 through 12. 102
3.5	Frequency distribution of the number of eggs in 179 complete clutches. 103
3.6	Mean clutch size reported for the wild turkey. 104
3.7	Percentage of 24 hens that laid their last egg one day before continuous incubation began (-1), the same day continuous incubation began (0), or the day after continous incubation began ($+1$). 106
3.8	Mean daily recess pattern of 22 incubating hens during 162 recess days monitored. 110
3.9	Sound spectrogram of the calling of poults and the responding hatching yelps of the hen, recorded simultaneously during hatching. 113

3.10   Sound spectrogram of the "hatching hoot" of a brood hen. Typical examples may have three syllables, as shown here, or only one or two syllables.   113

3.11   Sound spectrogram of the vocalizations of poults during the hatching period. A. Peeping notes, uttered singly or in groups of two to six.
B. A two-part call with rising and falling pitch.
C. A call similar to lost whistling—probably a distress call.   114

3.12   Hourly intervals that broods left their nests after hatching show a strong tendency to depart in the morning.   116

3.13   Investigator standing beside a turkey nest site in cypress woods.   119

3.14   Investigator standing beside a turkey nest site in palmetto-scrub ecotone.   120

3.15   The nesting season of 121 Florida turkey hens on Fisheating Creek and Lochloosa study areas.   121

3.16   Cumulative percentage of hatching by calendar date comparing adult and yearling hens.   122

3.17   Distribution of predation incidents ($N=27$) with respect to the stage of incubation.   122

4.1   Movement pattern of a one-day-old brood from the first night roosting place, to the woods, and to the second night's roost. Solid dots are positions of the brood each hour on the hour. The most rapid movement was across the open glade.   130

4.2   June range of a hen and brood.   146

4.3   June range of a hen and brood.   146

4.4   Summer range of a hen and brood.   146

4.5   Summer range of a hen and brood.   147

4.6   Summer range of a hen and brood.   147

4.7   June range of a hen and brood.   147

4.8   Weighted least squares prediction curve for poult mortality during the first 14 days of life.   152

5.1   Harvest estimates for the turkey and other major game species in Florida since 1969. (Data are not available for 1977 and 1978.)   169

5.2   The chronological distribution of the harvest by week of the open season during the study at Lykes Fisheating Creek WMA.   174

5.3   Roosting places of monitored turkeys on Thursday night, one day before hunters entered the management area.   180

5.4   Roosting places used by monitored turkeys on Friday night after hunters were allowed in the

	management area. Hunting was not permitted until the next day. 181
5.5	Roosting places used by monitored turkeys on Saturday night, after one day of hunting. 181
5.6	Roosting places used by monitored turkeys on Sunday night, after 2 days of hunting. 182
5.7	Roosting places used by monitored turkeys on Monday night after 3 days of hunting. The turkeys are widely dispersed as compared to prehunting locations, but they have not left the hunting area. 182
5.8	Roosting places used by monitored turkeys after 4 days of hunting. 183
5.9	Roosting places used by surviving monitored turkeys after 11 days of hunting. Many of the turkeys had been killed by this time, but not all survivors are plotted because of poor radio reception that evening. 183
5.10	Roosting places of monitored turkeys after 16 days of hunting. 184
5.11	Roosting places of monitored turkeys after 23 days of hunting. 184
5.12	Roosting places of monitored turkeys after 31 days of hunting. 185
5.13	Roosting places of monitored turkeys after 38 days of hunting. 185
5.14	Roosting places of monitored turkeys after 52 days of hunting, at the end of the hunting season. Survivors are in the same general vicinity they had been in during the open season. 186

Tables

1.1	Equipment and supplies for turkey trapping and handling.	27
1.2	Dosage, reaction time, and duration of anesthesia in tests of three drugs for capturing turkeys.	32
1.3	Hypnotic stages of narcotized turkeys.	36
2.1	Molt and plumage nomenclature for the wild turkey.	51
2.2	Comparisons of age determination methods applied to known age Florida turkeys.	53
2.3	Number and percentage of 125 juvenile turkeys in alternate (first winter) plumage that retained juvenal primaries, 9 and 10, 10 only, or neither 9 nor 10.	65
3.1	Wild turkey hens instrumented and monitored.	94
3.2	Mean clutch size, by year, for complete clutches only.	104
3.3	Summary of nest attendance by eight hens monitored daily during the period of continuous incubating behavior.	108
3.4	Consecutive nest recesses ($N = 67$) of five hens monitored during the period of continuous incubating behavior.	109
3.5	Mean length of recesses during the period of continuous incubating behavior.	110

3.6	Time intervals between events observed during the incubating periods of nine hens. 111
3.7	Elapsed time from first egg pipping until nest departure for three closely monitored broods. 112
3.8	Proportions of first, second, and third nests established in a single season, by habitat type. 117
3.9	Major plants occurring within 1.5 m of 63 nest sites, Fisheating Creek study area, 1968–1972. 118
3.10	Overhead cover of 82 nests in cypress woods and palmetto nesting habitats. 120
3.11	Percentage of successive nests in the same or different habitat types. 120
3.12	Number and proportion of 236 turkey nests in three habitat types, Fisheating Creek and Lochloosa study areas, 1968–82. 121
3.13	Fates of nests under observation. 123
3.14	Nest survival data used to calculate the probability of successful nesting (Mayfield 1961). 123
3.15	Number and percentage of hens returning to their nests after being deliberately flushed by an observer. 128
3.16	Number and percentage of hens by age class and habitat type that returned to their nests after being flushed by an observer during the laying and incubation periods combined. 128
4.1	Dates and age of 14 broods when first roosting in trees. 131
4.2	Characteristics of brood tree roosts used by turkeys in summer. 133
4.3	First day travel of 11 turkey broods. 134
4.4	Distances between successive nightly roosts of four broods. 134
4.5	Plant and animal foods of 21 wild turkey poults, one to 14 days old, Glades County, Florida, listed in order of importance. 139–40
4.6	Plant foods of 54 wild turkey poults 2 to 24 weeks old, Alachua and Glades Counties, Florida. 141
4.7	Animal foods of 54 Florida wild turkey poults, 2 to 24 weeks old, listed by common names of the orders and scientific names of insect families within each order. 142
4.8	Plant foods of 8 adult wild turkeys, 22 August to 1 November, Alachua and Glades Counties, Florida. 143
4.9	Animal foods of 8 adult wild turkeys between 22 August and 1 November, Alachua and Glades Counties, Florida. 144

4.10 Comparison of food types by age groups. 145

4.11 Summary of the number of poults counted in 61 known-age broods at different ages during the first 14 days of life. 151

4.12 Distance to release site and direction of subsequent travel of 16 turkeys tracked to test homing tendency. 159

5.1 Survival of radio-instrumented turkeys under heavy hunting pressure. 172–73

5.2 Proportions of 125 turkeys harvested/unharvested by age class in either-sex and gobbler-only years. 173

5.3 Proportions of 125 turkeys harvested/unharvested by sex in either-sex and gobbler-only years. 173

5.4 Features used by hunters to distinguish hens from young gobblers. 175

5.5 Summary of hen survival during spring hunting on Fisheating Creek and Lochloosa study areas. 200

Preface

The Florida Turkey (*Meleagris gallopavo osceola*) was named after the Seminole Indian, Osceola, by W. E. D. Scott (1890) from specimens taken near Tarpon Springs. It is a clinal subspecies that intergrades with the eastern subspecies (*M. g. silvestris*) in a zone from southern South Carolina, across southern Georgia, northern Florida, southern Alabama, southern Mississippi, to eastern Louisiana (fig. P.1) (Aldrich and Duvall 1955). The Florida form is differentiated from the eastern form primarily by the lesser amount of white barring in its wing feathers (Scott 1890). It is isolated geographically from the subspecies other than *silvestris*, all of which range farther west in the United States and Mexico (fig. P.2).

Florida had a sizable turkey population in early times (Wright 1915), but numbers were greatly reduced in some parts of the state by unregulated hunting, reaching a low ebb statewide around 1948 (Newman and Griffin 1950). This led to initiation of a restocking program in 1949 (Powell 1965) in which more than 6000 turkeys were trapped from protected populations and moved to suitable range that was not inhabited by turkeys. Completion of the program in 1970 gave Florida the distinction of being the first state to successfully conclude a statewide turkey restoration program. At the present time, Florida is the only state with turkeys and legal turkey hunting in all of its counties (fig. P.3).

P.1 The range of the wild turkey in early America.

- *M.g. osceola*
- *M.g. silvestris*
- *M.g. intermedia*
- *M.g. merriami*
- *M.g. mexicana*
- *M.g. gallopavo*

As the statewide restoration program proceeded during the 1960s, turkey numbers increased with estimates of the fall population topping 100 000 in late 1964. At that time, Florida had the third highest estimated turkey population in the United States, behind only Texas and Pennsylvania, and had the largest legal harvest of any state—about 25 000 taken by hunters each year. Then, for unknown reasons, the population plummeted to fewer than 50 000. The present study was partly an outgrowth of the initial investigation into the population decline.

As of 1967, no research had been conducted on the reproductive ecology of the Florida turkey and the information available from other populations was inadequate and not completely applicable to Florida. The objective of the resulting field study was to acquire reliable information on the

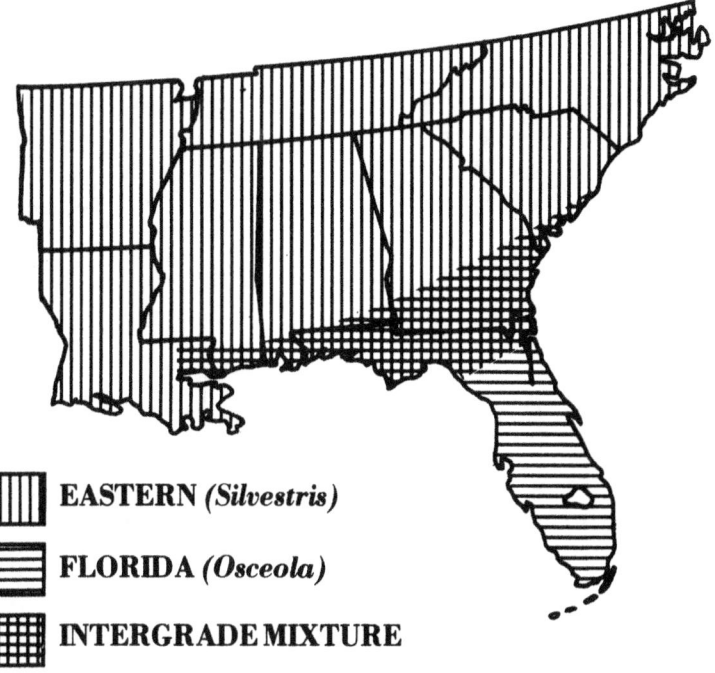

P.2 The range of the Florida turkey and the zone where it intergrades with the eastern subspecies.

major aspects of the nesting behavior and reproductive performance of the Florida turkey, from nest building through hatching, with emphasis on aspects of possible value in management. Also to be studied were the effects of various hunting regulations.

A survey of turkey parasites and diseases was initiated in 1969 following the previously mentioned statewide die-off. This work, by Donald J. Forrester and his students and associates at the School of Veterinary Medicine at the University of Florida, greatly enlarged our knowledge about the health problems of wild turkeys. This important work will not be reported in the present bulletin but the published reports are available to anyone who is interested.

This bulletin is written for a broad audience of biologists, conservationists, administrators, and laymen. Certain material will be of little interest to one or another of these groups. Some aspects of the study that were especially timely have been previously reported in journals. This bulletin updates certain topics to make the information more accessible, but contains mostly information that has not been previously published. It is not an attempt to review all the turkey work in Florida to date. Researchers are encouraged to refer to the technical papers listed in the Literature Cited section, most of which are available from the Wildlife Research Laboratory in Gainesville.

Preface

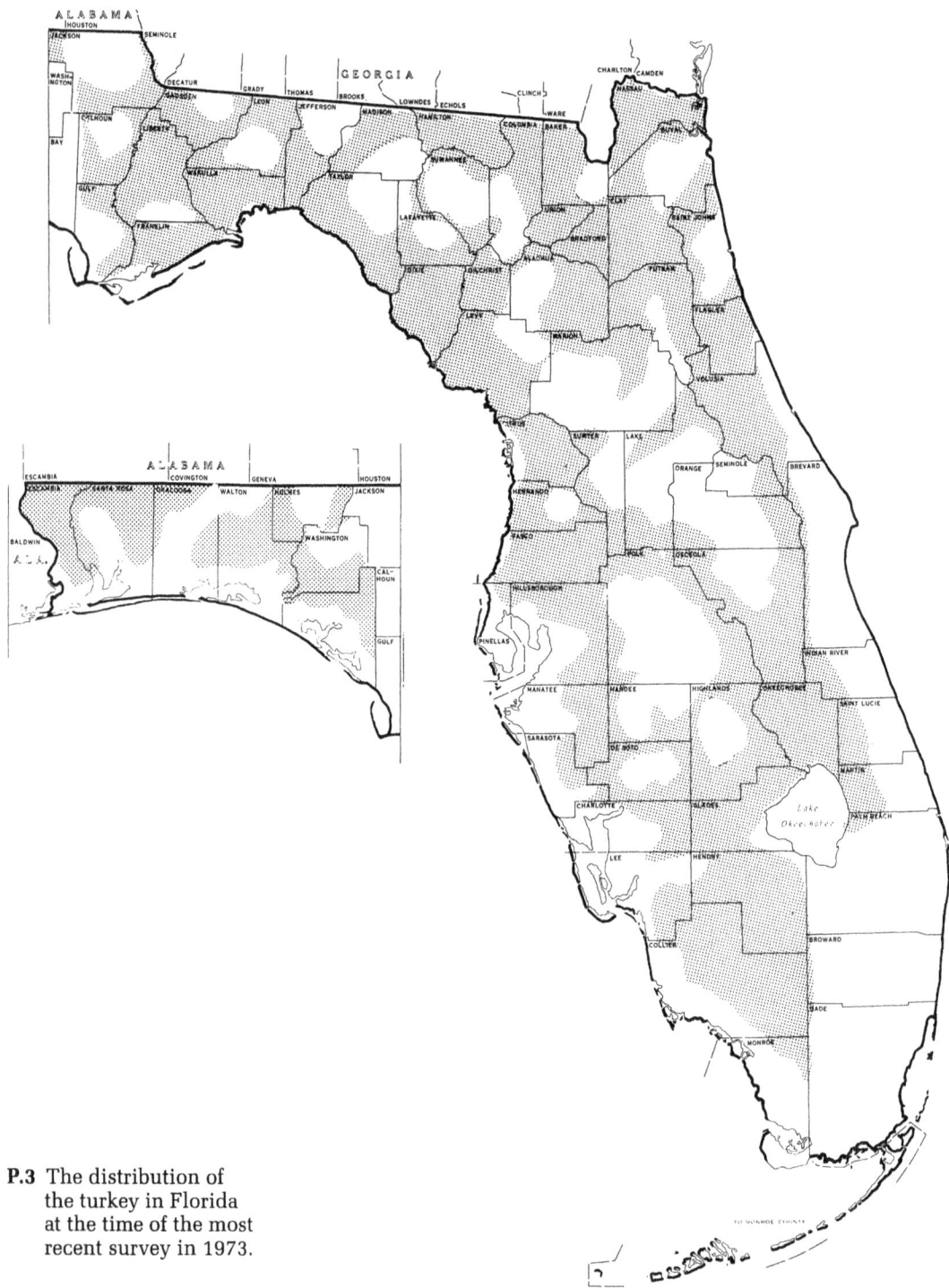

P.3 The distribution of the turkey in Florida at the time of the most recent survey in 1973.

Funding and administrative support for this project were provided by our agency, the Florida Game and Fresh Water Fish Commission, and the federal Pittman-Robertson Wildlife Restoration Program. Former Directors A. D. Aldrich and O. E. Frye, Jr. were particularly supportive as were Robert M.

Brantly, Harold E. Wallace, James A. Powell, Fred W. Stanberry, Allan L. Egbert and Tom H. Logan. Most of the field work was done on Lykes Fisheating Creek Wildlife Management Area with the support and cooperation of Charles P. Lykes, Sr. and Ben Swendsen of Lykes Brothers, Inc. We also thank Owen-Illinois, Inc., and tract manager Bill Schlitsgus, for use of their property on Lochloosa Wildlife Management Area as one of the study areas. Hank Webster generously gave his time and expertise in designing and constructing electronic equipment used to remotely monitor turkey nests. Bruce L. Akey, Larry H. Barwick, William Bess, Timothy A. Breault, David Z. Caudill, Neal F. Eichholz, M. J. Fogarty, D. J. Forrester, William B. Frankenberger, the late Herchell Haywood, Harvey L. Hill, L. Tipton Hon, Ray C. McCracken, Beverly Morris, Sandra Osceola, Jerry H. Peoples, Robert W. Phillips, Walter J. Sadinski, Jr., J. Scott Sanders, A. J. and Judy Wilson, and Linda Zimmerson all helped collect various portions of the data while they were assisting the project. Tom A. Webber assisted in making sonograms. A. G. Hyde of the U.S. Soil Conservation Service assisted with the identification of soil types on the study areas and T. F. Crossman assisted in the measurement of habitat acreages. Michael W. Collopy, Donald J. Forrester, J. W. Hardy, George W. Tanner, and Ronald F. Labisky reviewed the chapter on reproduction and made many helpful suggestions. Others who were helpful in other ways were H. Franklin Percival, Horace Gore, Peter R. Stettenheim, Larry D. Harris, George A. Hurst, Neal Weakly, James W. Glidden, Robert A. McCabe, Richard Gregory, and Daniel W. Speake. Dennis Wackerly, C. L. Abercrombie, and Roni Fuller provided statistical advice.

Secretaries Wanda Circy, Molly Shawver and Lynn Shaddock were much help at the Fisheating Creek study area during this project as were Mary Anne Lansberry and Lillian Davisworth at the headquarters in Gainesville. Terri Crown typed the early drafts of the manuscript. The artwork was by Mardell Moffitt, Barbara Harrison, and Rick Harrison. Bill Greer of the Commission's Office of Informational Services was helpful with photoprocessing.

This is dedicated to the memory of the late Tommie E. Peoples (frontispiece), our coworker and friend who worked on the project and died in late 1980 as the project was nearing completion. The manuscript was completed in 1984.

1

Study Areas and General Methods

Study Areas

Most of the fieldwork was conducted on study areas in Lykes Fisheating Creek Wildlife Management Area (WMA) and Lochloosa WMA (fig. 1.1). Both areas are privately owned with hunting rights leased to the Game and Fresh Water Fish Commission.

Fisheating Creek Fisheating Creek study area (fig. 1.2) is located in Glades County, about 12 miles (20 km) west of Lake Okeechobee. The terrain is flat, ranging between 30 and 55 feet (9 and 17 m) above mean sea level. The soils are predominantly sandy. The major soil associations are Freshwater Marsh and Swamp along the creek and about one m outward, Myakka-Pomello-Basinger on the higher areas adjacent to the creek swamp, and Oldsman-Wabasso-Felda in the prairies (Florida Department of Administration 1974).

The climate is subtropical. At Fort Myers, the nearest reference point for complete weather data, the mean maximum daily temperature in April is 28.9°C and the minimum is 16.3°C. The mean maximum in July is 32.8°C and the minimum is 22.9°C. The mean annual temperature at Moore Haven, about 30 km to the southeast, is 22.8°C. The mean date of the first night of subfreezing temperature at Moore Haven

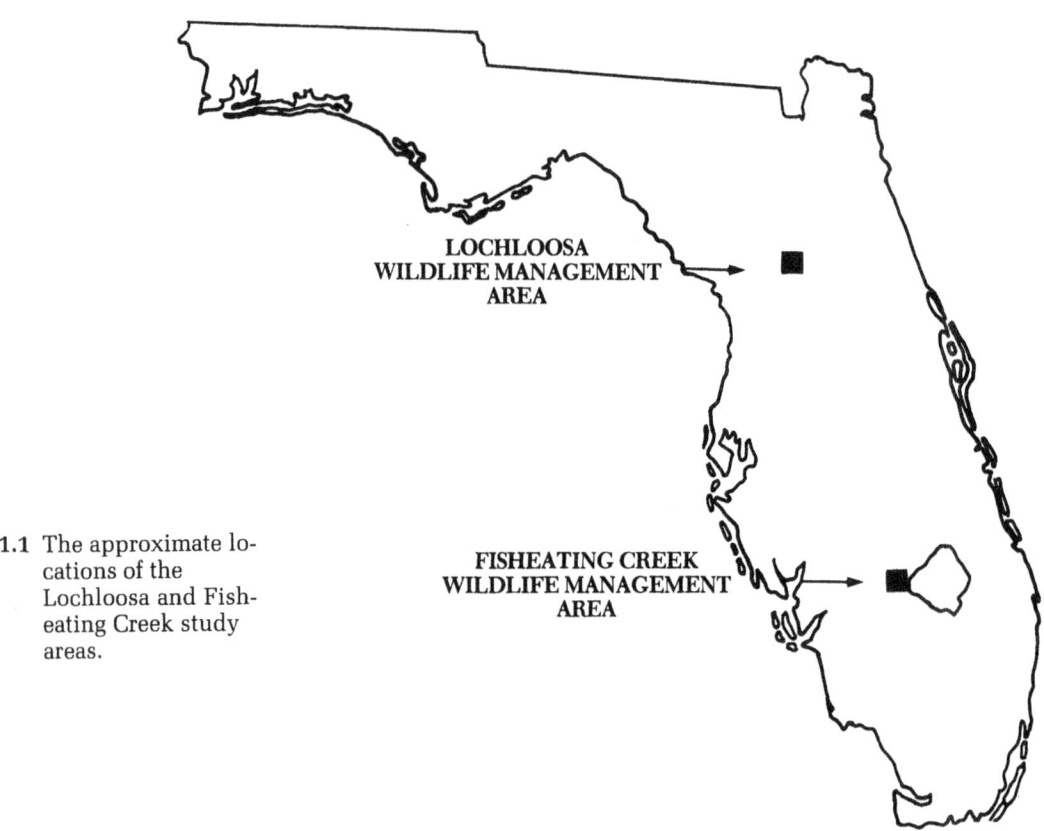

1.1 The approximate locations of the Lochloosa and Fisheating Creek study areas.

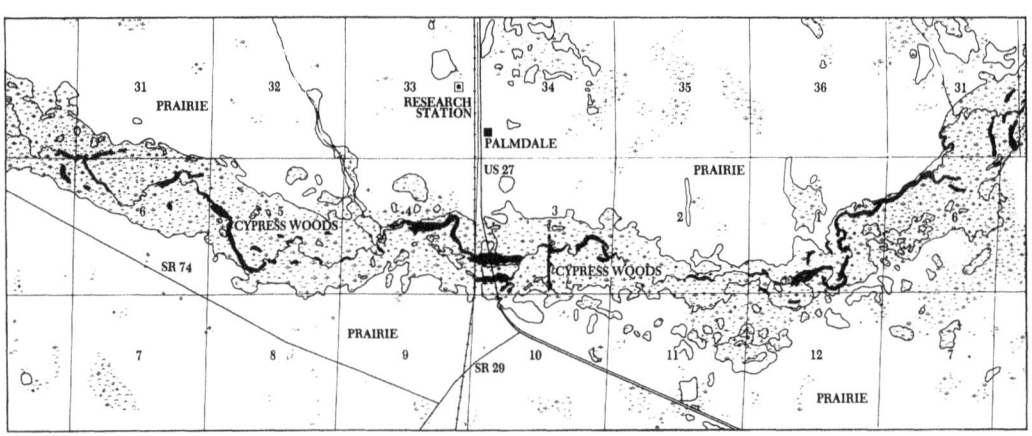

1.2 Lykes Fisheating Creek study area, Glades County, Florida.

is December 25 and the mean date of the last winter freeze is January 23 (National Oceanic and Atmospheric Administration 1978). Mean annual precipitation at Moore Haven is 50.4 inches (127.9 cm) and at LaBelle, about 15 miles (25 km) to the southwest, is 52.2 inches (132.5 cm). More than 60 percent of the annual precipitation, which is in the form of rain, comes during the summer months from convective thundershowers.

1.3 Cypress woods (Fish-eating Creek).

Six plant associations with narrow, ill-defined ecotones comprised the vegetation types on the area. Cypress woods, which made up 51 percent of the area, occurred along the creek (fig. 1.3) in continuous stands of cypress trees (*Taxodium distichum*). The soil there is sandy, overlain in places with humus and plant litter. The creek swamp has been subjected to frequent shallow flooding. Understory shrubs and midstory trees other than cypress were sparse; the groundcover of carpet grass (*Axonopus compressus*), smartweed (*Polygonum sp.*) mistflower (*Eupatorium coelestinum*), and other mainly annual herbs was dense by late April.

1.4 An open live oak hammock (Fisheating Creek).

Hardwood hammocks (fig. 1.4) consist of tree species that occur together at the higher elevations. They made up 12 percent of the area. Dominant trees are live oak (*Quercus virginiana*), laurel oak (*Q. laurifolia*), and cabbage palm (*Sabal palmetto*). Associated species include red mulberry (*Morus rubra*), hackberry (*Celtis laevigata*) and saw palmetto (*Serenoa repens*). The trees are draped with Spanish moss (*Tillandsia usneoides*) and other epiphytes. Many of the larger hammocks occurred where limestone was near or on the soil surface.

Glades (fig. 1.5) paralleled the creek, forming zones of short grasses (mainly *Axonopus compressus*) that were dotted with isolated live oak trees and small live oak hammocks. These open areas were heavily grazed by cattle and had the appearance of semi-improved pastures. Approximately 17 percent of the study area was in glades.

Broadleaf evergreen shrubs (e.g., *Myrica cerifera*), evergreen trees (*Gordonia lasianthus*, *Magnolia virginiana*, and *Persea* sp.), and vines (*Vitis* sp. and *Smilax* sp.) existed in

1.5 A grazed glade (Fish-eating Creek).

isolated "heads," which often contained surface water and supported dense, woody, understory vegetation. The soil contained a relatively high proportion of humus and litter. Heads made up 2 percent of the area.

Oak scrub (fig. 1.6), which covered 12 percent of the area, is an association of small, mostly evergreen oaks (*Q. chapmanii*, *Q. myrtifolia*, *Q. geminata*, and *Q. inopina*) and other short, woody vegetation (e.g., *Lyonia ferruginea*, *Befaria racemosa*, *Ilex opaca* var. *arenicola*) on deep, white, sandy soils at an elevation of about 45 feet (13 m). Scrub vegetation rarely exceeded 15 feet (5 m) in height. Sand pine (*Pinus clausa*) was not present.

The prairie is a wide, flat expanse of saw palmetto and wire grass (*Aristida stricta*) dotted with widely spaced pine trees (*Pinus palustris* and *P. elliottii*) and small islands of oak scrub. It made up 5 percent of the area.

Small patches of other plant associations, creeks, ponds, and marshes occurred among the major associations, com-

1.6 Oak scrub (Fisheating Creek).

prising less than 1 percent of the study area. The major plant associations form zones that lie approximately parallel to Fisheating Creek (fig. 1.7).

Cattle and feral hogs occurred on the study area. No special land management practice has been used for turkeys.

Lochloosa Lochloosa WMA is located principally in Alachua County in northern Florida (fig. 1.8) about 350 km north of Fisheating Creek WMA. The major landowner, Owens-Illinois, Inc. (Forest Products Division), managed the property for pulpwood. The study was conducted on a sector that comprised about one-fourth of the 31 000-acre (12 000 ha) area.

The terrain of Lochloosa is flat to slightly rolling, ranging from 55 feet (17 m) to 100 feet (30 m) above mean sea level. The main soil types on the sand ridges are Millhopper, Tavares, and Newnan sands. In the ponds and swamps, the main soils are Monteocha loamy sand, Pomona sand, and Samsula muck, and the main flatwoods soil is Pomona sand (U.S. Department of Agriculture 1982).

The mean annual temperature is 22.2°C at Gainesville, 10 miles (15 km) to the northeast. The mean date of the first frost is December 6 and mean date of the last frost is February 14. The mean annual rainfall is 52.5 inches (133.2 cm)

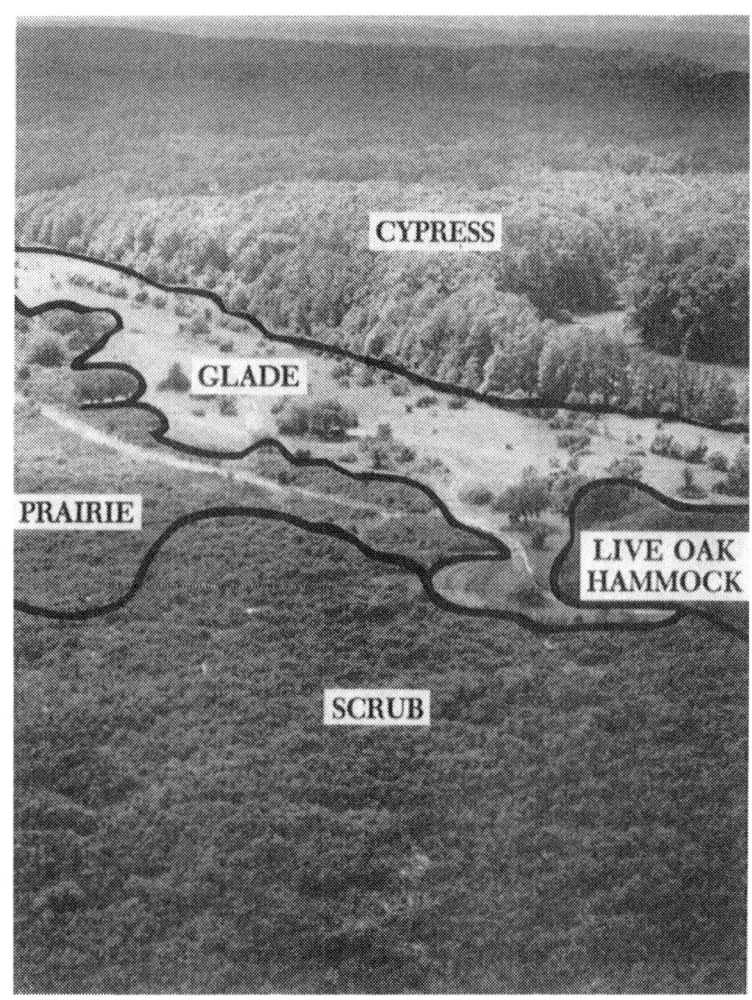

1.7 Aerial view of a typical cross section of the Fisheating Creek study area showing saw palmetto prairie, ecotone between prairie and grazed glade, grazed glade, and cypress woods.

with more than 50 percent occurring in summer (National Oceanic and Atmospheric Administration 1978).

The original plant associations were mainly longleaf pine (*Pinus palustris*) with turkey oak (*Quercus laevis*) and slash pine flatwoods (U.S. Department of Agriculture 1980). These associations were almost entirely replaced by slash pine plantations during the 1950s. Acreage to be planted was chopped, burned, and machine planted at a density of 764 seedlings per hectare. Pinewoods comprised approximately 50 percent of the area during this study; 9 percent was in natural slash pine. Many of the large live oak hammocks

Study Areas and General Methods

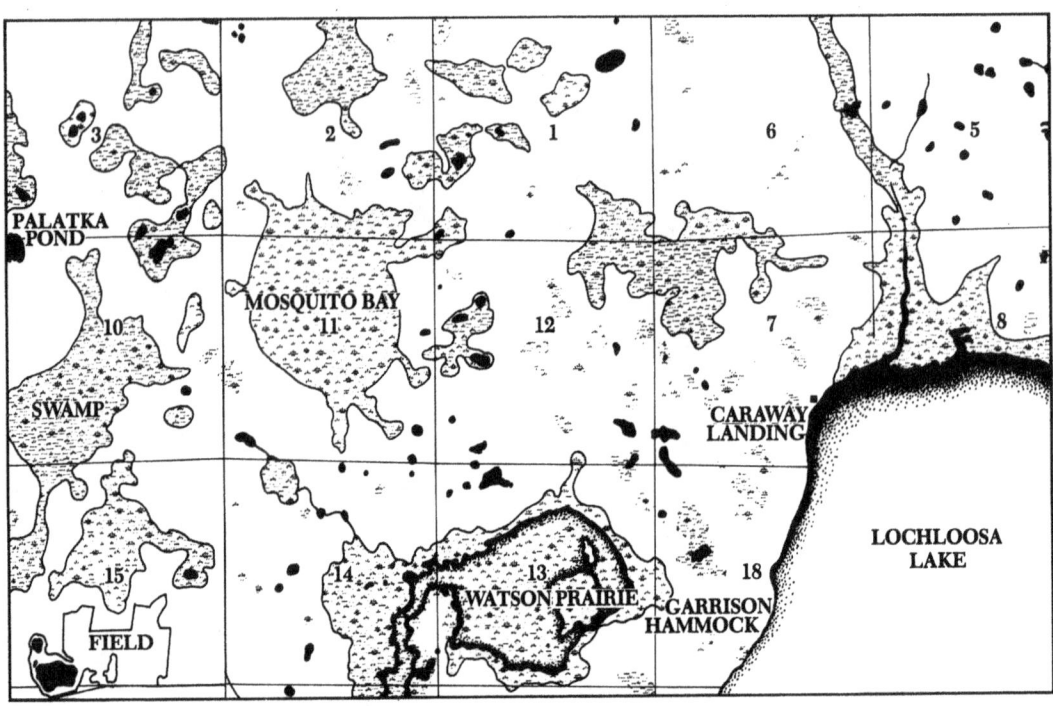

1.8 Lochloosa study area, Alachua County, Florida.

have been eliminated by commercial forest management practices; however, live oak and young laurel oak (*Q. hemisphaerica*) are still the dominant tree species in some of the remaining hardwood areas. A hardwood control program initiated during the 1950s was not entirely successful; consequently, the slash pine plantations have nearly as much young live oak and laurel oak as pine (fig. 1.9). Planted pine and oak associations occupied about 15 percent of the study area.

Recently clear-cut pinelands covered approximately 7 percent of the area and improved cattle pastures 2 percent. Cypress heads and hardwood swamps occupied 10 percent of the area, and open ponds comprised about 1 percent. Approximately 2 percent was in hardwood hammock; seasonally wet prairies made up the remaining 4 percent. There were no palmetto prairies or grazed glades as described for Fisheating Creek, but saw palmetto occurred abundantly. The area was grazed by cattle; feral hogs occurred in small numbers.

The wild turkey was eliminated by overhunting in the Lochloosa WMA between 1900 and 1950. The area was restocked with wild-trapped birds from Fisheating Creek WMA in the early 1960s. No other turkey management, except enforcement of hunting regulations, has been practiced on Lochloosa WMA. The area was open to year-round public

1.9 Pine woods (Lochloosa study area).

use. The spring gobbler season was limited to 16 days in late March during the study period 1969–75.

Capture Methods

Details about research methods will be given in the section to which they pertain, but a few general turkey research and management methods that were invented or refined in the course of the studies are discussed first. The accounts of capturing and handling turkeys have been presented in part in several papers cited in the text. The present account of capture methods contains information not presented in the original publications.

Procedures Common to Most Capture Methods

The more than 6000 turkeys that were captured during the turkey restoration and research programs, were taken primarily with cannon nets and oral tranquilizers (Austin 1965; Williams 1966; Williams, Austin and Peoples 1967; Williams et al. 1973; and Austin et al. 1973). Drop nets had been tested unsuccessfully in Florida before the study was initiated, and a type of drop-door trap (fig 1.10) was used routinely in the restoration program until about 1966 (Austin 1965).

Many of the procedures having to do with baiting and handling turkeys are the same regardless of the capture method. Bailey et al. (1980) made general recommendations on turkey trapping that will be of interest to some readers.

Establishing a Bait Site—Prebaiting habituates turkeys to a particular type of bait, makes them at ease around trapping devices and blinds, and attracts them to a site with regularity. We have tested wheat, sunflower seed, mixed

1.10 A drop-door trap—the first trap to be used successfully in the Florida turkey restoration program.

songbird seed, mule feed, chicken scratch, dogwood berries, shelled peanuts, white and yellow corn (whole and cracked), acorns, and sorghum, but have found no better bait than whole or cracked yellow corn.

Initially, corn is scattered where turkeys or their sign are regularly seen and run in thin lines up to one-fourth-mile long to intersect the turkeys' lines of travel. After turkeys begin to take the bait, as evidenced by field sign, a baited area can be reduced in size and a small site established.

It is best to use only the amount of corn that will be eaten in one day and to replenish it daily so the turkeys will not find the site unbaited. If large numbers of small birds use the site, whole corn may be a better bait than cracked corn because small birds will eat less of it. If deer or feral hogs use the site, cracked corn is better because it is less attractive to them. If other animals are using a bait site heavily, bait should be placed out immediately before turkeys are expected in early morning and widely scattered. Some of it should be covered with leaves and soil so that turkeys will find at least some bait by scratching in the event they visit the site after other animals have already been there.

Observation Blinds—An observer must be present for trapping turkeys because turkeys would injure themselves and be subject to predation in any automatic trap. Natural cover is sometimes sufficient for hiding, but the best practice is to use portable weatherproof blinds that have enough room for two people and their equipment, including folding stools or chairs. Portability is important when trap sites need to be moved frequently but less important when stationary traps (Sylvester and Lane 1946) are used. Insect-proofing is necessary during warm seasons.

We have used immobile blinds constructed at the site, small "pop" tents, cabana beach tents, pieces of canvas and netting to augment natural blinds, and several types of blinds made with umbrellas. The best has been one we designed with a skirt of camouflage vinyl cloth and insectproof netting fitted onto a tractor umbrella (fig. 1.11). The umbrella is held upright by a metal rod driven into the ground over which the hollow umbrella stem is placed. The blind can be made more sturdy by cords tied to nearby trees or to stakes in the ground.

The blind can be designed for seeing out of one or more side holes or through insect netting, but some opaque backing on at least one side is advisable. We usually pinned dark cloth against the netting to break the see-through effect in the event the wrong sun angles occurred during the trapping period. A floor is not necessary. In extremely hot weather,

1.11 Turkeys around an observation blind at a bait site.

one or more of the side flaps can be unsnapped for ventilation. Holes can be cut through the fabric for camera lenses, or zippered holes can be sewn in.

A tower blind (fig. 1.12) is heavy and difficult to transport but has many advantages. These blinds are made of three welded, cubical, angle-iron frames, stacked and bolted together. The tower is held in place by guy wires staked to the ground or tied to trees. A skirt, similar to the one used on the umbrella blind, is snapped on in one or more pieces and a large plastic cloth or a tractor umbrella is used as a roof. The gables can be left open for air circulation. The floor of the third level is a snugly fitted piece of ¾-inch marine plywood, reinforced in the middle. Ladder rungs are welded onto the lower two sections for climbing to the third level. The separate sections of a tower blind make sturdy, roomy blinds when used on the ground (fig. 1.13).

Handling Live Turkeys—Hand-held, living wild turkeys usually thrash with wings and legs, but they will rarely attempt to peck the handler. Care should be taken to have a firm initial grip because turkeys sometimes struggle violently when first touched. A turkey should be grasped by

1.12 A tower blind, especially useful in semipermanent situations.

1.13 The cubical sections of the tower blind can be used separately to make large, roomy blinds but are more difficult to transport than the umbrella type.

both legs firmly at the upper end of the tarsometatarsus and lifted off its feet while being held against the handler's hip or side (fig. 1.14). Another way is to grasp the bird by both humeri simultaneously (fig. 1.15). Care should be taken not to hold a turkey by one leg or one wing—the bird may rotate quickly and dislocate or break a bone. Turkeys are easily defeathered if grabbed around the body and will lose more feathers when handled wet than when they are dry. (Cannon netting is less satisfactory during rain for that reason.) Care must be taken to prevent adult gobblers from spurring themselves or the handler.

Confining Live Turkeys—Turkeys must usually be held for a few hours during recovery from drugs and to be banded and processed for shipping. Individual holding boxes are recommended. Turkeys will injure themselves in their efforts to escape if placed in wire pens or large containers. They become excited and tend to injure each other and to overheat when more than one bird is placed in the same small container. In individual boxes, the birds can be sorted by age, sex, band number, or other criteria when such information is posted on the boxes, whereas each bird may have to be handled repeatedly if several are in a common container.

We have used wooden, portable holding crates and wooden boxes built into truck bodies, but the best container

1.14 The best way to hold a turkey is snugly against your body or under one arm, grasping the intertarsal joints of both legs with the other hand.

has been a paraffin-treated cardboard box approximately 30 × 17 × 12 inches (76 × 43 × 30 cm) with overlapping ends for secure closing (fig. 1.16). A smaller box would be suitable for hens. The first cardboard turkey boxes were manufactured in 1964 to our specifications by St. Regis Paper Company of Jacksonville. These boxes resist moisture and can easily be carried into the field. They are strong, light, easily stored, reusable, inexpensive, and disposable for one-way shipment. Boxes of this type can be made in any dimensions by the manufacturer. A few turkeys have died from overheating when held in boxes in summer, but this can be prevented by placing the boxes in air-conditioned rooms.

Boxes received from the factory need to be stapled at one end with a stapler made especially for that purpose. The

1.15 An alternate way to hold a turkey is to grasp it by both humeri. One hand should hold both legs at the intertarsal joints.

other end can be fitted with a rivet on each flap and closed securely with a string, shock cord, or piece of rubber strung between the flaps (fig. 1.17). A less secure closure can be made with masking tape. Handholds and small air holes can be ordered from the box factory or cut in the boxes as needed. Care should be taken not to make holes large enough for the birds to stick their heads through.

Paraffin-treated boxes are bulky and pickup trucks will accommodate only a few at a time. Hauling capacity can be increased with light utility trailers (fig. 1.18).

Wooden holding boxes are too heavy for most field uses but may be satisfactory at headquarters. The tops and sides of wooden boxes should be padded on the inside and all sharp edges removed to prevent injuries to the turkeys' heads. Bottoms of one-inch galvanized mesh wire (that feces will fall through) have been satisfactory. Vertical front sliding doors are convenient where door space is limited, are usually

1.16 The paraffin-treated cardboard turkey transport box, in use in Florida since 1964.

stronger than swinging doors, and permit removal of live turkeys with less risk of their escaping.

If a paraffin-treated box is to hold a turkey for more than a few minutes, a conventional cardboard bottom pad should be added to absorb moisture. Without the extra cardboard, feces will ruin the box and soil the bird. Pads of nonparaffin-treated cardboard can be ordered from box manufacturers.

Turkeys can be safely held in individual containers for three days without food or water and force-fed water if held longer. On one occasion, we held a hen for five days without food or water and released her alive in apparent good health. Incubating hens will sometimes voluntarily go more than three days without water, even during the warm weather of

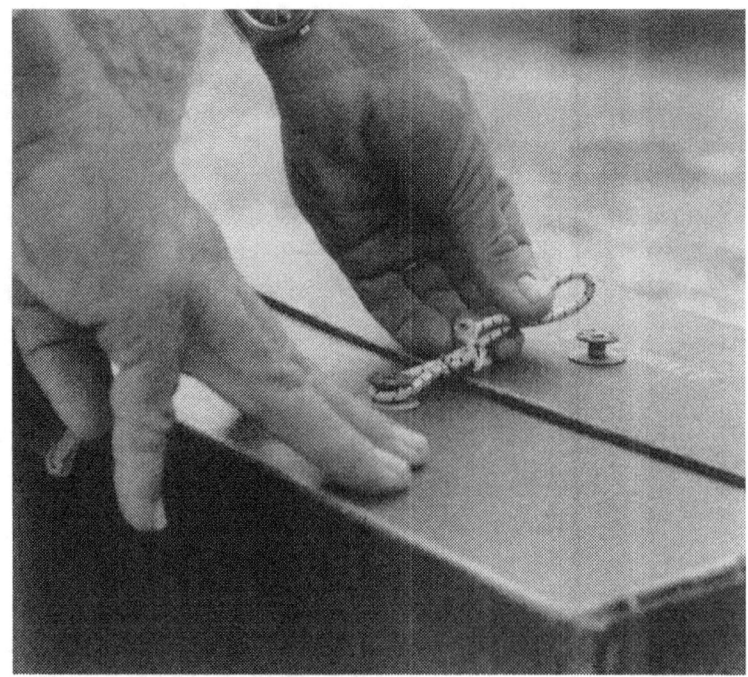

1.17 One way to close the end of a turkey box is with a piece of elastic cord strung between a rivet on each flap.

1.18 A light trailer designed for hauling turkeys in cardboard boxes.

June. We have never had a trapped turkey die from lack of water or from starvation while in captivity.

Turkeys can be held for a few hours in feed sacks or other strong cloth sacks if their legs are taped. The standard procedure is to cut off a corner of the sack for the turkey's head to stick out. The legs should be taped securely together, with the edge of the sack opening gathered and taped over the lower legs after the bird is inside so the feet stick out of the opening (fig. 1.19). Keeping the feet outside prevents damage to the nails and spurs. Turkeys will struggle if startled. Injuries can be minimized by loosely taping the sack to the body in the area of the wings so the turkey cannot open its wings inside the sack. If turkeys remain tied this way for more than about five hours, their legs may become temporarily (or sometimes permanently) paralyzed, and minor bleeding may occur at the alular region of the wings because of rubbing inside the sack. We do not use sacks when boxes are available.

When neither boxes nor burlap sacks are available, we

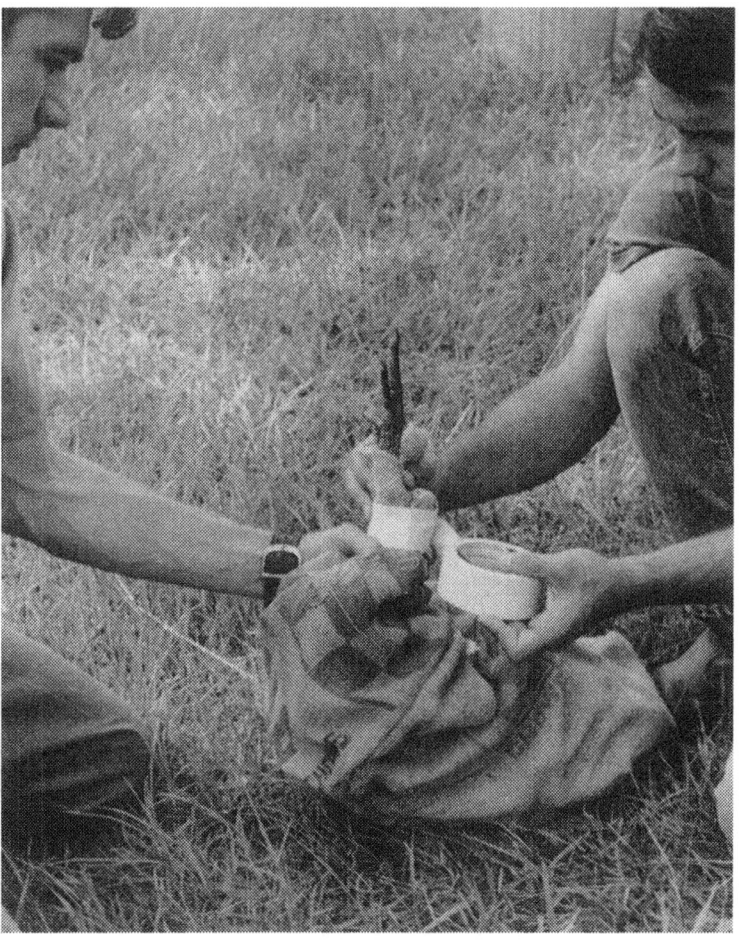

1.19 Turkeys can be held temporarily in feed sacks.

have immobilized captured turkeys by intramuscular and intraperitoneal injections of Brevane (Methohexital sodium, Corvel Laboratories). Injections were also occasionally used to completely immobilize turkeys for close examination. The proper dosage depends upon the level of narcosis the bird is experiencing, if the bird was drug-captured, and upon the size of the bird. A dosage higher than recommended for mammals (as printed on the vial) is usually needed for an unnarcotized turkey when injected intramuscularly in the mid-breast region. We have not attempted intravenous injections because a turkey's blood vessels are fragile. Depth and timing of anesthesia after an intramuscular injection cannot be accurately predicted. Intraperitoneal injections react faster than intramuscular injections but are more difficult for one person to administer. Lighter doses are required for intraperitoneal injections than for the intramuscular injections. We have experienced a small amount of mortality from injections.

Shipping—Live turkeys have been shipped routinely by airplane and truck. Small cardboard packing boxes are satisfactory during a brief flight and will permit more birds to be packed into the same airplane than can be in regular turkey boxes. A turkey cramped in a very small box will sometimes develop leg paralysis, as previously mentioned for cloth sacks. When turkeys are to be shipped by truck and may be in the boxes a day or longer, regular turkey boxes are necessary so that the turkeys can stand.

Releasing Live Turkeys—When released from boxes, turkeys sometimes fly against trees, vehicles, fences, and personnel. Fences in open areas are especially hazardous because turkeys sometimes enter long, low, gliding flight before landing on the ground and will occasionally strike a fence.

A hand-held turkey should be released quickly. It is better to open a holding box and permit the turkey to walk out and fly or run away than to remove it from the box by hand.

Using Cannon Nets

A cannon net was tested on turkeys in Florida prior to 1960 but there is no record of the results. The following account is based on a previous report (Austin 1965). A detailed description of the cannon netting technique as used in North Carolina (Bailey 1976) may be of interest to some readers.

Cannon nets were used again in 1960, this time a 40 × 60-foot (9 × 18-m) tarred fish net. The net was so heavy that it had to be fired at a high angle, which gave the turkeys time to fly out from under the leading edge before the net reached the ground. Only two turkeys were captured with it. In a test to correct this, two lightweight untarred nets were fired toward each other to entrap the birds quickly from both sides. The firing angle of one set was slightly higher than the other. These lighter nets were placed parallel 45 feet (14 m) apart and each projected by three Dill Cannon assemblies (Dill and Thornsbury 1950) powered by hand-loaded 12-gauge shotgun shells. Although the double net was more difficult to assemble and move, it resulted in the capture of 309 turkeys in 1962 and 1963.

After the 1963 season, a single 60 × 50-foot (18 × 15-m) untarred nylon net was used with four cannons. During the eight-week trapping seasons of 1964 and 1965, four trappers caught 625 turkeys with cannon nets. The now obsolete drop-door trap caught 227, and drugs, used experimentally for the first time, accounted for 208, for a total of 1060 turkeys.

Prebaiting—Prebaiting has been discussed. A few additional comments on baiting are needed in specific reference to cannon netting. For each trapper, several sites are needed. Clearings at netting sites should be large enough for a net to be spread with projectile lines extended. An area with short grass free of loose debris is preferred. The blind should be about 50 feet (15 m) from the net to permit a good view of the whole set.

"Dummy" nets, cannons, and blinds are placed at trap sites and baiting is started about two weeks before trapping is to begin. This will accustom the turkeys to seeing the paraphernalia. Dummy nets are approximately the same length as real nets. Turkeys become accustomed to dummy nets, and it was not necessary to conceal the real nets later. It is usually not advisable to leave real nets and cannons at the site because of deterioration, vandalism, and the expense of many inactive sets. A dummy net is usually gathered and permanently tied to make it easier to handle. Dummy cannons can be made from light metal or PVC tubing approximately three inches in diameter. We used discarded 2.7-inch military rocket tubes painted the same color as the real cannons.

The area around the dummy set is baited generously at first. As soon as turkeys are using the site, bait is confined to a string about a foot wide, approximately three feet (1 m) in front of the net, and 15 to 20 feet (5 to 6 m) on either side of the middle cannon but not directly in front of a cannon (fig. 1.20). Small amounts of bait seem to entice turkeys to be prompt in coming to the site, whereas too much bait, made available throughout the day, sometimes leads to erratic visitation. (Too little bait, however, can cause turkeys to stop using a site regularly.) Baiting just before daylight for two or three days before trapping will usually bring turkeys to the

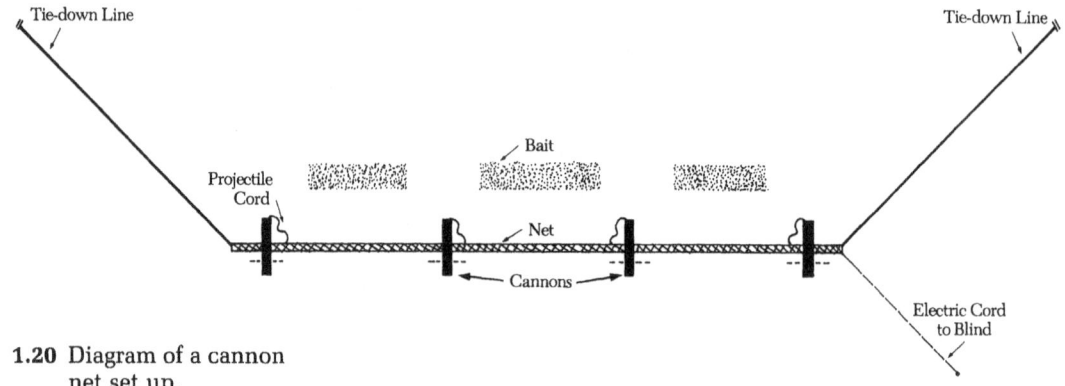

1.20 Diagram of a cannon net set up.

site very soon after sunrise. The morning the net is to be fired, the site should be baited with cracked corn to prolong the feeding time and permit a larger number of turkeys to arrive before the net is fired. It is advisable to accustom turkeys to cracked corn during the prebaiting operation so they will not be wary of it on trapping day.

Turkeys are usually ready to trap three to five days after they first visit the bait site. By baiting several widely separated sites, a choice is available for trapping each day. The best procedure has been to have two nets for each trapper, setting and firing each net on alternate days. By careful adherence to this tactic, a catch of turkeys can usually be made each trapping day by each trapper. Ideally, bait sites should be more than one-half-mile apart.

Setting the Net—When a suitable number of turkeys is using the trap site, the dummy set is replaced with a real net and cannon. The trailing edge of the net is anchored with steel stakes at each end, in the middle, and between the middle and ends to prevent turkeys from escaping under the edge. The net is fanfolded in a long, thin line about 18 inches (½ m) wide on top of the staked-down edge. Small bits of debris should be removed from the net. Cleaning and folding a net usually takes about five minutes.

Electric lamp cord for igniting the charges is placed along the staked-down edge, out of sight against the folded net, and led to the blind. Natural debris is used to cover the wire. Cannons are placed in position with the bases set into the ground firmly, each at a 15° to 17° angle above the ground. (A six-foot-tall man should be able to see directly down the center cannon barrel when standing 15 feet in front of it.) Outside cannons should be aimed about 3° lower. Projectiles are lubricated and placed in the cannon barrels. It is important that the projectiles be inserted all the way to the bottom of the barrels.

Tie-down lines, if used, are attached to the leading corners of the net and run 30 feet (9 m) forward at a 45° angle and staked down. Tie-down lines will prevent extreme lapping of the corners toward the middle. (Turkeys have escaped from nets not equipped with tie-down ropes, and a few have been killed when projectiles jerked back into the middle of the net.) Tie-down lines should be covered with soil or camouflaged in some way.

Cannons are pointed straight ahead if outside tie-down lines are used. If tie-down lines are not used, outside cannons should be angled about 5° outwards. Lines of the projectiles are attached to the loops on the leading edge of the net and placed in such a way as not to tangle when the net is fired.

Each cannon is charged by a 12-gauge shotgun shell with an electric match and a two-foot-long (0.6 m) wire inserted in the primer hole. Silicone sealant is used to waterproof the primer hole. The shell is loaded with 140 grains of FFFG black powder. A plastic overshot wad is inserted on top of the powder and sealed with silicone sealant. The electric match wires are attached, one to each of the two wires inside the cord to the operator's blind. It is safer to wait until the morning of firing before loading the cannons.

When the net is ready, the bait should be placed exactly as it will be at the time of firing. (No baiting should normally be done on the afternoon before a scheduled firing.) The firing set should appear identical to the dummy set. If there is any change, turkeys should be permitted to use the site again before firing is scheduled.

Firing the Net—Morning is usually the best time to fire a net because turkeys usually arrive at a properly prebaited site within one hour after sunrise. The net is fired by touching the bare ends of the electrical wire to the poles of a fresh 6- or 12-volt battery—one wire to each pole, it doesn't matter which.

After firing the net (figs. 1.21–1.24), the trapper should quickly pick up each turkey in a fold of the net, place his hands over the wings, twist the turkey in the net (fig. 1.25), and lay the bird back on the ground. After the turkeys are in boxes, the net may be reset. The projectiles are easier to load if wiped clean and loaded back into the cannons soon after they are fired. If the net is to be removed but the trap site is to be maintained, a dummy net and cannons should be set up.

Care of Equipment—Cannons should be cleaned before the trapping season so that projectiles will slide smoothly into the barrels. A rust-preventive paint on the outside helps preserve and camouflage them. During trapping, if projec-

1.21 A flock of turkeys approaching the trap site.

1.22 Turkeys on the bait line.

1.23 The cannon net is fired.

1.24 Turkeys flounce in the net while the trappers run to them.

Study Areas and General Methods

1.25 A netted turkey is secured by lifting it with a fold of net and twisting the net to bag the bird, after which the bird is placed back on the ground.

tiles become difficult to slide into the barrels, an automobile cylinder hone, powered by an electric drill, will clean them.

Projectile lines become frayed and should be checked regularly to see that they are strong and securely attached. Nets should be checked after each firing for torn places and before each firing for holes made by rodents during storage.

The electric wire should be checked for rodent damage by running a hand along the wire while picking it up. Nets should be stored in a dark, dry, cool place, secure from rodents. Cannons and projectiles should be cleaned and set in oil to prevent rust inside the barrels, and cleaned and repainted each season. The rubber O-rings on the projectiles should be cleaned occasionally and replaced every year.

Cannon Net Materials—Materials to operate one cannon net set are listed in table 1.1. We have used several types of cannon and rocket net assemblies and have found the Dill-type cannon assembly to be especially reliable. Such an assembly can be fabricated by most large welding shops. Cannons are 24 inches long (61 cm) with a 2½-inch (6.35 cm) inside diameter. The diameter can vary slightly as long as

Table 1.1 Equipment and supplies for turkey trapping and handling

Item	Quantity needed
General field work	
Blind	1
Flashlight	1
Food and water	Enough
Insect repellent	1 per person
Automatic baiting machine	1 per bait site
Corn	Enough and spare
Bucket	1
General turkey handling	
Cardboard box (or burlap sack)	1 per turkey
Masking or other tape	1 roll
Marking and banding supplies	As planned per bird
Cannon nets	
Dill cannon	4 per net
Cannon projectile	1 per cannon and spare
"Dummy" net	50 foot roll
Electric cord	150 (46 m) feet, on roll
Galvanometer	1
6v battery (or other device)	1 plus spare
¾ × 18 inch steel stake	7 per net
Cannon cartridges	1 per cannon and spares
50 × 60 foot nylon net	1 per set
Twine, 30 pound test	100 feet
⅜-inch nylon line	5 feet per cannon
¼-inch nylon line	30 feet, each end
Auto cylinder hone	1
Drugs	
Tribromoethanol	About 15 g per turkey
Plastic bucket	Several
Mixing spoon	1
Gram scales	1
Measuring cup	Several
Bottle of water	2 quarts
Brevane	About 5 cc (diluted) per turkey
Disposable syringe	Several
Needle	Several
Sharp knife/scalpel	1
Dip net	1

projectiles are made to the corresponding diameter. Projectiles should weigh approximately 2.20 kg. The best cannons are of stainless steel.

Cannon charges can be purchased ready-to-fire, but we have found that loading our own is easy, reliable, and less expensive. We obtained electric matches from Pyro Display Company, 1813 Bruin Road, Sebring, FL 33870. Other materials were purchased at various gun shops.

Using Oral Tranquilizers

Although cannon nets are effective for capturing turkeys, they have a few drawbacks. Their initial cost is high and they must be replaced from time to time. They are bulky and, to be most effective, they have to be left at the bait site to accustom turkeys to them, during which time they are exposed to deteriorating elements and possible vandalism. Two persons are required to use a cannon net for best results, and there are times and places that nets cannot be used, for example, during periods of widely fluctuating water levels and in heavy woods where there may not be large enough openings to fire a net. Orally administered drugs have none of these disadvantages and, when used in conjunction with cannon nets, will substantially improve the overall efficiency and flexibility of a large turkey trapping program. Oral tranquilizers themselves have a few drawbacks including the possibility of a serious overdosage incident. Only qualified trappers should use tranquilizers—drugs should not be considered as substitutes for trapping skill.

Early in the turkey research project, we tested oral tranquilizers as a trapping method for the statewide turkey restoration program and for research. The account that follows is an update of a previous report (Williams et al. 1973). This account is very explicit because experience has shown that any variance in procedures is likely to lead to unexpected results.

Orally administered narcotizing agents had been tested on many domestic animals but relatively few had been used to capture wild animals at the time this work began in 1963. Murton (1962) and Murton et al. (1963, 1965) used alpha-chloralose on wild wood pigeons (*Columba palumbus*) and other pest birds. Borg (1955) compared the effects of alpha-chloralose and beta-chloralose on crows (*Corvus corone*), magpies (*Pica pica*), pigeons (*C. livia*), pheasants (*Phasianus colchicus*), geese (*Anser anser, A. erythropus*), and gulls (*Larus argentatus*). Canada geese (*Branta canadensis*) and several species of ducks have been captured with alpha-chloralose and with alpha-chloralose mixed with diazepam (Crider and McDaniel 1967, 1968; and Crider et al. 1968). Murray and Dennett (1963) and Murray (1965) used diazepam to capture and handle three species of deer (*Cervus nippon, Dama dama,* and *Odocoileus virginianus*). Austin and Peoples (1967) reported on alpha-chloralose administered orally to feral hogs (*Sus scrofa*) in southern Florida, and Martin (1967) compared methoxymol, alpha-chloralose, secobarbital sodium, and methohexital sodium (Brevane) for capturing mourning doves (*Zenaidura macroura*). In Alabama, alpha-chloralose has been used routinely to capture turkeys since about 1968 (Speake et al. 1969). Smith (1967) used tribromoethanol on sea birds, and Evans et al. (1975) used the same drug on turkeys in Louisiana. Pomeroy and Woodford (1976) used alpha-chloralose on marabou storks

(*Leptotilos crumeniferus*). Bailey (1976) used several drugs on turkeys in North Carolina, including tribromoethanol and alpha-chloralose.

Henry S. Mosby and Dan E. Cantner were the first to suggest an oral, narcotic-like drug to capture turkeys and reported the capture of five turkeys with Avertin, an oral-basal anesthetic in which the active ingredient is tribromoethanol (Mosby and Cantner 1956). We were unaware of their work before we had undertaken similar research in 1963 using alpha-chloralose (Williams 1966).

After a satisfactory procedure for capturing turkeys with alpha-chloralose was developed (Williams et al. 1967), we tested other compounds and found one, called methoxymol, that was faster acting than alpha-chloralose on penned wild turkeys. When methoxymol proved to be distasteful to turkeys under most field conditions and difficult to obtain in sufficient quantities for adequate testing, we turned to tribromoethanol. Tribromoethanol proved to be palatable to turkeys, could be purchased in sufficient quantities, and approached methoxymol in narcotic characteristics. It was faster acting and caused a shorter period of narcosis than alpha-chloralose (Williams et al. 1973).

Although we have recently used tribromoethanol almost exclusively, alpha-chloralose remains a suitable drug for turkeys and is preferred by some game biologists. Alpha-chloralose can be purchased from large chemical suppliers. The availability of tribromoethanol is unpredictable; it is sometimes temporarily out of stock. For that reason, we usually purchased a large supply and stored it under refrigeration. Methoxymol is not on the market, as far as we know.

Bailey (1967) reported on the use of trichloroethanol (a compound chemically related to tribromoethanol) for capturing turkeys, but it was later (Bailey and Doepker 1978) found it to be too toxic.

Tribromoethanol (CBr_3CH_2OH) is a water-soluble, whitish crystalline powder with a pungent taste to humans. The powdered form is said to be unstable (Beckman 1961), especially at high temperatures in the presence of sunlight and air (Mosby and Cantner 1956). We have not measured the drug's stability but have experienced no serious deterioration of the compound the way we have used it. Alpha-chloralose is used in the form of a white powder and is chemically related to chloral hydrate. It is very stable and not soluble in water. Methoxymol is a white, finely powdered imidazole derivative with high solubility in water and a very astringent taste. At the time we tested it, methoxymol was a "new experimental drug" obtainable only from the sponsor (Vetco, a Johnson and Johnson Company affiliated with Jansen Pharmaceutical of Beerse, Belgium).

Dosages of each drug were tested on penned wild and domestic turkeys to establish a general dosage range, then used in the field and adjusted by trial and error to determine the heaviest dosage that could be used without undue mortality. During the testing phase, alpha-chloralose was used at 10 trapping areas, from 1964 through 1968; tribromoethanol was used on four areas, in 1969; and methoxymol was tried only occasionally on one study area, primarily in 1967 and 1968.

Bait Sites for Oral Drugs—Bait sites should be comparatively open with few trees or other ground-level obstructions within approximately 200 feet so that all the turkeys can be seen easily. When open areas are not available, that does not preclude the use of drugs—it simply makes it more difficult to keep up with any turkeys that leave the immediate site in a state of subeffective narcosis. Hazards associated with site location include danger of drowning by narcotized turkeys if sites are near water, disturbance by people who are not associated with the trapping operation if near roads, and harassment of narcotized turkeys by predators, livestock, and unnarcotized turkeys. Bait sites should be located close to roosting areas to maximize the possibility that turkeys will visit the bait in early morning when they are hungry, but should be far enough away from the roost to preclude disturbance of roosting turkeys during prebaiting operations.

Bait should be presented in piles of about ¼ cup. Coarse cracked yellow corn is recommended for bait and should be used exclusively in the final stages of prebaiting. Other baits may be satisfactory if turkeys will accept them, but adjustments in dosage may be necessary if smaller or larger particle sizes are used. Bait piles should be far enough apart to minimize antagonism among turkeys—three-foot (1 m) intervals are satisfactory in most situations, but greater spacing is desirable when separate social groups use the bait area together.

Prebaiting is best done in its final stages by personnel who will attempt to capture the turkeys. No change should be made in the site or in prebaiting procedures for at least three days before the capture attempt. Any variance will delay feeding and could affect the level of narcosis reached in the majority of the flock.

Best trapping success is had before 0930 hours. The main drawbacks of afternoon trapping are low appetite levels and uncertainty of the time of site visitation by turkeys. There is also the possibility that tribromoethanol will break down chemically during prolonged exposure to sunlight.

Preparing and Presenting Baits—The procedures described here have worked well, but variations in technique may be equally as effective under other circumstances. Evans et al. (1975) used weight, rather than volume, to measure bait and used wheat instead of corn.

We have used several methods of mixing drugs and baits, including adhesive compounds such as granulated sugar dissolved in water and Methocel (Dow Chemical Company). Ethanol, acetone, DMSO, and water have been used as solvents and carriers; of these, plain tap water worked best for preparing baits with alpha-chloralose, methoxymol, and tribromoethanol.

Treated bait has been presented in varying degrees of dampness with equal success. There appears to be no advantage in mixing baits in advance of the time they are to be presented in the field. To the contrary, if mixed in advance with water alone and permitted to dry, the surface coating of drug tends to flake off when handled. This results in administration of a lighter dosage than intended. We found it convenient to wet the bait with water in a clean plastic bucket at the bait site and permit it to soak for about one minute before draining off the excess water. The bait was allowed to stand for another minute to permit the surface water to soak in and the powdered drug was stirred in thoroughly. Longer soaking would permit a longer period of handling before the drug began to flake off from drying, a procedure that should be adjusted to individual trapping requirements. It is usually convenient to measure the bait and weigh out vials of drug in advance of mixing at the bait site.

The most satisfactory mixture for alpha-chloralose has been 1.8–2.0 g per cup of medium cracked corn mixed with water at the bait site and administered damp. Mixtures of 1.5 g or less were tested but too often resulted in subeffective narcosis. At mixtures greater than 2.0 g, the overdosage rate reached 10 percent. Dan W. Speake (personal communication) routinely uses 2.0 g per cup of cracked corn and sometimes removes the crop contents, by a surgical procedure, of any bird that is in very deep narcosis. Surgery is rarely necessary, however. Bailey (1976) recommended 1.5 g per cup—perhaps his turkeys ate more than ours.

A small loss of alpha-chloralose powder from the bait surface is inevitable when a sticking compound is not used; therefore, when mixed with water alone, the dose actually administered is less than 2.0 g per cup of bait. Lower dosage

Table 1.2 Dosage, reaction time, and duration of anesthesia in tests of three drugs for capturing turkeys

Drug	Recommended dosage per cup of cracked corn (grams)	Total number captured with recommended dosage	Mortality (percent)	Usual number captured per cup of bait	Average knockdown time (minutes)[a]	Approximate duration of anesthesia (hours)[b]
Tribromoethanol	10–11	209[c]	2.4	3–5	10–20	4–10
Methoxymol	4	113	6.3	3.5	7–10	3–4
Alpha-chloralose	2	1,600[d]	9.0[d]	1–3	30–70	20–40

a. Time from beginning to feed to time a bird could be captured with a long-handled net.
b. For birds reaching Stage III.
c. After these tests were concluded, approximately 1,200 turkeys were captured with tribromoethanol in routine trapping operations with a mortality rate of approximately 5%.
d. Because alpha-chloralose was being used for routine trapping, these figures are estimates from incomplete data and include mortality from all dosages tested in addition to the recommended dosage.

mixtures, in the range of 1.6 g to 1.8 g per cup of bait, should be used if a sticking compound is used.

Of the methoxymol mixtures tested (from 1.0 g to 12.0 g per cup of bait), 4.0 g proved to be the most satisfactory. The best dosage of tribromoethanol was found to be 10.0 g to 11.0 g per cup of medium cracked corn. Numbers of turkeys captured in the tests with each drug, recommended dosage rates and other data are presented in table 1.2.

The response to oral drugs is partly dependent upon bait particle size with larger particle sizes calling for lower drug mixtures. For whole shelled corn, about two-thirds as much drug is needed as with medium cracked corn. Of the turkeys that died from overdosage of tribromoethanol, some died on relatively low dosages (8.0 g and 5.0 g per cup) of whole corn. Other overdosage occurred on 12.0 g of tribromoethanol per cup of cracked corn administered during a light rain. In capturing approximately 180 turkeys during the initial tests of tribromoethanol, no turkey died of overdosage when less than 12.0 g per cup of cracked corn was used and only two of 22 were lost with the 12.0 g mixture.

We used several recovery stimulants including pentylenetetrazol (Metrazol) in the initial tests of oral drugs. While we did not conduct controlled experiments, we were not convinced that the compounds had any value in reducing the mortality rate (Williams 1967). Besides, the mortality rates we experienced were so low that research on potential antidotes did not seem warranted. Bailey (1972) reported on his use of stimulants as antidotes for drug overdosage.

Narcosis—The onset and duration of narcosis (figs. 1.26A–1.26D and table 1.3) differ for each drug. Alpha-chloralose produces gradual and continuously increasing induction

1.26A Stage I. After about 40 minutes, narcotized turkeys begin to stumble backwards.

from Stage I through Stage IV. With methoxymol, Stages I and II are brief and sometimes pass almost unnoticed before narcotized turkeys begin to stumble backwards as they enter Stage III. Tribromoethanol produces narcotic symptoms that are more like methoxymol than alpha-chloralose but is peculiar in the way that it causes dozing in Stages II and III while turkeys can still be easily aroused. Stage IV is similar for the three drugs.

Pickup and Handling—Paraffin-treated cardboard boxes were carried to the bait sites. Turkeys can be captured with long-handle dip nets (figs. 1.27A–1.27C) as early as Stage II, although they will normally progress into deeper narcosis if permitted to lie undisturbed. In most capture operations, various stages of narcosis occur simultaneously in a single flock. It has been our practice to permit even the least narcotized bird to reach Stage III (or else allow it to walk away in

1.26B Stage II. After about one hour, little dispersal occurs.

mild narcosis) before beginning to pick up those in deeper narcosis. When turkeys have not fed rapidly enough to reach Stage III on tribromoethanol, they tend to doze for periods up to 10 minutes and even lie prostrate for several minutes at a time. Such birds can be captured with a dip net if approached quietly from the backside. If a bird awakens upon being approached, it will usually lapse again into sleep a few minutes later, even if it runs away. Sometimes turkeys will reach Stage III on tribromoethanol and remain at that level for about two hours. If the pickup operation is delayed, birds narcotized earlier may recover and leave the area.

Once captured on tribromoethanol or methoxymol, turkeys are nearly impossible to capture on the same drug again, but they do not seem to taste alpha-chloralose and can be captured repeatedly with it. Such keen memory of a bad taste is not unprecedented—chickens will avoid drinking

1.26C Stage III. After about one and one-half hours, most turkeys are down.

1.26D Stage IV. After about three hours, general anesthesia.

Study Areas and General Methods

Table 1.3 Hypnotic stages of narcotized turkeys

Stage	Depth of hypnosis	Posture	Coordination	Escape response
I	Barely evident	Standing or walking (fig. 1.26)	Good, able to fly	Unwary until approached, cannot be captured with dip net
II	Sluggish	Standing, walking, or squatting (fig. 1.26)	Impaired but can run	Difficult to capture[a]
III	Shallow anesthesia	Not standing or walking (fig. 1.26)	Poor	Can usually be picked up by hand
IV	Deep anesthesia	Prostrate (fig. 1.26)	None	None

a. Turkeys can be captured with a long-handled dip net in Stage II if approached with extreme caution.

water with lithium chloride after a single experience with it (Genovese and Browne 1978).

Side Effects of Drugs—Concern has been expressed that anesthesia with drugs may alter the reproductive ability of turkeys, but we know of no reason to think so. A trial with domestic turkeys (Williams et al. 1966) revealed no serious adverse effects caused by alpha-chloralose. Furthermore, good turkey populations have been established in Florida and Alabama (D. W. Speake, personal communication) by turkeys captured with alpha-chloralose, methoxymol, or tribromoethanol, and these drugs have been used on turkeys in several other states without reports of ill effects. Tribromoethanol is also used in human medicine.

Response to Drugs by Age and Sex—Turkey poults weighing less than two pounds (1 kg) and younger than 10 weeks have been captured with tribromoethanol dosages of 8.0 g and 9.0 g per cup of cracked corn. After feeding only briefly and ingesting relatively little of the bait, poults were affected quickly by the drug and recovered sooner than older turkeys. Adult hens accompanying broods usually did not progress beyond Stage II narcosis on 8.0 grams of tribromoethanol per cup of bait and were difficult to capture. We do not know whether the deeper narcosis of young birds is due to the amount of bait eaten or to some physiological or other reason. D. W. Speake (personal communication) reported that in capturing summer poults with alpha-chloralose in Alabama, brood hens were easily captured when a 2.0 g per cup mixture was used.

Few data are available for dosages of tribromoethanol on adult gobblers, but 12.0 to 14.0 g per cup of cracked corn is thought to be an optimum mixture for them. A few gobblers have been captured on as little as 8.0 g per cup of whole shelled corn, but some were insufficiently narcotized at these dosages. More data will more accurately define the optimum

1.27A A dip net is used to catch a lightly narcotized turkey.

1.27B

Study Areas and General Methods

1.27C

dosages for different sex and age groups. It appears safe at this time to recommend 10.0 g to 12.0 g per cup for turkeys in fall and winter and 8.0 g per cup for poults during late summer. It may not be possible to use the same dosage satisfactorily for adult gobblers and hens and younger turkeys without risking underdosage of gobblers or overdosage of the others. Evans et al. (1975) reported similar uncertainty in their tests of tribromoethanol in Louisiana.

Weather Conditions—We have not deliberately administered drugs to turkeys during a rain; but when it began to rain unexpectedly during trapping, we found that the effectiveness of alpha-chloralose was not diminished and that the narcotic effect of tribromoethanol was actually enhanced. Bailey (1976) reported the same observation with tribromoethanol. The time to Stage IV narcosis on tribromoethanol was four minutes for the first turkey and seven minutes for the last in a family flock of six during a light rain, and there were a number of similar occurrences in light, early-morning rain. The quantity of drug washed off the bait by rain is evidently offset by an increase in the drug absorption rate with wet bait.

Capturing Flightless Poults—When radio-equipped

brood hens are tracked, their recently hatched poults can be captured by hand up to about nine days of age. The younger the brood, the easier the poults are to capture. Regardless of the age of the brood, it is more effective to approach the brood while it is still on its ground roost in early morning. After the brood has left the roost, the hen will often attempt to elude detection by moving and will sometimes hide the brood and run away.

One- or two-day-old broods are especially easy to capture. When three to five days old, the poults will usually run a short distance before hiding. After about five days of age, some poults may continue this "frozen" hiding behavior when approached but most will creep and run farther away, requiring a careful search. After they are about 10 days old, poults will usually fly into trees if pursued and cannot be captured by hand.

We held hand-captured flightless poults temporarily in containers that could be closed and darkened (fig. 1.28). The

1.28 A darkened, cloth box (in background) is used to temporarily hold hand-caught, flightless poults in the field.

brood hens usually remained away for 20 to 30 minutes while we worked on the poults. When they returned for the poults, we left the area. In approximately 70 times that this procedure was used, only one hen permanently deserted her brood.

Capturing Hens on Their Nests—On one occasion, an incubating hen was captured alive on her nest at night and two were captured this way during the day. Four persons approached the marked nest site, each holding a corner of a heavy mist net fully stretched between them. The size of the net was such that when the middle was over the nest, the investigators were about 30 feet from the nest. When the net was directly over the nest, it was lowered to the ground. When the hen flushed, one of the investigators bagged her in the net.

It seems unlikely that a hen captured on the nest would return to it, but in one case we made a test anyway. A hen was captured at night and gassed to general anesthesia with methane and placed back on her nest. She awoke and abandoned the nest during the night. In another netting attempt at night, the hen ran off the nest before the net was lowered but was captured by hand.

Banding and Other Marking

Captured turkeys were leg-banded for individual identification with National Band and Tag Company Number 213 aluminum, numbered, riveted bands (fig. 1.29) using size 11 for hens and size 13 for gobblers. The riveted feature was an effective safeguard against band loss. These bands have been known to last 12 years on turkeys in the wild, although one band that old was beginning to show signs of wear (fig. 1.30). Very few turkeys would ever live so long, however.

Patagial wing streamers (Knowlton et al. 1964) have been used with good success (fig. 1.31). Some turkeys retained streamers for four years. Specimens examined wearing streamers exhibited no significant abrasions where the buttons pierced the propatagium. Various plastic-fabric colors and lettering make individual identification possible.

We tested a type of coiled plastic leg band (National Band and Tag Company, "Bandette") on turkeys with a riveted aluminum band on the other leg but found that most of the bands came off after a few days. A good cement might have prevented the loss, but we have not attempted to test cements with plastic leg bands because the patagial streamers were entirely satisfactory for our purposes. Ellis (1961) tried the same plastic "Bandettes" on wild turkeys with poor success because of band loss and had only limited success when he attempted to remedy the problem with cements and wire locking devices.

1.29 Riveted leg bands have proven to be satisfactory. Different sizes are used for hens and gobblers. Bands are delivered flattened.

Poults one to 10 days old have been toe-clipped for identification by removing one terminal digit with fingernail clippers, scissors, or pocket knives (as described by Davis c. 1960). Blood loss was insignificant. The distal one-half of the last joint must be cut completely off to prevent the nail from partially regenerating. A system for individual identification can be worked out by clipping combinations of toes on each foot. Toe-clipping has been especially useful for marking preflight poults that were too young to band. They could be recognized when recaptured for leg-banding. We have toe-clipped more than 200 young poults this way; although there was no way to be certain about their survival, the minimal bleeding and completely normal behavior at the time of release, coupled with the recovery of many toe-clipped turkeys months later, suggest that the procedure was not seriously debilitating. Poults trapped later were easily recognized as toe-clipped specimens.

Chick dye (Columbus Vaccine Co., Columbus, Ohio) was

Study Areas and General Methods

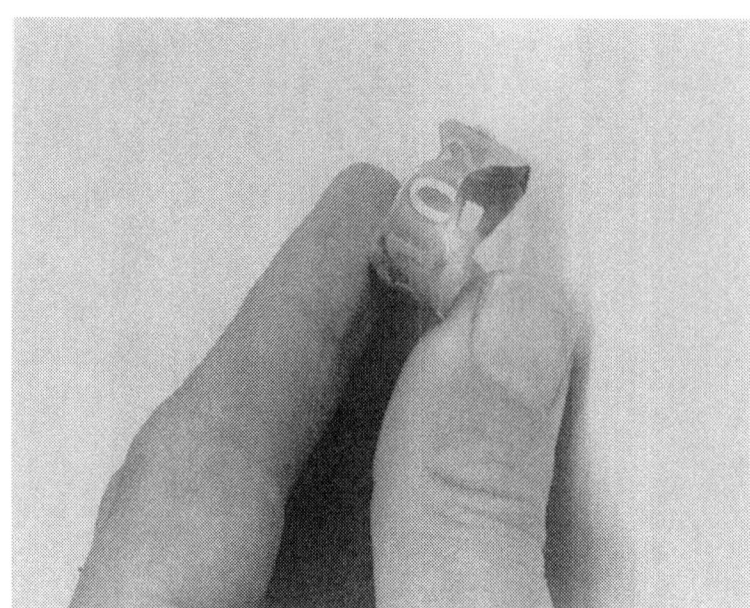

1.30 After 11 years on a wild turkey, this band had begun to show wear.

1.31 Patagial wing markers permit identification of turkeys at a distance.

tested for individually marking the plumage of young poults. The dye remained in the feathers, but the birds had to be examined in hand for positive identification and the coloring was lost as the dyed feathers were replaced during the normal molting process. Toe-clipping served the same purpose, was permanent, and was easier to perform.

Radiotelemetry has replaced many applications of leg-banding and color marking in turkey research. Radio tagged turkeys can be identified without being sighted and can be located at will. This permits direct observation of events that could not otherwise be seen. Home ranges and habitat use can be plotted with reasonable accuracy based on as many data points as needed.

We first tested radiotelemetry equipment on turkeys in 1966 using equipment manufactured by Markusen Electronic Specialities. Similar equipment by Dav-tron, Inc., AVM Instrument Co., Wildlife Materials, Inc., and Telonics, Inc., has also been used satisfactorily. The basic equipment was a small transmitter with a battery power supply (fig. 1.32), a portable receiver (fig. 1.33), and direction-finding antennas (figs. 1.34A–1.34B), on frequencies in the 150 MHz range. Such radio tags can be expected to transmit for at least one year if pulsed signals are used; under conditions of our study, range normally exceeded 1 km. Receivers with 24 or

1.32 A miniature transmitter with batteries and rubber tubing is ready to install on a turkey.

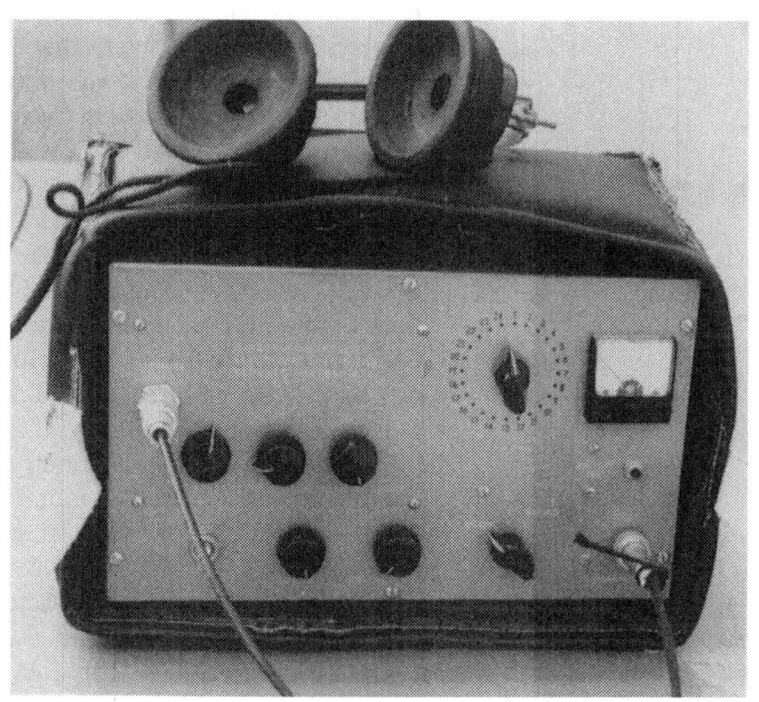

1.33 A portable telemetry receiver.

1.34A Double-element hand antennas are used when on foot or at close range.

1.34B Multi-element antennas are highly directional and necessary for distant signals.

more channels were used with as many as 50 transmitters simultaneously on the same study area. Signals on the same receiving channel were distinguished by different pulse rates.

The direction of the received radio signal provides a bearing on the source. Several bearings can be obtained by moving to a new position with the same receiving equipment, or with other receivers at other points. When plotted on maps, the bearings intersect near the point source of the signal, which is the approximate location of the turkey at that time.

Study Areas and General Methods

1.35 To affix a transmitter to a turkey, the bird is held firmly at the intertarsal joints by a helper and laid breast down on a flat surface.

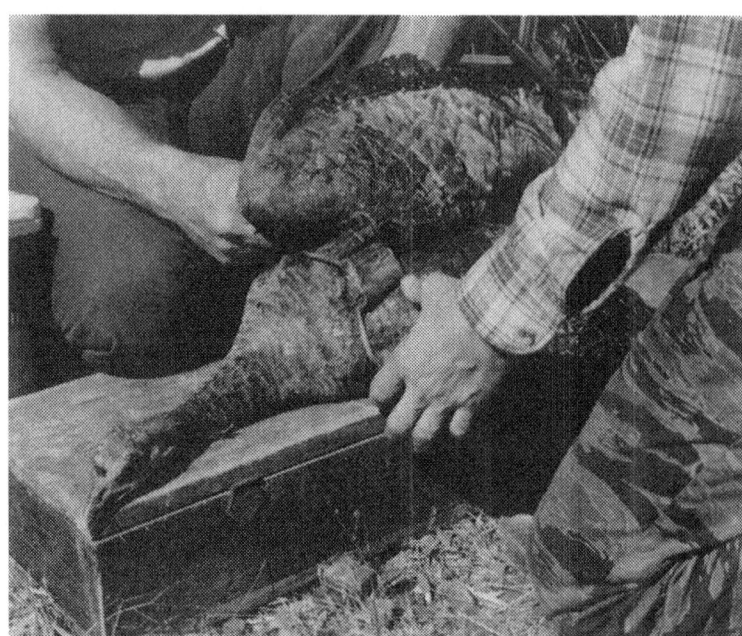

1.35A The transmitter is positioned in the midback area.

1.35B The ends of rubber tubing are tied in a square knot under each wing.

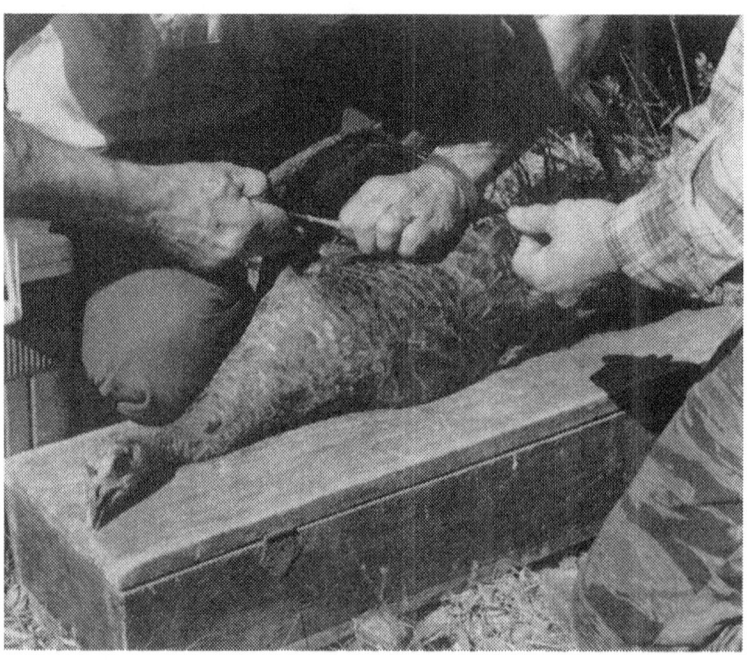

1.35C The harness fit is tested before the knots are firmly tied—it should be unstretched even with a wing partly extended.

1.35D Excess tubing is cut away.

Study Areas and General Methods

The least error is had when the bearings intersect at nearly 90-degree angles. In many applications, such as finding nests, the signal source can simply be approached on foot or in a vehicle without plotting bearings on maps.

Transmitters weighed 30 to 60 g; with the additional battery weight the package weight did not exceed 100 g, which is little more than the weight of a turkey egg and less than 3 percent of the weight of the hen. Nenno and Healy (1979) observed turkeys' behavior with and without 140-g transmitters and concluded that there was no difference. Their transmitters weighed nearly 4 percent of the body weight of the hens.

Rubber tubing was attached to the transmitter-battery assembly with fiberglass reinforced tape, and the radio packages were affixed in the mid-dorsal region of the turkeys with under wing loops of natural latex surgical tubing (figs. 1.35A–1.35D). Square knots were tied under the wings and the excess rubber was trimmed at the knot. The rubber loops were not so tight as to require the rubber to stretch when the birds flew. Some transmitters fell off, due to deterioration of the tubing and to accidents, but most remained on for one year or longer. The nearly flat transmitter was usually covered with feathers and was difficult to detect on a living turkey (fig 1.36).

1.36 The hen on the right is wearing a transmitter.

Receivers were light and portable, operating on dry cell

batteries. Some new models had scanners. Receivers with sensitivity controls and ammeters were especially useful when signal sources were close but not conspicuous to the eye, such as turkeys on their nests and loose transmitters at the site of a predation incident.

2

Physical Characteristics

Molts and Plumages

The molts of the juvenile eastern wild turkey have been described by A. Starker Leopold (1943). Since Leopold, research on turkey molt has focused on plumage features to determine the age of specimens for game management purposes (Knoder 1959, Nixon 1962, Kelly 1975, and Healy and Nenno 1980). Like Leopold's studies, recent research has dealt only with *M. g. silvestris*. Published information on molting of the Florida subspecies (*M. g. osceola*) consists of two brief notes pointing out differences between the Florida and eastern turkey with respect to primary molt (Williams 1961, Williams and Austin 1970). As far as we can determine, molts and plumages have not been described for any of the subspecies except *M. g. silvestris*.

In the following descriptions, emphasis is on the major feathers of the wing and tail, other plumage that affects the appearance of the bird as it matures, and on certain external features that correlate with age and maturity. Comparative statements about *M. g. silvestris* are based on Leopold's paper (Leopold 1943) unless otherwise stated.

Approximately 67 living or freshly killed known-age specimens between one and 209 days old were examined. Notes on the entire plumage were made on 15 of these at different molting stages, and partial data were recorded from 30. The other specimens in this group were siblings in the same molting stages. Eight additional freshly killed specimens between 14 and 27 weeks old were examined. Seventy-three summer and 45 early fall poults were captured alive, examined with respect to tail and wing molt, and released. The approximate ages of all unmarked specimens were determined by comparison with marked known-age specimens.

Data on retention of juvenal primaries 9 and 10 during the first winter were obtained from a sample of 125 specimens examined at Fisheating Creek between 1970 and 1980. Twenty-one adult specimens were examined during their annual molt. Approximately 300 other dead and living turkey specimens were examined at various times of the year to pinpoint the time that certain stages of molting occur. Approximately 150 poults were examined immediately after they hatched in artificial incubators and from time to time during the first few days of life. The specimens examined represent M. g. osceola (Aldrich and Duvall 1955). In addition to the specimens examined for molting, 608 tarsometatarsi were examined in a study of their color characteristics. The tarsi were from localities in Florida and the eastern and midwestern United States.

The molt and plumage terminology of Dwight (1900) has long been used satisfactorily on gallinaceous birds and will be used in the present discussion along with the newer terminology of Humphrey and Parkes (1959), as modified slightly by Lucus and Stettenheim (1972) (table 2.1 and fig. 2.1).

The major feathers of the wing and tail are numbered in the approximate sequence in which they are molted. This is from the most proximal primary outward, from the most distal secondary inward, from proximal to distal in the alula, and from the middle of the tail outward on both sides. Major wing coverts are numbered the same as their corresponding primaries or secondaries.

Table 2.1 Molt and plumage nomenclature for the wild turkey

Molt Number	Old name for molt[a]	New name for molt[b]	Feather generation	Old name for plumage[a]	New name for plumage[b]
—	—	—	1	Natal	Natal
1	Postnatal	Prejuvenal	2	Juvenal	Juvenal
2	Postjuvenal	First prebasic	3	Postjuvenal	First basic
3	First winter[c]	Prealternate	4	First winter	Alternate
4	Annual	Prebasic	5	Adult	Basic[d]

a. Dwight (1900).
b. Humphrey and Parks (1959) and Lucas and Stettenheim (1972).
c. Leopold (1943).
d. The same cycle is repeated annually thereafter.

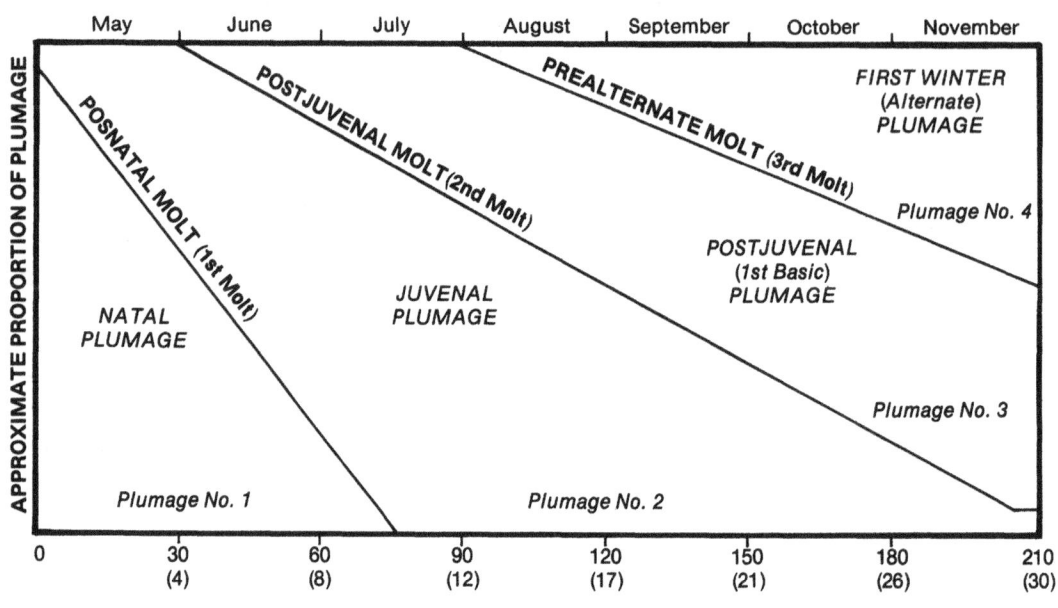

2.1 Diagram of the molt of the Florida turkey, showing old and new terminology.

Age Determination Methods

An attempt was made to use the age determination method of Healy and Nenno (1980), but their specimens had longer primaries than our known-age specimens of the same age which caused the method to consistently underage Florida turkeys. Knoder's (1959) method is in closer agreement with the known-age material available in our study (table 2.2), evidently because his turkeys were smaller than Healy and Nenno's.

Natural variations in food supply and quality, diseases, and other factors are known to affect the growth rate of feathers. Knoder (1959) found that blackhead disease seriously retarded feather growth in some of his captive turkeys and there is little doubt that numerous other diseases would do the same thing. Most juvenile Florida turkeys are infected with fowl pox, at least three blood parasites, and several other parasites and diseases during the period of major molting activity in summer. One would expect, therefore, to find more growth variation and perhaps slower average feather growth rates among wild-living turkeys than among carefully managed, disease-free, well-fed, captive turkeys such as those used by Healy and Nenno (1980). Feather growth of healthy, captive turkeys will approach the intrinsic growth rate rather than the rate that is likely to be observed in na-

Table 2.2 Comparisons of age determination methods applied to known age Florida turkeys

Florida[a]		Knoder[b] method		Healy & Nenno[c] method		
Known age (days)	Sex	Calculated age	Age difference (error)	Calculated age (days)	Equation number	Age difference (error)
59	M	—	—	55	11	− 4
64	M	—	—	65	11	+ 1
133	F	136	+ 3	124	29	− 9
133	F	129	− 4	113	29	−20
133	F	135	+ 2	121	29	−12
133	M	135	+ 2	117	22	−16
133	M	137	+ 4	123	22	−10
133	M	123	−10	120	22	−13
133	M	123	−10	122	22	−11
135	F	120	−15	107	29	−28
135	F	118	−17	109	29	−26
144	F	144	0	129	30	−15
172	M	165	− 7	152	23	−20
198	M	203	+ 5	174	23	−24

a. Marked, wild poults of M. g. osceola from Glades County, Florida.
b. Knoder (1959), based on captive turkeys of a semiwild strain of M. g. silvestris.
c. Healy and Nenno (1980), based on captive human-imprinted wild M. g. silvestris.

ture. Thus, many wild-living turkeys are probably older than captive turkeys of any given feather size. This, in addition to smaller body size in M. g. osceola, probably contributed to the discrepancies revealed in table 2.2.

General Plumage and Molts

At one stage or another, the turkey has down feathers, semiplumes (especially in the abdominal region), bristles (especially on the head and neck), and contour feathers (almost completely covering the body). It does not have powder down or a brood patch, and we were unable to find feathers that can be considered filoplumes. The turkey has a well-developed preen gland and spends considerable time tending its plumage, which is not waterproof.

The general molting sequence of M. g. osceola is similar to M. g. silvestris. At hatching, the poult is covered with down and undergoes a gradual and complete molt of the down during the postnatal (prejuvenal) molt. This is followed by a nearly complete molt of the juvenal plumage during the postjuvenal (first prebasic) molt, and a partial replacement (prealternate molt) of its late summer (first basic) plumage before it acquires its first winter plumage. After that, there is an annual (prebasic) molt that renews the adult (basic) plumage (fig. 2.1). The flying ability of turkeys is not impaired by molting.

Plumage at the Time of Hatching—The newly hatched poult is covered with wet down held hairlike in thin sheaths

2.2 The egg tooth remains on the tip of the upper mandible of the poult for two or three days after hatching.

matted against the pinkish skin. The egg tooth is prominent (fig. 2.2). As the down dries, the sheaths are shed, and within about six hours the down becomes fluffy. The only bare areas are the yellowish flesh-colored bill, tarsi, and feet.

The plumage color pattern is mottled whitish-yellow and whitish-tan over much of the body. The crown is brown with a mid-dorsal strip of varying width from the snood to the middle back. Underwings are dirty white with dark mottling. Primaries 1 through 7 and secondaries 3 through 13 are in juvenal blood sheaths that are tipped with natal down. Juvenal rectrices are not present at this time. During the first day, the white tips of some of the primaries and secondaries begin to erupt from their sheaths.

Postnatal Molt and Acquisition of Juvenal Plumage—The postnatal (prejuvenal) molt begins before hatching, as evidenced by the tufts of down feathers attached to the sheath tips of the incoming primaries and secondaries at the time of hatching. By four days (fig. 2.3), the first seven juvenal primaries are 25–40 mm long, the longer being the more proximal, with sheaths making up about one-half their length. Secondaries 3 through 13 are erupting from sheaths. The major primary and secondary coverts are conspicuous, protruding up to 10 mm from their sheaths. Three of the four alula feathers are beginning to erupt, the longest being about 1 cm. The rest of the skin is covered with down. No juvenal rectrices have emerged by this time, but there are 12 in the down stage. Leg, foot, and bill colors have darkened slightly and have lost their yellowish tinge. The egg tooth has been shed by this time.

The variation in plumage development within the same brood during the first few days after leaving the nest is due to the difference in age among the poults. The interval between the hatching of the first and last eggs is more than one day.

By 10 or 11 days of age, 8 primaries are protruding beyond

2.3 Wing of a four-day-old turkey poult.

their sheaths, and number 9 is emerging in its sheath. Primaries are 35–50 mm long, the longer (and older) being the more proximal. Thirteen secondaries (3–14) have by now erupted beyond their sheaths and measure 12–48 mm, the longer being numbers 3 through 6 and the smallest being number 14. Secondary 15 is in a small blood sheath; 16 through 19 cannot be seen. Secondaries 1 and 2 are not present at this time. A definite gap can be seen in the wing where these secondaries will later emerge. The number 2 greater upper secondary covert is already conspicuous. The primary coverts are stationed between the primaries in such a way that each lies distal to its corresponding primary. The greater upper secondary coverts are squarely on top of their corresponding secondaries. The first eight pairs of rectrices have erupted from their sheaths and pair eight is in blood sheaths. The other rectrices are of the down stage. Feathers of the humeral tract (tertials) are developing rapidly; some have broken their sheaths by this time. Leg, foot, and bill color have not changed since about three days of age. Poults can fly at 10 days but they will not roost in trees for about four more days (Barwick et al. 1971).

Around the ninth or tenth day, the first pinfeathers are seen on the body and legs and in the femoral tract, then in the major (first rank) upper tail coverts, and finally in a thin line running the length of the lateral breast area. By the eleventh day, a few pinfeathers are coming in on the back.

Feather development in two female 23-day-old siblings was remarkably uniform. Primaries 1 and 2 were fully grown, number 3 was just reaching full size (but still had a blood sheath at the base), and numbers 4 through 9 were growing with blood sheaths. Number 10 had not yet emerged. Primary coverts 1 through 7 were fully grown, number 8 was nearly grown, and 9 was breaking out of its sheath (and slightly larger than primary 9). Primary covert 10 was not found in one of the specimens but was breaking the tip of its sheath in the other. Secondaries 3 and 4 were fully grown, and 5 through 18 were growing in, in that order—number 18 was just breaking the tip of its sheath, with a down feather still on the tip. Number 19 was in a small down-tipped sheath without noticeable blood at the base. Greater upper secondary coverts 2 through 14 were fully grown, and number 1 and 15 were nearly grown. Sixteen through 19 were in blood sheaths and growing. The lesser ranks of upper wing coverts (the feathers of the dorsal wing) were almost grown and all apparently had begun at nearly the same time. The feathers of the dorsal propatagium were about one-half grown. The ventral propatagium had only a small amount of down.

The lesser rank of feathers immediately posterior to the primary coverts was mostly in the down stage except for the two most proximal which were about one-half grown, and the two or three distal to them that were in closed blood sheaths.

In the same 23-day-old female specimens, under wing primary coverts 1 and 2 were breaking their sheaths, in that order. Numbers 3 through 6 were in blood sheaths; 7 and those distal to it were in the down stage. Secondary under wing coverts 1 through 8 were growing well beyond their sheaths. The covert for secondary number 1 was smaller and newer than those adjacent to it. Covert number 2 was as large as number three. It had not been delayed (by waiting on its corresponding covert) as the greater upper wing coverts had been. Secondary under wing coverts 9 through 19 were still of the down stage.

The four feathers of the alula had come in from proximal to distal. Numbers 1 and 2 were fully grown while numbers 3 and 4 were almost grown. Their coverts were nearly grown.

In one male and one female 28-day-old siblings examined, the tenth primaries of both specimens were about 5 mm long, in sheaths; and secondaries number 2 and 1 were coming in, in that order. Primaries 3 through 6 were fully grown and numbers 7 through at least 16 were coming in, in that order. The tails had nine pairs of rectrices with the central pair being recently shed in both specimens. By this age, poults are strong flyers and have been roosting in trees for about two weeks (Barwick et al. 1971).

Postjuvenal Molt and Acquisition of First Winter Plumage—The postjuvenal (first prebasic) molt begins in the fourth week when the central pair of rectrices is dropped, as in *M. g. silvestris*, and ends in about the thirty-second week in most males when postjuvenal primary number 9 reaches full size. Females finish this molt about three weeks earlier than males. Three conditions exist with respect to the molting of primaries 9 and 10. Some specimens molt both of these primaries during the postjuvenal molt while others molt only one and yet others molt neither. This will be discussed more fully later. In male specimens that do not molt primary number 9, the wing is fully grown in about 29 weeks. In such cases, juvenal primaries 9 and 10 are both retained in the first winter plumage. When primary number 10 is molted, the wing of the young male is not complete until soon after the thirty-fifth week, when primary 10 reaches full size. Most of the juvenile population will have its complete first winter plumage by early December, 29 to 32 weeks after hatching.

The first juvenal primary drops in the sixth week as in *M. g. silvestris*. Molting of the primaries proceeds in an orderly and consistent pattern permitting the age of fall juveniles to be determined from measurements of ingrowing first winter primaries with error of no more than about five days. The measurements by Healy and Nenno (1980) are not accurate for *M. g. osceola* for reasons previously discussed.

Data from known-age *M. g. osceola* specimens indicate that primary number 1 is shed in the sixth week, number 3 in the seventh week, and number 4 in the eighth week by both sexes. Primary number 5 and secondary number 8 are shed at 10 or 11 weeks. Four primaries are usually in active growth at the same time with the fourth emerging in sheath about the same time the first of the active group reaches full length.

Five female specimens of 18 weeks had just dropped primary 8. Most males were 19 weeks old before shedding number 8. Females molt their primaries nearly a week ahead of their male siblings after about the fourteenth week. In a marked male specimen of known age, primary number 9 was molted in the twenty-fifth week and in another male specimen, primary 10 was molted in the twenty-eighth week.

There is considerable individual variation in the timing and order of the tail molt with as much as four weeks difference in the age at which corresponding juvenile tail feathers are shed. The central pair is usually molted first with the process spreading "centrifugally" (from inside to out), usually in sequence. The second pair is followed by the third and so on until by the eighth week most specimens have molted all but the two or three outer pairs (fig. 2.4). By the eleventh week, two of the remaining pairs have been dropped in most specimens and the major upper tail coverts are at this time being replaced, centrifugally, as were the rectrices. By the fifteenth week the outer pair of rectrices is being replaced.

Atypical molting in the tail includes specimens with the central pair and the outermost pair still juvenal after the others have been shed, specimens with one side of the tail far ahead of the other, and examples of several adjacent rectrices falling at the same time. In all immature specimens, however, tail molt began somewhere toward the middle of the tail and finished somewhere near the outer edges.

After about fourteen weeks, no juvenal tail feathers remain. It is at this time that the central pair of postjuvenal rectrices is shed, initiating the third molt that Leopold (1943) called the "first winter molt". In the terminology of Humphrey and Parks (1959) it should be called the prealternate molt, and the plumage that is commonly called "first winter" is the alternate plumage. This molt is only partial and does

2.4 An eight-week-old poult with two pairs of juvenal outer rectrices.

not occur again in the life of the bird. The Coturnix quail (*Coturnix coturnix*) has a similar molt (Lyon 1962).

The shedding of the central pair of postjuvenal rectrices is followed by the adjacent pair within a few days, again centrifugally. This produces a temporary notch in the spread tail. The shedding of rectrices during the prealternate molt of the tail may stop at this point or it may continue. It involves three pairs of rectrices in the majority of Florida specimens and commonly proceeds until four central pairs are replaced. Occasionally, more rectrices, up to and including all nine pairs, will be replaced. When the new central rectrices are fully grown, the characteristic extended middle tail of the winter juvenile is seen (fig. 2.5). Both sexes have extended

Physical Characteristics

2.5 Extended central tail feathers of a young gobbler in first winter plumage.

central tail feathers in their first winter, but the trait is much more pronounced in the young male. The growth of the first winter tail is complete in most specimens between the twenty-second and twenty-seventh weeks, depending on how many middle rectrices are molted. If only three central pairs are replaced—the most frequent condition—the tail is fully grown by about the twenty-second week, or by mid-October in most individuals.

Comparisons among preserved specimens of various age reveal that the brown terminal edge of the rectrices is paler in the juvenal plumage than in the new first winter or the adult plumage. This is especially noticeable after the new extended tail feathers are in place in the winter juvenile at which time these feather generations can be seen side by side. Comparisons among preserved specimens of various age reveal that the paler coloration of the tip of the postjuvenal tail is not caused by fading.

The first caruncles of the neck, below the dewlap, begin to enlarge noticeably and in males by the tenth week, and, by the eleventh week, males begin to show less feathering of the head and neck than the hens. These secondary sexual characteristics will continue to become more pronounced for about one year. The head of the female remains essentially feathered at 11 weeks and will continue throughout life to be more heavily feathered than the male's (fig. 2.6). The heads and necks of female *M. g. osceola* seem to have more feathering than *M. g. silvestris*, even in adults. By 11 to 13 weeks, there is a pink tinge of color on the side of the male's head. While hens sometimes will have pink coloration in the larger throat caruncles, neither adult nor juvenile hens have pink skin on the side of the head.

By the end of the eleventh week, the back is in a mixture of juvenal and postjuvenal feathers and is molting heavily. The advanced maturity of some of the new plumage suggests that the postjuvenal back molt began in the middle back region. The breast still holds more juvenal than postjuvenal feathers but molt is very active there at this time, proceeding dorsally and ventrally from the lateral breast area. The neck has a conspicuous lateral streak of juvenal feathers (fig. 2.7).

About one-half of the juvenal feathers of the lower leg have molted by the eleventh week, beginning on the anterior (leading) edge near the intertarsal joint and proceeding around and up the leg. The upper leg (thigh) begins molting later than the lower leg.

The period from 14 to 17 weeks is especially eventful. This age is reached in September by most Florida turkeys. The last of the juvenal rectrices have recently been shed and

2.6 Sexual differences in the feathering of the head and upper neck of turkey poults are evident by 12 weeks of age and become more pronounced for about a year. The hen (upper) and gobbler (lower) are the same age, in midsummer.

the tail is growing rapidly. Primary number 7 sheds around 14 weeks and primaries 1 through 3 (or 4) are by now fully grown. Secondaries 3 through about 8 have reached their full length, 9 through 11 are still growing, and 12 through 15 are still of the juvenal feather generation. This is the time when the beard begins to emerge from the breast skin of the young gobbler and the greater upper secondary coverts 2 and 1 are shed. Molt is very active all over the young turkey at this time. The most conspicuous remaining juvenal feathers are in the upper neck and mid-breast areas. The juvenal feathers of the rump, including the lesser ranks of upper tail coverts, have been replaced and the new feathers are growing. The mixture of postjuvenal and first-winter (alternate) plumage is becoming conspicuous on the breast. The head remains mostly in juvenal plumage.

2.7 A female poult in midsummer showing mixed juvenal and postjuvenal plumage. The postjuvenal plumage will be mostly replaced in the next molt which occurs in late summer and early fall.

Greater upper secondary covert number 1, the last in the series to be replaced, is shed about the sixteenth week, somewhat ahead of its secondary, and is fully grown by about the twentieth week. The last of the juvenal under tail coverts are dropped by the twenty-first week. The four feathers of the first winter alula series are fully grown by the twenty-fifth week. In the underwing plumage, the major rank of primary coverts is molted from proximal to distal by about the thirty-third week. The under secondary coverts and most of the other underwing feathers seem to molt almost simultaneously in each series and are completely replaced by the thirty-third week. Two known-age 19-week-old hens exam-

Physical Characteristics

ined alive in mid-October had molted more than one-half of their juvenal plumage, but many juvenal feathers were still scattered across their bodies with the greatest concentration of juvenal plumage in the midbreast area. Little or no juvenal plumage remains in the body area after 21 weeks.

The beard of the young male, which typically emerges from the skin in the upper breast area between the sixteenth and twentieth weeks, is at first only a cornified epidermal protuberance. It reaches about 3 mm in length before beard filaments begin to emerge from its tip. By the time it is 40 mm long, it is about 10 mm wide—a typical size in fall specimens. These first beard filaments are usually translucent and amber colored.

First Winter Plumage—The first winter (alternate) plumage of the juvenile turkey resembles the basic plumage of the adult. The breast feathers of the young male are not as lustrous as the adult gobbler's, and many juveniles of both sexes retain one or sometimes two distal juvenal primaries during the first winter whereas adults do not. The more striking differences are the extended central tail feathers previously discussed (fig. 2.5) and the distinctive configuration of the greater upper secondary coverts of the juvenile, which will be discussed shortly. The prealternate molt involves a large part of the plumage, but its extent in *M. g. osceola* cannot be accurately determined from the material available. It is clear, however, that it involves primarily the body plumage and that many other parts of the plumage are not affected.

Many galliform birds retain the two most distal juvenal primaries (9 and 10) during the first winter and do not replace them until the first annual (prebasic) molt, when the bird is more than one year old. Petrides (1942) said that this is true of all races of the turkey but later made a correction with respect to the Florida subspecies by saying that Florida turkeys show a tendency to retain only the tenth primary (Petrides 1945). Later it was pointed out (Williams 1961) that retention of only the tenth juvenal primary is the normal condition in the Florida turkey and that a substantial proportion of Florida turkeys replace also the tenth during the postjuvenal molt. Replacement of primaries 9 and 10, when that occurs, is in numerical order.

In a sample of 125 Florida turkeys in alternate (first winter) plumage, the ratios of those retaining 2, 1, or 0 juvenal primaries were 9:90:26 (table 2.3). The small differences between the sexes were not significant (Chi-square = 0.5074, 2 df, $p = 0.05$). Thus retention of two distal juvenal primaries in the alternate plumage, which has been reported as the normal condition in northern populations of *M. g. silvestris*,

Table 2.3 Number and percentage of 125 juvenile turkeys in alternate (first winter) plumage that retained juvenal primaries, 9 and 10, 10 only, or neither 9 nor 10.

	Retained numbers 9 & 10	Retained only number 10	Retained neither number 9 nor 10
Males	2 (5%)	30 (73%)	9 (22%)
Females	7 (8%)	60 (71%)	17 (20%)
TOTAL	9 (7%)	90 (72%)	26 (21%)

is the least frequent of the three conditions in the Florida turkey. It would be useful to know how this ratio varies among turkeys in other populations. There is no reason to expect the trait to be closely, or at all, associated with subspecific designations. Retention of distal primaries is probably a genetically controlled clinal characteristic that varies from the lowest frequency in the extreme south to the highest frequency in the extreme north. Populations at intermediate latitudes probably exhibit a mixture of conditions between the two extremes. This may be true also of the bobwhite quail (*Colinus virginianus*), which usually retains its two most distal primaries in the first winter plumage in northern populations (Stoddard 1931) but molts them in southern Florida (Frye 1954).

The molting of both distal juvenal primaries is made especially obvious in the male turkey because of his associated immature secondary sexual characteristics, but it is not as obvious in the young hen. Until the juvenal primary molt is more carefully studied throughout the range of the wild turkey, biologists that use distal juvenal primaries to indicate the age class of turkeys may be erroneously classifying juvenile hens as adults. That error can be avoided, however, by using the greater upper secondary covert method (Williams 1961) to assign hens to age classes.

Since the more distal primaries are not replaced until near the end of the first basic molt, specimens with juvenal distal primaries can be distinguished from older or younger specimens until about 1½ years old. In 1½-year-old birds, the distal juvenal primary will be faded and active primary replacement will be evident in the proximal part of the wing. Specimens with faded adult type distal primaries in late summer or fall are at least 2½ years old. Thus specimens trapped in early fall can be placed in three separate age classes based on plumage characteristics: (1) juvenile, (2) 1½ years, and (3) at least 2½ years old. Any error would be proportional to the frequency of the complete primary molt in juveniles. North of Florida, where the frequency of complete primary replacement in the first prebasic plumage may approach zero, late summer and early fall specimens should be separable into three age classes without substantial error.

Many fall specimens appear to be retaining juvenal primaries 9 and 10 if their first prebasic molt is not complete in the wing at the time they are examined. This condition is indicated by the incomplete growth of primaries seven and eight.

In any series of feathers that is acquired sequentially by turkey poults during the rapid growth period of summer, there is an age-dependent size, color, and shape gradient from small, dull brown, and pointed in early acquired feathers, to large, lustrous, and blunt in later acquired feathers. The earlier acquired body feathers of the first winter plumage (feathers that come in following the prealternate molt) and all feathers acquired earlier and held during the first winter, have a distinctively immature appearance. The earlier they were acquired, the more immature their appearance will be. The greater upper secondary covert series provides a good example of this.

Many gallinaceous birds retain their juvenal greater upper secondary coverts during the first winter, but the turkey replaces the juvenal generation of these feathers during its first prebasic molt. Secondary covert number 3 is shed first, followed by number 4 and the others in the series in the proximal direction, each covert shedding several days before its corresponding secondary. It is not until around the fifteenth week that coverts 2 and 1 are shed, in that order, and the replacement feathers do not reach full size until about the twentieth week. The delayed molt of coverts 1 and 2 and the sequentially larger size of numbers 3 through 8 create the characteristic covert patch configuration of the juvenile (fig. 2.8a) that can usually be detected in living turkeys at a distance (fig 2.8b). No difference between *silvestris* and *osceola* has been found with respect to this part of the molt, and it almost certainly holds for other wild turkey populations as well. The newer feathers tend to resemble in color and size the general plumage state as of the time they are acquired.

There is a late summer stage, near the end of August, when the covert patch of the juvenile resembles the adult type due to incomplete growth of the recently molted rank of lesser coverts immediately dorsal to the greater upper secondary coverts. The lesser coverts will cover the bases of the greater upper secondary coverts after a few weeks growth and produce the typical juvenile shape of the covert patch.

A few specimens of *M. g. osceola* replace all greater upper secondary coverts before the first winter.

The replacement of the body plumage during the prealternate molt is an adaptation of the turkey that is necessary to provide adequate covering and insulation for a bird's body

2.8A Wing of a juvenile male in first winter plumage, showing two distal juvenal primaries and the typical configuration of the juvenal greater upper secondary wing coverts.

that has increased very greatly in surface area since the first juvenal feathers were acquired. The central tail feathers, which are also replaced, were the first in the series to be acquired and would not be large enough for flight by a winter-sized turkey; they are therefore replaced. Although most of the juvenal plumage is replaced during the prealternate molt, a few traces usually remain in the winter plumage, most no-

Physical Characteristics

2.8B Adult (foreground) and juvenile hens. Arrows point to the greater upper secondary covert patch which is broader and shinier in the adult.

ticeably on the breast. These are probably the newer and larger feathers of that generation and fit the larger body size adequately.

Annual Molt—In both sexes there is a single prebasic molt involving the entire plumage. Leopold (1943) tentatively reported a prenuptial molt in the turkey, which has been quoted widely in the literature; but it has been found that no such molt takes place in the turkey (Williams and McGuire 1971) although it is said to occur widely in other gallinaceous birds. Although beardless adult gobblers are occasionally seen, the beard is not shed during molt. Beardless specimens have scars where the beard normally emerges from the breast which suggests that the beards were lost by accident.

The timing of the annual molt is partly dependent upon the mating status of the individual in question. Juvenile male *M. g. osceola* are seldom seen strutting. They probably do not mate and are, as a group, the first to initiate the annual molt, which they begin by shedding primary number 1 in

March or early April while the mating season is underway for the adult males and hens. In more than 90 juvenile gobblers examined during February, only one had begun the annual molt as indicated by a molted primary number 1, but this was only in one wing and could have been due to an accident in which the feather was pulled.

When a new primary number 1 has grown to about 40 mm, number 2 is shed and a few days later the greater upper secondary coverts begin to molt, starting with number 3. The vacant space created by recently shed coverts 3 and 4 is detectable in living turkeys at a distance. It has been confirmed repeatedly from baited blinds that many juvenile gobblers reach this stage by mid-April, well in advance of other turkeys in the population. Molt was underway in the lower legs, upper legs, and middle back in 8 juvenile male specimens examined in April.

Evidence of recently shed greater upper secondary coverts has been seen in a few adult males ($N = 10$) in mid-May indicating that some of them also begin molting while mating is still in progress in the population. Although adult gobblers sometimes strut and gobble after beginning to molt these coverts, we do not know whether the birds were still copulating. Raitt and Ohmart (1966) found that molting was "concurrent" with gonadal regression in the gambel quail (*Lophortyx gambelii*) but found a few exceptions, which, they said, indicated that at least a small number of the quail were molting and mating simultaneously.

As previously described, the annual molt begins with the shedding of primary number one. Leopold (1943) reported that in *M. g. silvestris* all the primary coverts are shed before their corresponding primaries. In our *M. g. osceola* specimens, the molt in this feather series began with the coverts shedding after the corresponding primaries had shed. In the middle of the molt, the shedding of primaries and their coverts was more or less synchronous; but by the end of the molt of this series, the coverts were being shed ahead of their corresponding primaries.

By mid-May, most of the one-year-old males (juveniles of the previous winter) have shed primaries 1 through 5, and some of the older adult males have shed primaries 1 through 2 or 3. (Many of the hens are still nesting in May and are not yet molting.) The primaries and their coverts continue to molt in the same proximal-distal direction as in the postjuvenal molt. All 10 primaries are replaced during the annual molt.

The Florida turkey has 19 secondaries. Proceeding proximally from number 11, each secondary is substantially smaller and there is a distinct color gradient in the series after number 10 or 11. Secondaries 12 through 19 are similar in color and pattern, almost lacking the white bars that are characteristic of the primaries and the more distal secondaries. Number 19 is not much longer than its greater upper covert. Leopold (1943) reported only 16 secondaries for the eastern turkey. It is possible that he simply did not consider the last three feathers of the series to be secondaries because of their very small size.

The first secondary to shed is usually number 3. This happens about the time the second or third primary is shed but there is so much variation in the molt of the secondaries that it can be discussed only in broad terms. The next secondary to molt is usually the fourth, after which the molt skips over secondaries 6 through 11 to secondary 13 or 14 and proceeds in the distal-proximal direction. While molt is active in that region, number 12 is molted in many but not all specimens. Numbers 5 and 6 are molted (usually in that order) about the same time as numbers 15 and 16 (also in that order). Thus at this stage, molt is active in distal parts of the secondary series with little or no molting in secondaries 6 (or 7) through 11 (or 12). Secondaries 2 and 1 are replaced next, and those in the middle of the wing, numbers 6 or 7 through 11 or 12, are replaced last. Specimens that completely violated this pattern were one adult gobbler which, in September, was replacing simultaneously numbers 2, 10, 14, and 18 (and no others) and an adult hen that had replaced numbers 5 through 9, in that order, and number 12 (and no others). There was more variability among the adult hens ($N = 12$) examined than among the adult gobblers ($N = 9$).

Typical replacement of the greater upper secondary coverts during the annual molt is similar to the postjuvenal replacement pattern: beginning with number 3, proceeding proximally, and ending with numbers 2 and 1, in that order. But there is some irregularity with respect to whether the covert sheds before or after its corresponding secondary. These coverts are usually replaced about the same time as the corresponding secondaries. A hen that was about one year old in June had molted greater upper secondary covert 4 in both wings but no other coverts or secondaries. We have too few data to deal with this at greater length.

The ranks of lesser primary and lesser secondary coverts on the dorsal part of the wing are not molted until the greater upper primary and greater upper secondary converts have been mostly replaced. The second rank of lesser coverts is the first to molt. These are followed by the first and third ranks, and so on, in such a pattern that adjacent ranks do not molt simultaneously. This tends to maintain a thin, almost continuous covering of feathers on the skin while the molt is in progress. Many of the lesser coverts in a given rank are molted about the same time rather than in the proximal-distal sequence of the major coverts. The molting pattern seen in the lesser coverts suggests that the lesser coverts function as a skin covering rather than in flight.

The four large feathers of the alula are replaced from proximal to distal. Number 1 reaches full size before number 4 is molted. The first alula feather is not shed until some time after the first secondary. The fourth and last alula feather is shed about the time the primary number 9 or 10 is shed.

The feathers of the underwing surface are among the last to be molted. The first to be shed are in the propatagium, followed by some of the lesser underwing coverts. The largest primary underwing coverts are shed ahead of the secondary coverts, but both of these series of large underwing feathers are shed only after the smaller underwing feathers are. Many of the underwing feathers are shed simultaneously. It appears that the feathering of the underwing surface has minimal function since this is the least feathered part of the plumaged skin and is the only region where the molting pattern has not evolved in a way to prevent temporary nakedness during the annual molt.

The breast does not begin to molt until the annual molt is well along in other parts of the plumage. It reaches a peak of activity in the adult male about the time that primaries 7 and 8 are shed in August. The back, which began molting about the time the second or third primary was shed, also reaches the height of activity about this time. Molting begins across the midback and spreads anteriorly and posteriorly at the same time. In both the breast and back, the molting pattern is distributed evenly throughout each tract in a pattern that prevents partial nakedness and loss of insulation on any part of the body surface during the molt.

The first rank of upper tail coverts molt centrifugally (more or less) early during the annual molt and is completely replaced by the time primary number 8 is shed, nearly two months before the molt is completed. The lesser upper tail coverts molt later without a strong centrifugal pattern.

The crural tract (the lower leg) begins to molt a few days after the first primary is shed and reaches a height of activity about the time the third or fourth primary falls. These feathers are completely replaced by the time new primary wing feather number 5 reaches full size.

The head and upper neck are only sparsely feathered with bristles and semibristles. There are more of these in the head and neck of a juvenile of either sex than in the adult. The male has a few unspecialized contour feathers in the head region that form a thin line tapering anteriorly up the back of the neck. These small feathers are among the last to be replaced in the annual molt. The female also has numerous small, contour feathers up the neck to, and including the crown, giving her head a more feathered appearance than the male's (fig. 2.6).

The bristles and semibristles of the head and upper neck appear to be molted during a relatively short period in summer. June and July specimens show no evidence of head molt, but in late September specimens head plumage has been replaced.

The small feathers surrounding the ear opening evidently are molted very gradually. We have found no specimens showing evidence of substantial ear molting at any one time. In an adult male examined in August, the feathers of the ear opening had been partially replaced before the new facial bristles had appeared. Our material was not adequate to be very conclusive about molting in the head region.

The majority of Florida turkeys have nine pairs of rectrices; a very few have 10 or only 8. Leopold (1943) reported an occasional unmatched central rectrix, which resulted in a total of 19 feathers (9½ pairs) in *M. g. silvestris*; and we have examined a specimen from southern Alabama (*M. g. silvestris* near the intergrade zone with *M. g. osceola*) that had 10 pairs. Nine and one-half pairs have not been reported in *M. g. osceola*.

The rectrices of 9 adult males and 12 adult females in annual molt were examined. The adult pattern was not as consistent from bird to bird, and it differed from the juvenile molt by proceeding in a centripetal (inward) rather than centrifugal (outward) direction. This is similar to the situation in *M. g. silvestris* (Leopold 1943). The rectrices were shed with strong bilateral symmetry although both members of a pair rarely fell out on the same day.

In the adult gobbler, the first rectrices to drop are usually 8, 7, and 6, in that order, followed later by 9, and then by 5, 4, 3, 2, and 1, in that order (fig. 2.9A–2.9C). There is a pause between the molting of the first group (8, 7, and 6) before the shedding of number 9 and another pause before the central five pairs (5 through 1) are molted. The tail does not begin to molt until about the time that primary number 6 or 7 is shed, which is usually in late June or July for most males and late July or August for many females.

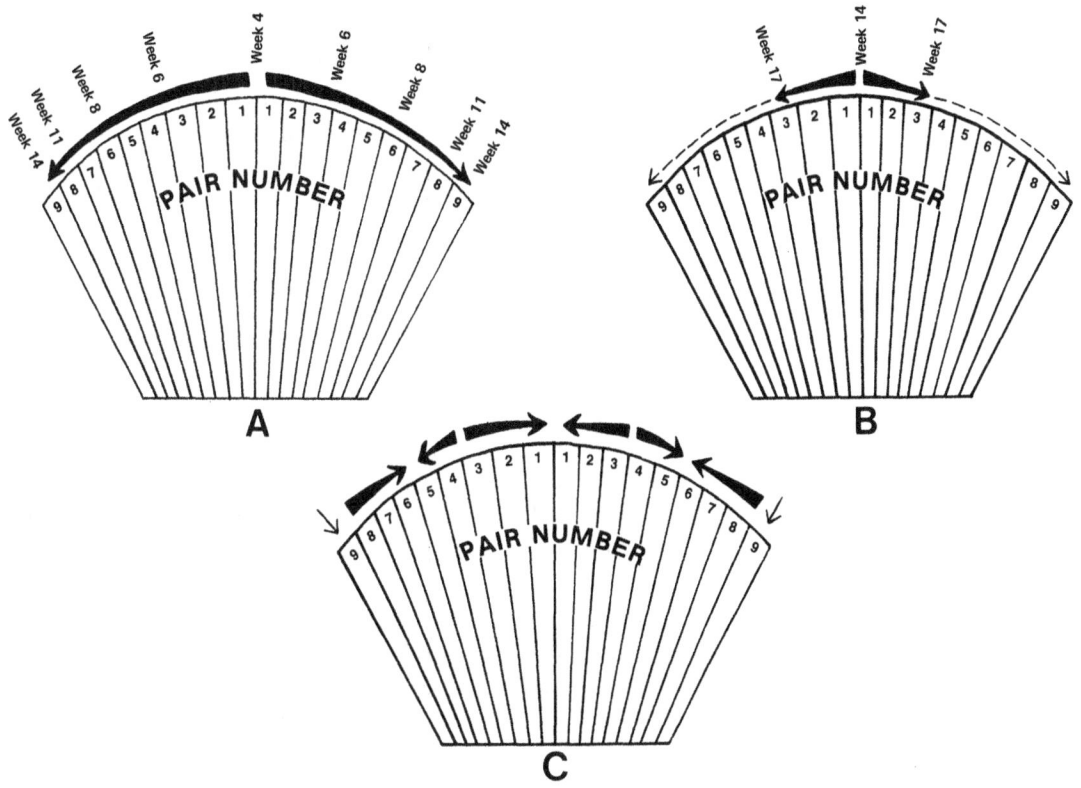

2.9A The typical juvenal pattern. The molt begins with the middle pair (number 1) in the fourth week.

2.9B The typical juvenal pattern of molting the central rectrices during the prealternate molt.

2.9C The most common annula molting pattern seen in adults begins with the shedding of rectrices eight, seven and six, followed by nine, four, and five, and finally three, two, and one, in that order.

The tail molt of the hen does not as often begin with pair number 8 as it does in the gobbler. Of the 12 hen specimens examined in active annual molt, one had first shed pairs 1 through 5 and 9 almost simultaneously; another had first shed number 3; and three other specimens had molted the middle pair before molting pairs 7 or 8. In general, hens dropped more rectrices more nearly simultaneously than gobblers did and exhibited greater variability in the tail molting pattern.

In a sample of 62 adult turkeys (17 hens, 45 gobblers) taken by hunters on three Florida wildlife management areas in mid-November through December, 42 percent of the gobblers had acquired their full basic plumage but only 24 percent of the hens had. The delayed molt by the hens is probably because late nesters (including those that nested more than once) did not begin to molt until after they had nested for the last time that season.

In examining more than 248 nests, we found no evidence that turkey hens begin to molt before the brood leaves the nest. If they did, there would be numerous shed feathers at the nest. In fact, the only shed feathers found in nests were a very few contour feathers and semiplumes from the breast area. This indicates that significant molting does not occur in the hen until after the incubating period. That delays the process at least four weeks after a hen's last clutch is laid. Since early nesting hens begin laying in March and late nesters are still incubating as late as June, hens may begin the annual molt any time between May (early successful nesters and those that do not nest) and July (renesters). The latest nesting hens would be almost two months behind the adult gobblers when beginning to molt.

Any advantages of renewing the plumage before winter should apply to both sexes. Since many late-nesting hens do not begin to molt until a month or more after the adult males, they could not be expected to follow the same pattern and timing and still acquire their plumage before winter. This is borne out by our observations that molting of hens does not follow the same timing or the same pattern as the molting of gobblers.

The variation in the tail molt among hens may be dependent on the different times that this molt is initiated (which is determined by the time the hen finishes nesting) with the late-nesting hens condensing the pattern by molting more feathers almost simultaneously.

At least some of the time lag between the sexes is made up by the faster rate at which the hens grow their new plumage (possibly because their feathers are smaller). At the end of the postjuvenal (first prebasic) molt, juvenile females are molting ahead of the males by about three weeks, and it is plausible that adult females would also exhibit this faster pace.

There are known instances of accelerated late-season molt of the females of other bird species. Female gambel quail are said to begin molting later than the males and to make up for lost time by molting faster and finishing only slightly later (Raitt and Ohmart 1966). Late-hatched redhead (*Aythya americana*) ducklings of both sexes exhibit accelerated maturation rates in their primary wing feathers (Smart 1965).

The tail molting pattern in *M. g. silvestris* as described by Leopold (1943) is more systematic than in *M. g. osceola*. The Florida specimens do not correspond closely to Leopold's description except that they molt pair number 8 first. It would appear that one consequence of the briefer molting period available to *M. g. silvestris* in the short, northern summer would be less opportunity for variation among individuals.

A feather is often dropped on one side before the corresponding feather on the other side, and it is common to see a tail feather of the new generation nearly half grown before its counterpart on the other side of the tail is shed. This asymmetry is much more frequent in the tail than in the wings probably because some semblance of bilateral symmetry in the wings is necessary for satisfactory flight. When three or four distal primaries are plucked from each wing, a penned turkey is still able to fly, but when the same feathers are plucked (or cut) on one wing only, the bird will move in a circle and be unable to achieve directional flight. A wild turkey would presumably have a similar problem if the molt were not approximately bilateral. We have observed turkeys that were able to fly well after all their tail feathers had been pulled by accident when they were trapped. They were unable to land on the ground without flipping over head first, however. Thus, bilateral symmetry appears to be more important in the wings than the tail for flight.

Fighting, which occurs immediately before and during the mating season, would damage the fragile blood sheaths of ingrowing feathers and deform the new feathers. It may be that molting is delayed until summer in the male for that reason and in the female for a different reason. In the female the delay may be an adaptation to avoid an undue demand on energy resources while hens cannot feed regularly (during continuous incubating behavior).

Leopold (1943) estimated that the annual molt in Missouri turkeys he studied took about four months to complete. Although we have not examined the same turkey specimens at the start and end of their molt, the evidence suggests that the prebasic molting period for *M. g. osceola* is longer, perhaps as long as five or six months for individuals and at least nine months for the population. Since the nine adult gobbler summer specimens we examined were well into the annual molt by early June, and 58 percent of the sample of adult males from hunting areas previously mentioned had not completed their molt by mid-November, it would appear that June through November, a period of six months, is the major period of molt for most adult males. (It is possible that individuals molt in much less time, which needs to be checked by retrapping the same birds in June and October or November). In the population as a whole, however, Florida turkeys molt from March (one-year-old gobblers) through December (hens and adult gobblers)—a period of about nine months.

The longer molting period in Florida than in Missouri is probably a climatic adaptation. A shorter molting period northward in the same species is certainly not unprecedented in birds. Mewaldt and King (1978) showed a clear-cut latitudinal effect in white-crowned sparrows (*Zonotrichia leucophrys*), and there are other examples. In Florida, turkeys have a longer warm season, with an abundant summer and fall food supply, and they apparently take advantage of it by having a prolonged molting period. This may be of practical importance in applying age determination methods to turkeys in other latitudes.

The opportunity to molt at a more leisurely pace relieves turkeys in the south of some of the demand for especially rich energy resources and allows the population to channel a larger part of its resources into other activities and physical processes. This could be a determinant of population size and species success at different latitudes, particularly if the requirements of the species farther north cannot be satisfied adaptively. In this regard, it is of interest to note that turkey population densities in Florida, where soils are sandy and relatively poor in plant nutrients, are at least as dense as they are on much richer soils elsewhere.

Molting Differences Among Populations

The more noticeable molting differences between M. g. osceola and M. g. silvestris are that the Florida turkey usually molts the ninth and sometimes also the tenth distal juvenal primary during the prealternate molt while many eastern populations retain both 9 and 10. There is probably a zone between typical M. g. silvestris and M. g. osceola where the condition is intermediate. M. g. osceola also has a more extensive prealternate molt of the rectrices, and the annual molt of these feathers exhibits a more variable pattern than M. g. silvestris. The wing and tail molting differences and their variability in M. g. osceola are probably related to the longer molting period available in Florida, which permits time for more juvenal feathers to be replaced during the prealternate molt. The longer period would not demand as tight a molting pattern. Thus, as might be expected, the major differences between the Florida and eastern turkeys are dependent upon differences in climate. It would be further expected that a latitudinal gradient affecting the period of molt, and therefore its extent and tightness of pattern, exists throughout the natural range of the species.

In comparing the molting patterns of wild Missouri and domestic (M. g. gallopavo) turkeys, Leopold (1943) described a more extensive molt in the domestic turkey, particularly in the number of rectrices molted during the first prebasic molt and also reported less regularity of the tail molt in the domestic strain during the annual (basic) molt. He noted that the domestic turkey regularly molts the ninth primary before acquiring its first winter plumage. These differences also exist, as we have found, between M. g. silvestris in Missouri and M. g. osceola in Florida.

Leopold (1943) described a juvenile wild specimen of M.

g. gallopavo from Mexico which had molted all its rectrices before the first winter, as Florida turkeys sometimes do, and had replaced all of its greater upper secondary coverts as well and, like 7.2 percent of Florida turkeys, had retained distal primaries 9 and 10 from the juvenal plumage. Thus, the wild Mexican specimen was exhibiting some of the differences that we would expect to find in the molting pattern of turkeys at lower latitudes; namely, a more extensive and more variable molt.

We question Leopold's (1943) belief that molting patterns that are at variance with *M. g. silvestris* from Missouri indicate interbreeding with domestic turkeys. A better argument can be made for a natural south-north gradient in the extent and variability of molting in turkeys. The domestic turkey has evidently retained some of the molting patterns it evolved at its place of origin in Mexico or the southwestern United States. The similarities between Mexican (including domestic) and Florida turkeys have probably come about through convergent adaptation in similar climates rather than close genetic affinities between *M. g. osceola* and *M. g. gallopavo*.

It is plausible that the tightness of the molting pattern described for Missouri turkeys by Leopold (1943) must be maintained by the forces of natural selection. When a tight pattern is not important, as in the Florida turkey (because of a warmer climate) or the domestic turkey (because of human care), the pattern will become "looser" and molting will be more variable and take longer, thereby lessening the physiological stress associated with more rigorous molting pattern requirements.

Indicators of Age and Sex Other Than Plumage

Droppings The shapes of turkey droppings (feces) sometimes indicate the sex of the individual that made them. This was pointed out by Bailey (1956) and has been confirmed in our work. Repeated observations at bait sites have indicated that most curled droppings are made by hens and those that are straight or J-shaped are made by gobblers (fig 2.10). Bailey (1956) did not know the age at which the characteristic dropping configuration first occurs and wondered whether dropping shape might be useful in determining sex of poults. Our field observations indicate that there is no clear and consistent difference between males and females in dropping shape or diameter until well after other secondary sexual characteristics have developed. Furthermore, dropping configuration is not infallible even in older birds except in the very typical

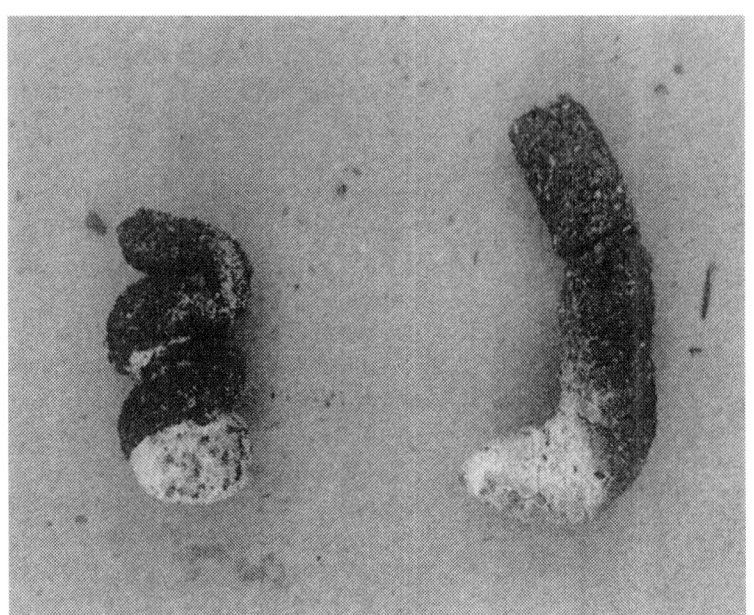

2.10 The characteristic shapes of hen and gobbler droppings. The nearly straight "j-shaped" dropping is the gobbler's.

examples. The degree of overlap in the intermediate configurations is especially frequent in younger turkeys. We think hens allow fecal matter to accumulate in the cloaca before evacuation and that the spiral effect is the result of packing of the small-diameter, tubular dropping. On the other hand, gobblers frequently evacuate directly through the cloaca from the large intestine without the feces accumulating and becoming coiled.

Beard and Spur Length

Kelly (1975) studied spurs and beards of known-age male specimens and concluded that spur length was a better age criterion than beard length but that a combination of spur length, beard length, and body weight was more accurate for estimating age than any single character. Our data on beard and spur length are not sufficient for analysis at this time.

Color of the Beard Tip

The first beard filaments to emerge in the young gobbler contain less dark pigment than the basal portion of the same filaments will have as the beard continues to grow. The increase in black pigmentation occurs rapidly after the beard is 3–4 cm long and that produces a terminal zone of translucent amber in the young male that will be evident until the tip wears off. Since the beard tip does not wear appreciably until it begins to drag on the ground while the bird feeds, and since that length is not attained until late in the second year of life, the amber beard tip is a useful character in distinguishing the age class of males well past the age that plumage characters can be used. Although the age at which the amber tip wears away has not been accurately determined, our preliminary data indicate that one-year-olds have beards about 100 mm long and that the beard grows about 130 cm (5 inches) per year thereafter. The beard does not begin to wear appreciably until it is about 250 mm (10 inches) long. Thus, adult gobblers having amber-tipped beards about 250 mm long (10 inches) are probably younger than otherwise identical specimens not having amber beard tips. The amber tip wears away during the third year of life. This has been described in a preliminary way (Williams 1981:24 and color figure facing p. 118).

Head and Neck Coloring and Feathering

A glimpse of the head and neck area is sufficient to distinguish grown male and female turkeys in the field. The neck and throat of the hen is partially feathered and the skin is gray; the neck and throat of the male are bare and the skin is reddish. The head of the hen is moderately feathered, including the back of the crown, and is grayish-blue; the head of the male is nearly bare, especially on the cheek, and is predominantly reddish with some white and blue. Even in fall these features can be used reliably to distinguish males from females (fig. 2.11–2.11B).

By 14 weeks of age, young males have pink coloration in the bare skin of the face and have nearly bare throats with prominent pink caruncles. A few adult hens have small pink caruncles and some may have only sparse head feathering, but they will not have enough pink in the face or bare enough necks to look like young males.

Color of the Tarsometatarsus

Writers have discussed the tarsometatarsus with respect to age, sex, and subspecies, but there is considerable misunderstanding about their color characteristics. Schorger (1966: 120) in a single paragraph, quoting from others on the subject, said that tarsus color varies with season and sex, that old scales are silvery, that there is a definite season for shedding scales, that leg scales of older turkeys are thick, rough, and horny, and that leg color continues to change as adult turkeys grow older. None of these statements is true.

In the present study, approximately 300 living or recently killed turkeys and 130 museum skins were examined. Additionally, 186 severed tarsi, mostly collected by hunters, were air-dried for varying lengths of time and examined.

Four specimens were examined alive and dissected im-

2.11 Head feathering and coloration differences by sex.

2.11A Adult gobbler.

mediately after death. One tarsus from each specimen was permitted to dry in an air-conditioned room, with no special treatment; the other tarsus from each was frozen and compared, after three months, with the air-dried tarsus of each pair and with tarsi from living turkeys. Each pair of frozen and air-dried tarsi was dissected and examined under a low-power microscope.

Five tarsi were permitted to age for about one year in a dry place, with occasional exposure to sunlight and to the outdoor atmospheric conditions in Florida. Eleven fresh tarsi were examined regularly while they were drying in the Florida air. Other tarsi that had been dried for varying periods of time were compared. The oldest had been preserved in the U.S. National Museum specimen cabinets for 86 years.

2.11B Adult hen.

Age, Sex, and Subspecies of Material Used

The ages of 75 live *M. g. osceola* poult specimens (from 0 to 124 days) were known (the poults were being radiotracked and examined in connection with another study or were hatched in an incubator). One hundred sixteen other live poults up to eight months old were aged by plumage criteria (Leopold 1943, Knoder 1959). Turkeys in first winter plumage were classified as juvenile by their upper secondary coverts (Williams 1961). Fifty-five living or recently killed juveniles and 30 living or recently killed adults were also examined. One banded male at least six years old and one hen at least five years old were examined. Other adult turkeys of known age were examined as follows: two years, six males and three females; three years, four males and four females; and four years, three males and two females. All adults of known age were *M. g. osceola*. Age-classes were determined for the 130 museum specimens by characteristics of distal primaries, greater upper secondary coverts, or leg spurs.

The sex of all whole specimens, except poults younger than four months, was determined by the black (male) or brown (female) tips of the breast feathers, by other obvious secondary sexual characteristics, or by dissection and inspection of the gonads. The sex of poults younger than about 14 weeks was not determined; but all, representing both sexes, had tarsi of similar color. When the same groups of marked poults were reexamined after secondary sexual characters had developed, both sexes were found to be about equally represented.

Specimens were assumed to represent the subspecies that occur in the geographic area where they were taken. Based on Aldrich and Duvall's (1955) geographic distribution, the following specimens were examined for each race: *M. g. osceola*, 364; intergrade between *M. g. osceola* and *M. g. silvestris*, 110; *M. g. silvestris*, 109; *M. g. intermedia*, 29; *M. g. merriami*, 3; *M. g. gallopavo* (or *M. g. mexicana*), 1. These specimens were from Florida; Alabama; South Carolina; Mississippi; Tennessee; Missouri; New York; West Virginia; Texas; Oklahoma; New Mexico; and Jalisco, Mexico.

Two adult female and two juvenile male domestic turkeys of a common barnyard mixture of predominantly "bronze" ancestry and a series of 12 captive specimens from crosses between this stock and wild *M. g. osceola* were also examined. Living and freshly killed turkeys and dried museum skins of both sexes and all age-classes were examined each month of the year.

Color Changes After Death

Preserved specimens of the tarsi of adults did not change markedly in color upon drying except where air spaces developed under the scales causing these areas to appear light brown or silver-colored. Dissection revealed that the red color, which is in a tissue layer immediately under the podotheca, was being masked by light refraction in the separated scales. The external color of four juvenile tarsi became paler after drying. Dissection revealed that the normally pinkish layer of tissue immediately under the leg scales had faded to a light orange.

Death, freezing, or refrigeration caused no immediate change in the color of tarsi; however, tarsi exposed to sunlight and to outdoor conditions developed a silvery cast caused by the physical breakdown of the outer surfaces of the scales. Dried museum specimens that had been kept up to 86 years in museum cabinets compared closely in color with fresher specimens.

Color Changes With Age of the Bird

The tarsi of newly hatched poults were pinkish-brown. Examination and dissection of the tarsi of poults between 0 and about 150 days old revealed a gradual darkening in external color caused by deposits of blackish and brownish pigments in the scales and a gradual reddening in the pigmented tissue layer under the scales.

The blackish and brownish pigments in the scales gradually diminished after the juveniles were about eight months old. Before this time, the underlying reddish color was partially masked, producing the typical dark tarsi of the juvenile turkey. The scales of the foot continued to exhibit considerably more dark pigment than the tarsi, even in older adults.

The leg scales of turkeys of both sexes contained some brownish and blackish pigmentation until about 10 months old but to a degree noticeably less than seen in younger turkeys. While the dark color was disappearing from the scales, the underlying color layer was becoming more reddish. The combined effect produced a more reddish and brighter-colored tarsus in turkeys one year old than in younger turkeys.

Further reddening of the tarsi and feet with age after one year varied considerably among individuals of *M. g. osceola*, even within the same brood. Few specimens had noticeable pigment in the scales (except in the toes) after one year, and the underlying reddish color was only slightly redder after one year. Variation beyond 1½ years is probably due to individual differences rather than to age.

Gradual color changes with increasing age were noted in all poults of *M. g. osceola* that were examined alive. (Live poults were not available for other subspecies, but the appearance of preserved older juveniles representing the other subspecies suggested that the process of color change is similar in all races.) Melanin in the leg and foot scales of young turkeys may add strength during early life when the scales are thin in the same way it is supposed to strengthen feathers (Averill 1923). The fact that the foot remains darker than the tarsus in adults would seem to support the idea that strength is a function of melanin because the foot experiences more contact with the substrate and low vegetation than does the tarsus and the scales of the foot would therefore be subject to more wear were it not for the heavier deposits of melanin.

Color Variation of the Tarsus Caused by Other Factors

No consistent differences in color were found between the sexes or among specimens examined at different seasons. There was no change of color soon after death, and fresh-frozen and refrigerated tarsi remained within the normal range of red shades observed in other specimens.

No subspecific difference in tarsus color of adults was evident, but the number of specimens of *M. g. merriami* and *M. g. gallopavo* was small. An inadequate number of juvenile *M. g. intermedia* and *M. g. silvestris* was available for comparison with young of *M. g. osceola*. The tarsi of juvenile turkeys from southern Florida were sometimes much darker than tarsi of juveniles from farther north in the same state. There is a tendency for the tarsi of turkeys in northeastern Florida (St. Johns, Flagler, and Volusia counties) to be whitish, even completely white in a few cases.

The tarsi of the four domestic birds examined were brownish-gray, and none of the 12 tarsi of specimens from crosses between domestic and Florida strains were as red as those of the wild type. However, all the hybrids were raised in pens and had some loose scale layers on the podothecal surface, which masked the underlying coloration. The loose surface layers on the podotheca of wild turkeys probably wear away smoothly from daily contact with vegetation, whereas conditions in captivity permit the dead layers of the scales to accumulate on the tarsi. Occasionally a wild turkey will exhibit heavy sloughing of the leg scale surfaces, but this is observed so infrequently that it is doubtful that it represents a true scale replacement process. Year-round examination of hundreds of tarsi has indicated that there is no single period of especially heavy wear or shedding. Evidently the surface of the scales wear away gradually as they grow. Spurs longer than 4 cm are extremely rare, even on older specimens. Wear probably causes the dead, cornified spur cap to become sharper with age.

Anomalies in Tarsus Color

Of the specimens examined, only two *M. g. osceola* completely lacked reddish pigment in their tarsometatarsi and were white. The plumage and other body parts of these specimens were colored normally in every respect.

Spur and Nail Color

Leg spurs and toenails varied in color from nearly white to black, with the darker shades predominating. Most spurs and nails were brownish-gray. Nail and spur color and shade of red in the tarsus seemed to vary independently. The nails and spurs of *M. g. osceola* appeared to be darker, on the average, than those of the other subspecies, but there was considerable overlap among the subspecies. Specimens from Missouri, New York, and West Virginia tended to have claws that were worn off on the tip and therefore shorter in length than others. This was evidently due to scratching in abrasive soils.

Summary of Tarsus and Foot Coloration

Usually the tarsometatarsi of adult wild turkeys are red. There is no marked variation in color because of race, sex, season, or age in adults. Dried museum specimens change color only slightly and remain red in general appearance. If the drying scales become separated from the underlying tissues or if weathering on the surface occurs, the underlying red color will be masked; but removal of separated or weathered scales reveals the normal reddish color underneath.

The red color of turkey tarsi is in a layer of tissue under the scales and is not caused by pigments in the scales themselves or by blood. The color is seen through the transparent scales of adults but is masked somewhat in juveniles, especially very young ones, by brownish and blackish pigments in the scales. The characteristic dull, dark color of juvenile tarsi results from the effect of a paler red layer under the scales that is partially obscured by dark pigments in the scales.

Anomalous Physical Characteristics

In the course of these studies, a number of unusual turkey specimens have been examined. Off-colored plumage has been the most frequently seen.

Plumage Coloration

A "smoke gray" plumage color mutant (fig. 2.12) has been described in both juvenile and first winter plumages (Williams 1964 and Williams 1970). Florida specimens are known from Baker, Clay, Bradford, Nassau, and Volusia counties. Similar specimens have been reported (in lit.) from Alabama, Georgia, South Carolina, Mississippi, Arkansas, and Virginia. The similarity among smoke gray specimens is striking. Specimens may appear almost white at a distance but in hand are seen to be grayish with faded dark markings. The eyes are dark. The general impression is that one or more of the metallic brown color components of the plumage is missing. The condition is much more frequently seen in hens than in gobblers, but a few smoke gray gobblers have been examined. Although these specimens have been found in most eastern states (including the subspecies M. g. *silvestris* and M. g. *osceola*), the condition has not been reported from the west. Two smoke gray hens were known to produce broods containing both smoke gray and normal colored poults and

2.12 Female smoke-gray color mutants from Baker County, Florida, about four months old.

smoke gray poults have been seen in broods without a smoke gray brood hen.

An erythristic adult hen was obtained from Sarasota County, Florida, in 1965 (Williams 1967). The feathers of the breast were chestnut-brownish red, tipped with light tawny. These same feathers in normal specimens are blackish brown, barred subterminally with black and terminally with light shades of tawny and buffy brown. Most of the hen's plumage was reddish. Most of the reddish feathers in this specimen were in parts of the plumage that are normally a lighter shade which suggests that the abnormal red color is caused by the addition of a red pigment rather than the mere unmasking of a normal red due to the loss of a darker, overlying one.

Erythrism of a more subtle type has been observed in a number of Florida specimens from Gadsden, Leon, Wakulla, Columbia, and Santa Rosa counties. Redness was most noticeable in the secondaries, and there was disarrangement of the color pattern in the secondaries as well.

There were turkeys with both red and white feathers in a population at Baldwin Bay, Florida (on the Duval-Nassau County line) in 1963 and 1964 from which were obtained representative feathers from a single specimen that had been shot by a hunter. Live specimens were seen there on occasion, but efforts to collect one were unsuccessful. Only gobblers were seen. The feathers obtained in 1963 represented a distinctly different expression of erythrism than the Sarasota County hen previously described. There was an almost complete disarrangement of pigments and pattern. Some of the wing feathers had a combination of red and white on the same feather and the breast feathers were brighter red than in the Sarasota County hen. The live examples of this mutation in Baldwin Bay showed almost as much white as red in their plumage.

A unique adult gobbler color mutant was taken in Levy County in 1979 and mounted in the collection of the Florida Chapter of the National Wild Turkey Federation. Much of its plumage is normal, but it is speckled throughout with white and partly white feathers. The eyes, skin of the head, and legs and feet were normally colored.

Single or bilaterally matched white feathers are sometimes seen in Florida turkeys. This is most noticeable when it occurs in the large feathers of the wing or tail but is also known to occur in the body plumage. Sometimes primary wing feathers exhibit no white barring; occasionally all the primaries of both wings are unbarred. Reduced wing barring was one of the taxonomic characters upon which the naming of the Florida subspecies was based (Scott 1890), but the complete lack of white bars is not an example of that character because the completely black condition sometimes occurs in one or more feathers independently of the amount of barring in the other primaries. We have seen it in specimens of *M. g. silvestris* from Georgia.

Off-color beards have been reported. Don Frowick, of Gainesville, Florida, showed us a beard from an adult gobbler that had a 6-cm-long midsection of translucent amber color. Both the base and tip were normal colored. Neal F. Eichholz of Tallahassee, Florida showed us a completely blond and a partially blond beard from young gobblers. The straw-colored beard tip sometimes seen on young gobblers is a normal condition that usually disappears as the beard grows out and wears at the tip.

The amber zones in the beard appear to be weaker than the normally pigmented black areas and there is a tendency for beards to break in the weaker zones. When a beard has such a weakened zone extending across the entire beard, it may break off cleanly, leaving a much shorter and somewhat blunt-tipped beard. Sometimes the weaker zone extends through only part of the beard and results in only a portion of it breaking off, as if cut by a knife.

There is no known connection between off-colored turkeys and the crossing of wild domestic turkeys. Aberrant specimens examined in these studies were in all other ways typical wild turkeys. Obviously, turkeys, like other animals, experience genetic mutations affecting their external coloration. Such mutations (or rare gene combinations) tend to recur in a given locality even after many of the specimens have died or been killed, indicating a tendency for that particular off-color trait in the genetic makeup of the population. It is probably not harmful, and in any case it cannot be eliminated by shooting the specimens that exhibit the trait because they carry only a relatively small proportion of the population's genes that are affected. The next generation is likely to produce additional off-colored birds despite the removal of all such specimens at any one time.

Hens with Spurs and Beards

At hatching, turkeys of both sexes have an enlarged leg scale on the lower medial surface of each tarsometatarsus. This becomes the spur cap in the male but remains little more than the largest leg scale of the series in the normal hen. Several other galliform birds, including the domestic chicken, have similar metatarsal spurs.

Turkey hens with well-developed metatarsal spurs have been reported from *M. g. osceola* (Williams and Austin 1969) and *M. g. intermedia* in Texas (Pattee and Beasom 1977). Enough Florida females with leg spurs have been found to permit calculation of the trait's frequency. Of 608 adult hens examined for this trait in south Florida between 1968 and 1982, eight (1.5 percent) had a spur on one leg and four (0.7 percent) had spurs on both legs for an overall frequency of about 2 percent with at least one spur. The longest hen spur was 17 mm and was sharp. Two hens with well-developed spurs that were being radiotracked were known to have nested successfully.

The spurs of the normal adult male consist of an external cap of hard keratin resting on and loosely attached to a conical core of bone which is attached firmly to the tarsometatarsal bone. (The spur caps of the young gobbler are not firmly attached to the tarsal bone until after it is one year old.) The spur of the hen has a similar makeup; one well-developed hen spur that was examined was not attached to the tarsometatarsus.

Normal adult gobblers and a few hens have beards. In a sample of 608 adult *M. g. osceola* hens from south Florida that were examined in hand, four (0.7 percent) had beards. The longest was 177 mm. McDowell (1956) found almost the same proportion (.0657) in a sample of 557 hunter-killed wild turkeys of both sexes in Virginia. Since approximately one-half of them could be expected to be gobblers, the frequency of bearded hens in the Virginia sample was about twice as high as in south Florida. Beards are even more frequent (up to 8.9 percent) in hens of some strains of domestic turkeys (Schorger 1957) and in pen-reared "wild" turkeys (McDowell 1956).

There was no apparent association between beards and leg spurs in hens.

Hen beards are smaller in diameter (having fewer and thinner filament strands) and are shorter than gobbler beards on similar aged birds and those over about 4 inches are usually kinked (while gobbler beards seldom are). When incubating her eggs, a hen's beard would be pressed against the ground and, at times, folded. It may be in this way that the hen's beard takes on its characteristic kink.

Multiple Spurs on Gobblers

An adult male wild turkey normally has one metatarsal spur on the lower posterior edge of each tarsometatarsus (tarsus). These spurs vary in size depending upon the age of the individual and probably some genetic factors, but are usually about one inch long in individuals more than two years old. Adult male turkeys lacking a spur on one or both legs, and numerous spurs of intermediate size and various shapes suggesting arrested development, have been observed, but only six turkeys with more than one spur (fig. 2.13) on either leg have been reported.

In April 1965, a two-year-old male from Wakulla County, Florida, with two spurs on each tarsometatarsus was obtained (Williams 1966). The lower spur on the right leg was slightly larger than the spur on the left leg. Both spurs had bony cores as normal spurs have. Comparison with normal specimens suggests that the lower spur is the extra one. Since 1965, five additional male specimens with two spurs on each tarsus have been found: three from the same general locality in Wakulla and nearby Leon counties, Florida; one

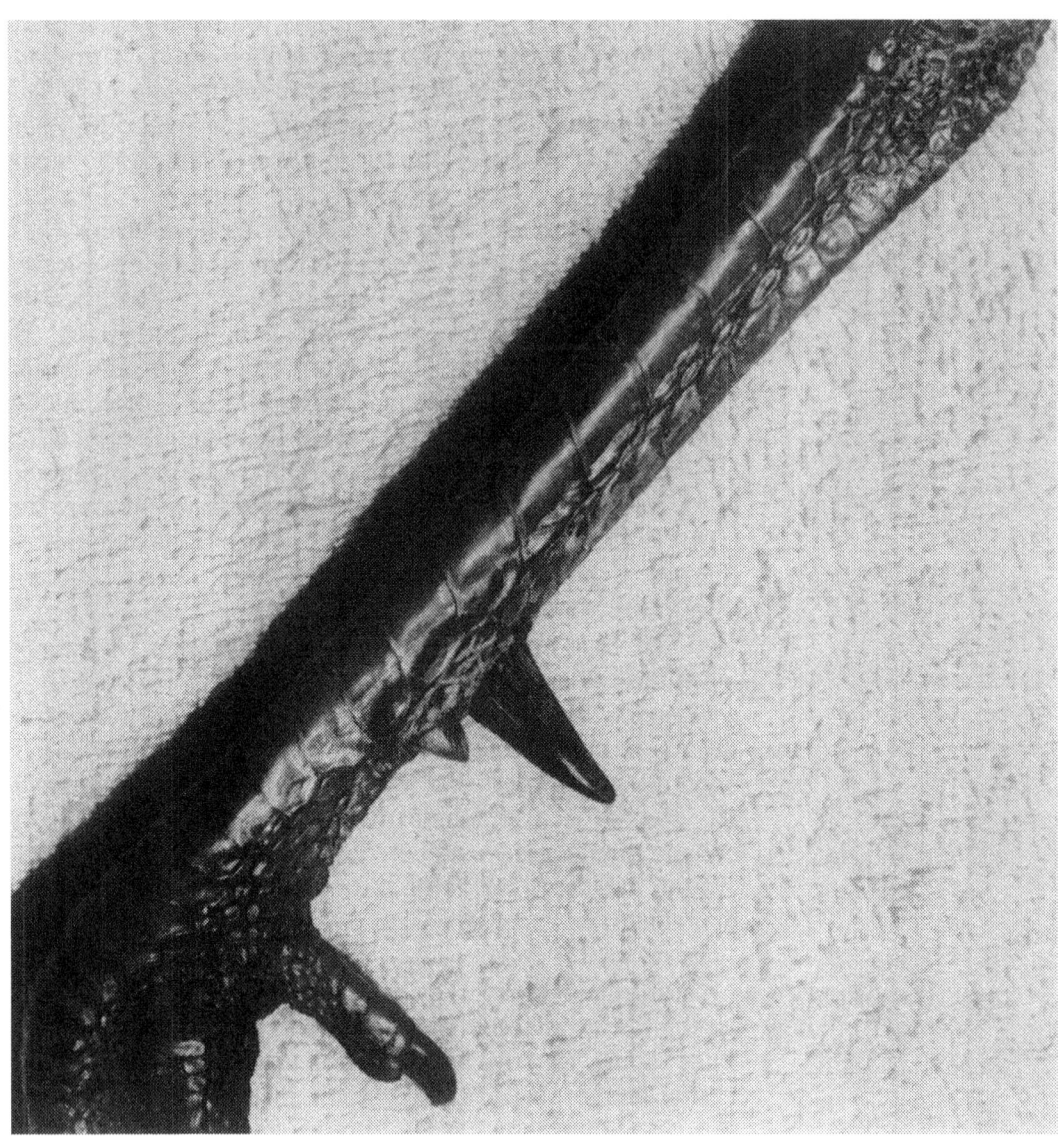

2.13 A tarsometatarsus of an adult gobbler that had two spurs on each leg.

from Sumter County, Alabama (Kennamer 1982); and one from Minnesota (Williams 1981).

The extra spur appears to be an enlarged, modified member of the series of conspicuous scales (numbering six to nine in most specimens), which extends in decreasing size along the posterior edge of the tarsus from the spur to the foot. The first scale below the spur is the largest of the series. None of the normal scales has a bony core.

In a strain of chicken that frequently has multiple metatarsal spurs, the development of an additional spur is first indicated by an enlarged scale at the site where the spur will later emerge (Hutt 1949). In one of the aberrant Florida turkey specimens, the scale immediately above the normal spur was markedly enlarged and may have been on its way to becoming a third spur when the bird was killed.

Wetmore (1931) described a new species of extinct turkey from Pleistocene fossils of Florida (Pinellas County) that he called *Meleagris tridens*. The diagnostic character of the species is the presence of three spurs on the lower tarsometatarsus in place of the normal single spur. Although we have not examined Wetmore's specimen, we wonder whether *M. g. tridens* may have merely been a *M. g. osceola* specimen with three spurs.

One of the tarsometatarsi with two spurs from a Wakulla County specimen taken in 1965 was deposited in the Smithsonian Institution.

Multiple Beards Multiple beards are too common to be considered truly anomalous. A Rio Grande gobbler with five beards was taken in Texas where as many as nine beards have been seen on one gobbler (Schorger 1966). Numerous Florida specimens having two or three beards have been examined. In most, but not all cases, the beard in front is the longest.

Absence of Beard and Spurs in Males A few adult gobblers do not have beards. A gobbler's beard is not difficult to detach by pulling. It is possible that beards are occasionally pulled off living turkeys in some way. Close examination of two beardless adult gobbler specimens revealed a scar where the beard had emerged from the skin. In one case, when a marked adult gobbler under observation somehow lost his 8-inch beard, he grew two new beards—one from immediately above and one from immediately below the point of removal of the original beard, but there was no new growth where the old beard had emerged before. Such beard losses and regrowth above and below the old scar could account for some of the multiple beards that are seen in turkeys. It is doubtful that this would account for all multiple beards.

A few adult gobblers have no spurs or may be missing a spur on one leg. Enlarged scale spur caps are present in such cases, but no observable development of the underlying bony spur core can be seen. Although a metatarsal spur can be twisted off a living turkey with strong fingers, the bony core would remain. No wild specimen has been found exhibiting that condition.

Schorger (1966: 119) reviewed the literature on castration of turkeys and concluded that the growth of spurs is generally not retarded by castration. Kozelka (1929) transplanted spur potential tissue of chickens to other chickens and found that subsequent spur development depended on the sex of the donor and not on the sex of the recipient of the tissue, suggesting genetic rather than endocrine control. The successful nesting of spurred hens in Florida (Williams and Austin 1969) indicates that spur development does not require high levels of male hormones.

Male-type Plumage in Females

Several female turkey specimens with typical male plumage have been taken at Fisheating Creek and one was examined alive by us in Escambia County, Florida, in 1984. McIlhenny (1914: 116–117) reported a similar specimen taken on the Trinity River of eastern Texas. Two such specimens we collected in the winter of 1967 at Fisheating Creek weighed 7 and 7½ pounds (3.2 and 3.4 Kg) and had the typical body proportions of hens. They had neither beard nor spur. Their heads and necks had less than normal feathering, for hens, but the other head features (snood, dewlap, and caruncles) were not as well developed as in the adult gobbler. Upon dissection, no macroscopic evidence of an ovary could be found, but there appeared to be a shriveled oviduct in both specimens. Two additional hens of this type were seen at Fisheating Creek during the 1960s. It is puzzling that so many of these specimens were encountered at Fisheating Creek during the period between about 1961 and 1969—only one has been seen there since despite the fact that many more turkeys have been examined in the same area and all personnel handling turkeys have been alert for such specimens.

If a specimen of this type had a beard, it is doubtful that an observer would think that it was anything other than a dwarfed gobbler. It is possible that specimens such as these are the basis for the stories sometimes told about miniature strains of wild turkeys.

3

Reproductive Behavior and Performance of the Hen

HENS were captured with cannon nets, rocket nets and orally administered tribromoethanol or alpha-chloralose and were age-classed by the configuration of the greater upper secondary coverts (Williams 1961). All were weighed and banded prior to being radio instrumented. Handling procedures have been described previously.

Radio transmitters were attached to 414 hens, 35 on the Lochloosa study area and 379 on the Fisheating Creek study area (table 3.1). Data were obtained from 248 nests of 202 hens that nested one or more times. Because of the small number of nests on the Lochloosa study area ($N = 15$), no attempt has been made to compare the turkey populations on the two areas.

Transmitters were spaced across the frequency band (150.815 MHz to 151.210 MHz) to provide 24 channels separated by 10 to 15 KHz. Transmitters weighed from 65 to 90 g, measured approximately 50 × 25 × 80 mm, and exceeded the performance requirements of a 2-km range and six-month signal transmission without battery change. Transmitters were fitted to the turkeys as described earlier under general methods.

Field monitoring was accomplished with 24-channel, crystal-controlled, portable radio receivers. Receiving antennas included ¼-wave whips on trucks, hand-held yagis for

Table 3.1 Wild turkey hens instrumented and monitored

Year	Number instrumented	Found dead before nesting season	Contact lost before nesting season[a]	Monitored during nesting season	Nests found
1968	30	0	0	30	20
1969	26	0	4	22	14
1970	34	0	3	31	19
1971	33	5	4	24	14
1972	35	2	6	27	14
1973	30	1	0	29	20
1974	33	1	4	34	25
1975	25	1	2	22	20
1976	20	0	3	17	12
1978	18	0	1	13	12
1979	21	3	1	17	13
1980	43	5	8	30	28
1981	54	9	4	41	32
1982	12	1	3	8	5
TOTAL	414	28	43	345	248

a. Not including those found dead.

work on foot, and large multielement directional antennas mounted on trucks. Nests were found by radio signals when instrumented hens were present. Data were collected at nests while the hens were absent. Methodology was the same as for other radio telemetry applications discussed in this bulletin.

Electronic devices were used to record nest attendance. The low-power signal from the transmitter was monitored by a battery-powered receiver hidden near the nest. This signal was retransmitted to the field station on a different frequency by a directional antenna; maximum transmission range was 8 km. The sensitivity of the receiver at the nest was adjusted to restrict the radius of signal reception to within 1 m, which made the equipment function as a proximity detector. At headquarters, the incoming signal activated an electronic switch and was recorded on a 30-day time-calibrated Esterline-Angus event recorder, thereby making a continuous record of the time the hen was on the nest. A maximum of 20 nests could be monitored simultaneously. Nests were monitored by these automatic recorders for about 8000 hours and for about 400 hours manually. Visual observations confirmed the reliability of the nest monitors.

Behavior of hens was observed with telescopes and binoculars from portable cloth blinds located about 30 m from the nests. Microphones were placed within 1 m of seven nests to monitor and record the sounds of hatching on a ¼-inch open reel Uher tape recorder. Sound spectrograms of recorded hen and poult vocalizations were made on a Sona-Graph model 7029A instrument (Kay Electric Company).

All vegetation within five feet (1.5 m) of each of 57 nests found on the Fisheating Creek study area in the five years from 1968 to 1972 was identified and its coverage estimated visually to the nearest 5 percent; coverage of the overhead vegetation was visually estimated for these nests. The habitat within 45 m of 236 nests was classified by the most abundant vegetation present—palmetto, cypress woods, or other. Habitat acreages were measured from aerial photographs (scale: 600 feet = 1 inch) with a Mode 11211–H–1 Nemonics Corporation electronic digital planimeter.

The Mayfield (1961) method, which permits the use of data from nests that were observed during only part of the laying or incubation period, was used to calculate nesting success. The Wilcoxon Rank Sum test was used to compare clutch sizes of first, second, and third nests and of nests in which incubation began before 1 May, between 1 May and 20 May, and after 20 May. Chi-square analysis was used to test for differences in renesting tendencies of hens whose nests were disrupted during the laying versus the incubating periods; differences in the proportions of nests located in the three habitat types and the success and predation rates in each habitat type; differences in predation rates of nests that hatched before 1 May, between 1 May and 20 May, and after 20 May; differences in the tendencies of hens to return to their nests when flushed; differences in return-after-flushing tendencies of hens nesting in three habitat types; and differences in the proportion of yearling versus adult hens that abandoned their nests after being flushed. The T-test procedure was used to compare renesting rates of adult and yearling hens and mean length of recesses of incubating hens. The Kolmogorov-Smirnov Z test (Zar 1974) was used to test for differences in the distribution of seasonal nesting curves for adult and yearling hens. Fisher's least significant difference test (SAS Institute, Inc. 1982) was used to compare length of recesses during four segments of the period of continuous incubation behavior. The confidence interval on the proportion of recesses hens took in the afternoon followed the form $p \pm 1.96\sqrt{\dfrac{p(1-p)}{N}}$

The mating system of the Florida turkey fits Oring's (1982) description of "male-dominance polygyny with intermediate dispersal." Hen flocks dissolved before nesting began. Gobbling and strutting activities in early February, before the hen flocks dissolved, indicated that gobblers were receptive to mating earlier than hens. Hens, upon attainment of sexual receptivity, visited the gobblers for mating.

Before nesting, hens established new home ranges and

often roosted alone in small, isolated hammocks and bayheads where gobblers and non-nesting hens seldom ventured and rarely roosted (Williams et al. 1974). Hens were seen frequently traversing the edge of saw palmetto prairies and the oak scrub-palmetto ecotone as if searching for nesting sites. Tracking effort was concentrated in these areas so a few nests could be found early in the laying cycle.

Egg Covering and Nest Construction

Four hens were monitored by telemetry as they established their nests and laid their first eggs. When a hen approached the nesting area, she would spend approximately 5 to 20 minutes moving in a restricted area before becoming still. This suggests that she was in the process of selecting a place for the nest.

The deposition of the first egg followed a definite pattern. Hens scratched shallow depressions in the soil, laid the eggs, placed a few dried leaves over the eggs, and departed. The mean length of time spent on the nest while laying the first egg was 70 minutes ($N = 4$, $SE = 28.4$). Freshly laid eggs were clean and chalky, with a thin layer of sand adhering only to the side in contact with the ground.

Five additional nests were found at the time the second or third egg was being laid. In two of these nests, shallow, scratched-out depressions were found within 10 m of the nests in what appeared to be suitable nesting places, indicating these hens had scratched shallow depressions in more than one place before selecting the place they would lay.

Evidently, hens did not transport nesting material an appreciable distance to cover their eggs but used debris present at the site. Two hens observed while laying covered their eggs with plant debris picked up from beside their nests; no hen was observed carrying nesting material. About a century ago, an observer reported to Bendire (1892) that Florida turkey nests were lined with dead leaves and grass that were so like the surrounding debris that he wondered whether the material was placed there by the hen or was already present under the eggs.

Although numerous patches of bare ground were available in the vicinity of most nests, only a single nest was established on such a site. The availability of nearby dried plant material may be a factor in nest site selection.

Twenty nests that were observed a total of 90 times during the laying period were always sparsely covered with dried leaves (fig 3.1). Approximately 160 different nests were inspected at least once while the hens were on recess during the incubating period; none of these nests was covered (fig. 3.2). These observations indicate a tendency for hens to

3.1 Unattended nests are partially covered with leaves by the hen before she departs after laying.

cover their eggs while away during the laying period but to leave them uncovered while on recess during the incubation period. Although many writers (e.g., Audubon 1831, McIlhenny 1914, Mosby and Handley 1943, Bailey et al. 1951) have stated that turkey hens cover their eggs with leaves, they did not specify that this is done only during the laying pe-

3.2 Unattended nests during incubation are not covered with leaves.

riod. Green (1982) noted that hens in Michigan did not cover their eggs before taking incubation recesses.

Camouflage, rather than insulation, appears to be the function of egg covering by the turkey. If insulation were required, it would also be needed during the incubation period when embryos are more vulnerable to chilling; however, turkeys do not cover the eggs during incubation recesses. Furthermore, the fact that hens use only debris from beside the nest to cover their eggs suggests that the purpose is to blend the nest with the immediate surroundings.

Egg covering is also the means by which a turkey nest is constructed. When the hen returns to the nest to lay each egg, she does not uncover the nest before laying, which causes more debris to accumulate with the laying of each egg. When the hen turns the eggs, the debris settles to the bottom and sides of the nest and, by the time the last egg is laid, the nest depression is well lined with leaves. A typical nest measures 2 cm deep, 20 cm wide, and 24 cm long (Williams et al. 1968).

Laying Posture   Three hens were observed while in the process of laying a total of 11 eggs. Hens sat on or crouched over their nests before laying. The laying of the egg was accomplished from a partially erect body position. They trembled as they laid, with wings drooped slightly and tails raised. The back feathers were ventilated. Eggs were laid on the ground beside the other eggs and not on top of them. Of the more than 2000 turkey eggs examined, only two were cracked in a manner that would suggest one egg had struck another while being laid.

Multiple Nesting   Some bird species, such as the ring-necked pheasant (*Phasianus colchicus*), have very large clutches when more than one hen lays in the same nest. Multiple nesting has been reported for the wild turkey (Bent 1932, Mosby and Handley 1943); however, the only evidence presented is Bendire's (1892) report of a turkey hen seen on a nest while another hen was seen standing close by and presumed to be waiting to lay in the same nest; Audubon (1831) also mentioned three hens on the same nest.

In the present study, two hens were observed visiting the same nest on three occasions. Both were seen sitting on the nest, although never at the same time. Telemetry data indicated that these hens did not associate with each other. More than one egg per day was laid in the nest on two occasions. It seems almost certain that both hens laid in this nest. The nest was deserted after the twelfth egg was laid.

Another nest was photographed after the hen had been flushed deliberately. When the nest was examined about two hours later, one egg had been added. The sitting hen had passed the twentieth day of incubation behavior; therefore, the extra egg must have been laid by another hen.

The potential for multiple nesting exists in Florida turkey populations; however, it is probably not a common behavior. If multiple nesting depends upon chance encounters, it should be expected to be more prevalent when nest density is higher, which would partly explain the much higher incidence of multiple nesting observed in the ring-necked pheasant (Labisky 1968).

Egg Dropping Some birds occasionally lay single eggs where there is no nest. Stoddard (1931) reported this phenomenon as common in the northern bobwhite (*Colinus virginianus*). Single eggs that were never incubated constituted a minimum of 8 percent of the annual egg production of ring-necked pheasants in Illinois (Labisky 1968). In the present study, only seven turkey eggs not associated with a nest were observed in approximately 30 000 man-hours of field work during the nesting season, indicating that egg dropping is not prevalent among Florida turkeys.

Nest Attendance During the Laying Period Blakey (1937) provides the only reference about the pattern of egg laying by the wild turkey by saying: "Study of artificially propagated wild turkey shows that, when . . . (egg laying) . . . becomes regular, one egg is laid daily, approximately one hour later each day beginning at about one hour after sunrise and continuing until sundown terminates the cycle. Then the hen may skip a day and begin over again at the early morning hour and repeat the cycle."

In four nests monitored from the deposition of the first egg, the hens came to lay between 1120 and 1300 hours ($\bar{x}$ = 1234 hours). Only eight of 74 eggs were laid before 1100 hours. Two of these hens skipped laying the day after laying the first egg, and one also skipped laying the day after laying the second egg. The other two hens skipped laying early in the laying period—one skipped the day after the third egg, and the other after laying both the second and third eggs. In 103 laying events by 22 hens, the only additional skipped days observed were after the first, fourth, and ninth eggs. There was no tendency for hens to skip laying late during the laying period.

Blakey (1937) reported that after laying by turkeys becomes regular, each egg is laid approximately one hour later each day. To test this hypothesis for wild turkeys, the time of laying of 29 pairs of consecutively laid eggs was compared. This comparison revealed that 50 percent were laid within the same hour as the previous egg, 17 percent were laid at least one hour earlier and only 24 percent were laid one hour later. Furthermore, in 65 percent of the laying events monitored, hens came to the nest to lay between 1000 and 1500 hours. This pattern of laying in midday compares closely with the pattern reported for the domestic turkey (Stockton and Asmundson 1950) but not with the pattern reported for wild turkey by Blakey (1937).

In 74 observations of laying events in 22 nests, two days were skipped after the fourth egg was laid. In neither of these cases was laying resumed in the early morning of the following day.

In summary, the first egg of the Florida turkey is usually laid in midday and is followed by a skipped day; the second egg is laid on the third day and is sometimes followed by a skipped day. A few hens skip laying one additional day after the third egg, but very few skips occur later in the laying period. The fourth through final eggs are usually laid on consecutive days with a tendency to lay a few minutes later and to remain on the nest longer each day. The clutch is typically completed in late afternoon (fig 3.3). Hens failed to lay only four of 78 times they were observed visiting their nests.

Hens remained on their nests an average of 55 minutes while laying each of eggs one through five. The slight decrease ($\bar{x} = -7.3$ minutes, SE = 11.3) in mean attendance during the laying of each of the first five eggs was not significant ($p = 0.531$) (fig. 3.4). Hens remained on their nests an average of 50 minutes (SE = 12.0) longer as they laid each of eggs 5 through 12. Hens were remaining on the nest about 348 minutes with the laying of the eleventh egg. Thus, incubating behavior began gradually with the laying of the sixth egg and the length of incubating sessions increased with the laying of each successive egg. The first egg was subjected to about 25 hours of incubation on the average before the twelfth or last egg was laid.

No hen began continuous incubating behavior with fewer than five eggs. This finding, coupled with the observed tendency of hens to begin incubating with the laying of the sixth

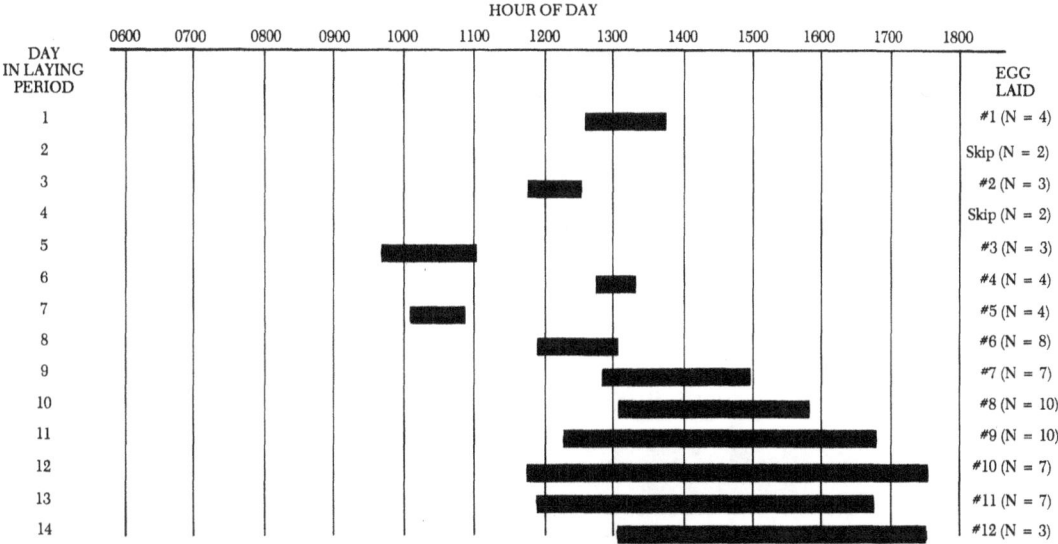

3.3 The pattern of egg laying by Florida turkey hens.

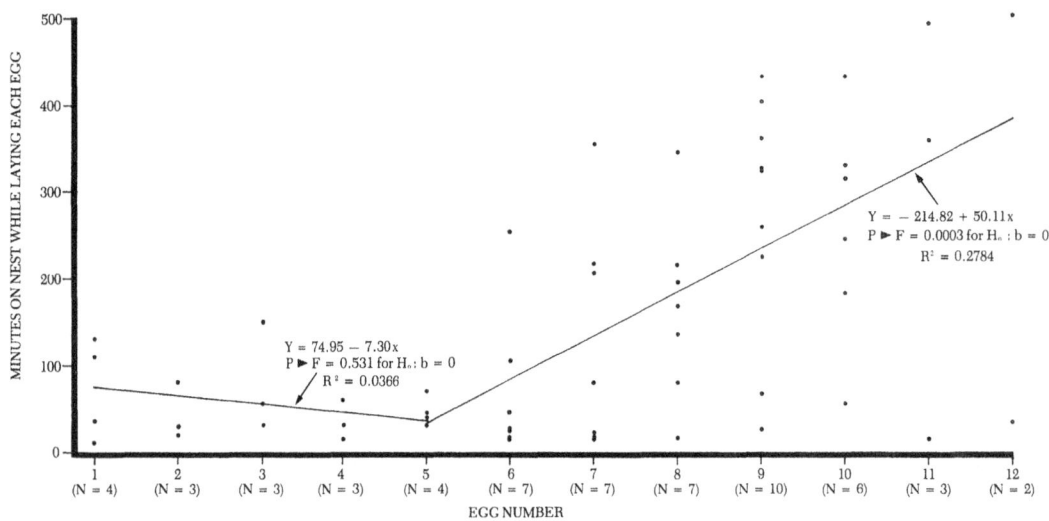

3.4 Time spent on the nest with the laying of each egg. The lines are separate least square linear regression curves for eggs one through 5 and 5 through 12.

egg, suggested that at least five eggs are required to stimulate the gradual onset of incubating behavior observed. This hypothesis was tested by manipulating eggs in three nests during the laying period. In one nest, four eggs were removed from a clutch of seven, and then one egg was removed each day to maintain the clutch at three eggs. The hen abandoned this nest after laying the ninth egg. In another nest, three of six eggs were removed at the time the nest was found; this clutch also was held to three eggs. This hen abandoned the nest after laying 12 eggs without initiating continuous incubating. The electronic monitor indicated that the hen did not exhibit the normal pattern of gradually lengthening incubating behavior late in the laying cycle; she remained at the nest no more than 34 minutes while laying any egg, thereby demonstrating behavior typical of a hen in the laying cycle. Another nest was found with four eggs and the clutch was held at that number by daily removal of eggs during the remainder of the laying period. This hen abandoned the nest after laying the ninth egg.

Abandonment of the three manipulated clutches supports the hypothesis that approximately five eggs in the nest are required to stimulate the gradual onset of incubating behavior.

If the turkey were a so-called "indeterminant" layer (Cole 1917), these hens would have laid a greater number of eggs than represented in normal clutches. The result indicates that the wild turkey is a "determinant" layer and will not continue to lay indefinitely merely because its eggs are removed as they are laid.

The gradual onset of incubating behavior is stimulated by

five eggs, probably through visual or tactile cues. Termination of laying occurs several days after the onset of gradual incubation, probably caused by increasing prolactin secretions as incubating behavior progresses (Eisner 1958). A daily increase in the secretion of prolactin would effectively determine the clutch size in the species by terminating laying.

Clutch Size A clutch is completed when no additional eggs are laid. Clutch size averaged 10.3 eggs (SE = 0.14) in 179 complete clutches (table 3.2). Clutch size of yearling hens, which averaged 10.0 (SE = 0.28), differed significantly (Wilcoxon two-sample test, S = 2248, Z = 1.6245, p = 0.104) from those of adult hens, which averaged 10.5 (SE = 0.16) eggs. Sixty-seven percent of the complete clutches had 9, 10, or 11 eggs; the modal clutch size was 10 eggs (fig. 3.5). No complete clutch contained fewer than five eggs. Mean clutch size did not vary significantly among years (F = 1.50, df = 178, p = 0.12).

The Wilcoxon Rank Sum test indicated that mean clutch size of the first ($\bar{x}$ = 4, N = 150), second ($\bar{x}$ = 10.2, N = 26), and third ($\bar{x}$ = 9.8, N = 4) of the same hens within the same year did not differ significantly (first versus second: Z = 0.088, p = 0.93; second versus third, Z = 0.751, p = 0.45; first versus third: Z = 0.088, p = 0.40). Mean clutch size among nests in which incubating behavior began before 1 May ($\bar{x}$ =

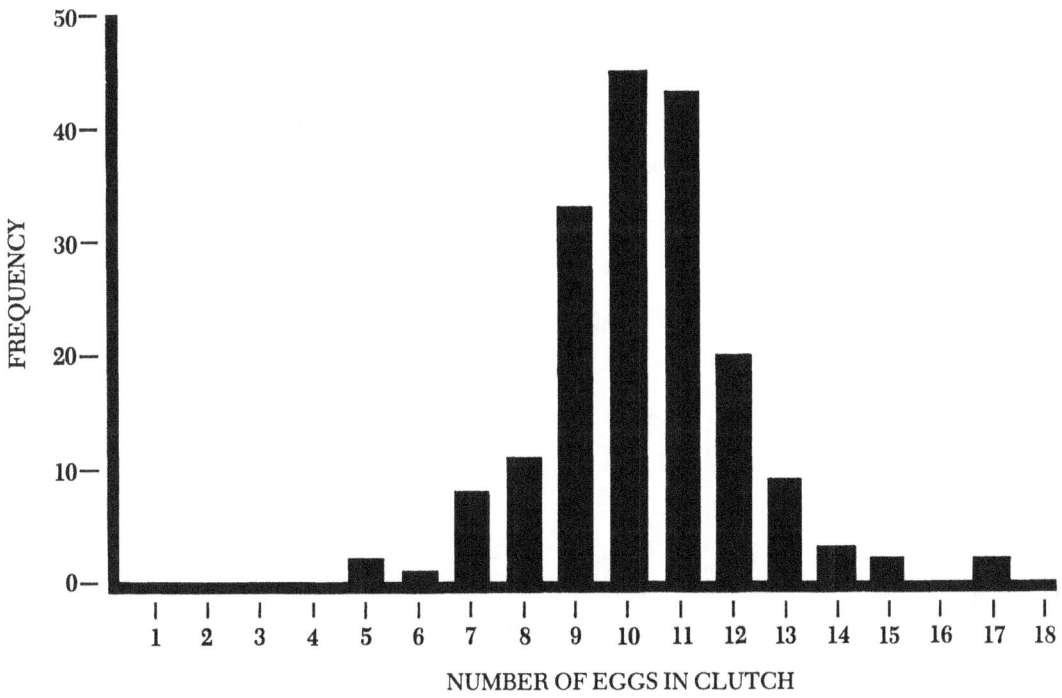

3.5 Frequency distribution of the number of eggs in 179 complete clutches.

Reproductive Behavior and Performance

Table 3.2 Mean clutch size, by year, for complete clutches only

| | Adult | | | | Yearling | | | | Overall[a] | | | |
Year	N	x̄	SE	Range	N	x̄	SE	Range	N	x̄	SE	Range
1968	9	9.9	0.72	5–12	3	9.7	0.33	9–10	12	9.8	0.53	5–12
1969	3	9.0	1.15	7–11	3	10.3	0.33	10–11	12	9.0	0.51	5–11
1970	14	9.9	0.44	6–12	2	9.5	1.50	8–11	16	9.8	0.47	7–12
1971	5	10.6	0.40	10–12	7	9.3	0.71	7–12	12	9.8	0.47	7–12
1972	7	10.6	0.84	7–14	2	10.5	0.50	10–11	9	10.5	0.65	7–14
1973	15	10.9	0.40	9–13	1	15.0	—	—	18	11.1	0.42	9–15
1974	7	10.7	0.57	9–13	2	11.0	1.00	10–12	14	10.5	0.39	8–13
1975	14	10.4	0.39	7–13	2	11.0	1.00	10–12	16	10.5	0.35	7–13
1976	5	10.2	0.73	8–12	2	10.0	1.00	9–11	7	10.1	0.55	8–12
1978	6	10.3	0.76	8–13	–	—	—	—	6	10.3	0.76	8–13
1979	7	10.3	1.06	7–15	1	8.0	—	—	8	10.0	0.96	7–15
1980	19	11.4	0.55	8–17	1	10.0	—	—	21	11.2	0.51	8–17
1981	19	10.3	0.40	8–14	6	9.5	0.43	8–11	25	10.0	0.32	8–14
1982	2	10.5	0.50	10–11	–	—	—	—	3	10.3	0.33	10–11
TOTALS AND MEANS	132	10.5	0.16	5–17	32	10.0	0.28	7–15	179	10.3	0.14	5–17

a. Includes clutches of hens of uncertain age (N = 15, x̄ = 9.4, SE = 0.46, range = 5–12).

10.2, N = 99), between 1 May and 20 May (x̄ = 10.0, N = 33) and after 20 May (x̄ = 9.6, N = 8) also did not differ significantly (Kruskal-Wallis X^2 = 1.25, df = 2, p = 0.54).

Mean clutch sizes of the wild turkey in other regions of the United States indicated that clutches in Florida populations may be smaller than in Alabama, Mississippi, Missouri, and Virginia, but larger than those in populations of the Rio Grande turkey in Texas (fig. 3.6). Comparisons using the Student's T-test indicated no significant difference, however, between mean clutch sizes in Florida and Mississippi (Schumacher 1977) (t = 1.15, df = 189, p = 0.01) or Florida and Texas (t = 0.73, df = 213, p = 0.01). The clutch size reported in one of the Virginia studies (McDowell 1956) was

3.6 Mean clutch size reported for the wild turkey.

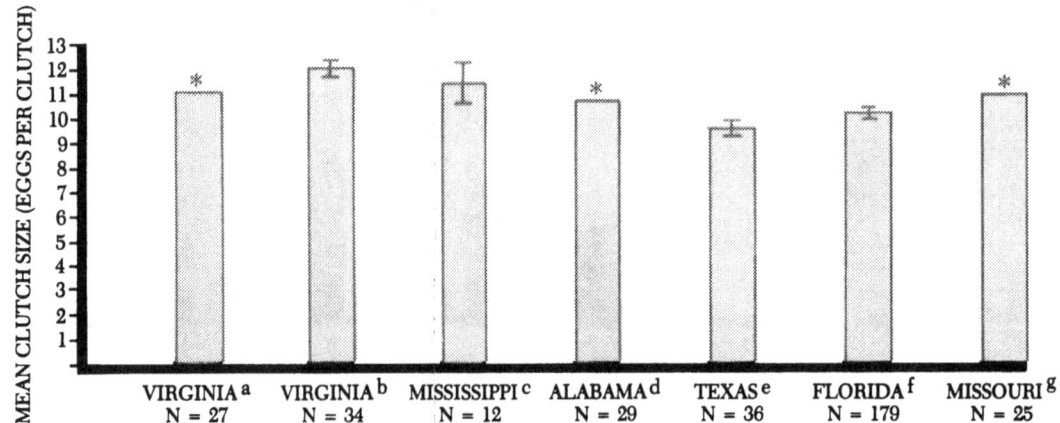

much larger than in the present Florida study (t = 2.77, df = 211, p = 0.01).

Mean clutch size in the turkey may be under genetic control and may vary among populations, but the genetic component is outweighed by the combined effects of experimental error and small sample size in the data presently available from other regions.

Renesting Hens carrying transmitters emitting weak signals and those that moved away from the study areas were not monitored closely. Some of these hens probably nested but had their undetected nests destroyed by predators. Consequently, the renesting statistics are minimum estimates.

Fifty-seven percent of 30 hens that had their nests disrupted during the laying period renested, whereas only 28 percent of 93 hens renested after their nests were disrupted during the period of continuous incubating behavior ($N = 123$, $X^2 = 8.223$, df = 1, p = 0.004). No hen renested after incubating more than 18 days. Adult hens renested with greater frequency than yearlings; 44 percent of 80 adults nested at least twice in the same year, whereas only 22 percent of 23 yearlings renested (t = 2.1, df = 1, p = 0.05).

Nest Disturbance by Man Sixty-two percent of 38 hens that were flushed from their nests during the laying period did not return. Since 43 percent of 30 hens whose nests were disrupted did not renest, the loss to the population of potential reproduction was 0.27 (0.62 × 0.43) nests per hen flushed during the laying period. During the incubation period, 40 percent of 38 hens that had been flushed abandoned their nests and 72 percent ($N = 93$) of them did not renest, representing a loss of approximately 0.29 (0.40 × 0.72) nests per hen flushed. Thus, the net impact on annual reproduction would differ little if a hen was flushed during the laying or the incubation period. Five (2 percent) of 218 nests were deserted for no apparent reason.

Incubating Behavior The term "incubation" is commonly used to mean either the behavior of the hen sitting on or standing over the eggs or the embryonic developmental processes that take place inside the egg shell, or both. These components are independent— a hen can carry on "incubation" behavior whether or not embryonic development takes place (as with infertile or artificial eggs), and the embryo can develop without a parent incubating it (as in artificial or natural incubators). When the term "incubation" is applied to the behavior of the hen, it is a presumption that embryonic development is occurring in the eggs, which may not be the case. Therefore, sitting of the hen would better be called "incubating behavior" to distinguish what the hen is doing from the incubation process that occurs only within the egg. Since the length of time a hen will sit is indefinite, the expression "incubation period" should be reserved for the period of incubation required for an egg to hatch.

In the Florida turkey, incubating behavior consists of gradually lengthening afternoon incubating sessions after the fifth egg is laid followed by continuous, day and night incubating sessions upon completion of the clutch.

Twenty-four hens began incubating overnight on either the day before laying the final egg, the same day of laying the final egg or the day after laying the final egg (fig. 3.7). Two eggs were laid in four of the 24 nests after continuous incubating behavior began. Of these eight additional eggs, only one was left unhatched despite the fact that the last laid egg in each nest had been incubated at least two days less than the rest of the clutch.

Stoddard (1931:29) said that northern bobwhite leave their eggs unincubated after the last egg is laid for as long as one week. No turkey clutch went unincubated for a single day after the last egg was laid. None of the 24 hens observed laying their last eggs took a recess between the time of laying the final egg and the first overnight incubating session. This behavioral trait of the turkey would minimize the risk of nest predation by lessening the time the nest is exposed to predators.

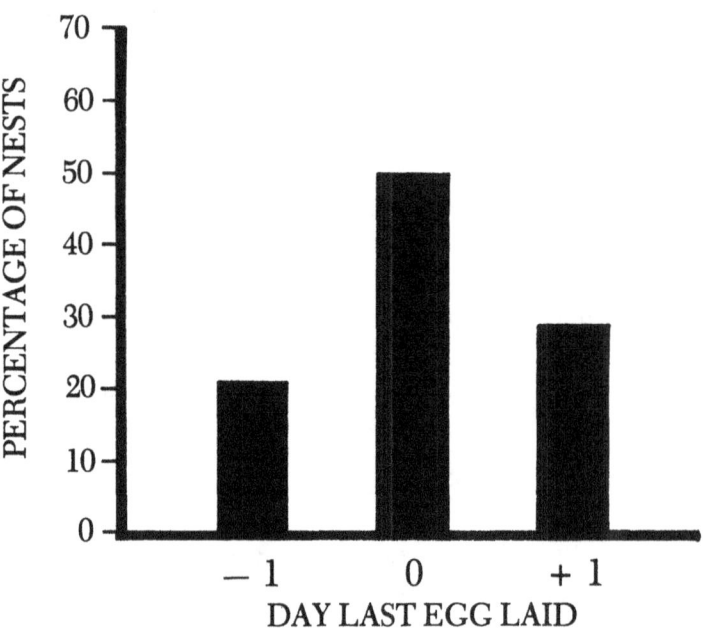

3.7 Percentage of 24 hens that laid their last egg one day before continuous incubation began (−1), the same day continuous incubation began (0), or the day after continuous incubation began (+1).

Approximately 400 man-hours were spent observing nine different hens on their nests during continuous incubating behavior. While sitting, each hen's body parts were positioned as in standing, except that their legs were folded at the upper tarsal joints forward under the breast. While sleeping in the nest during daylight hours, the head and neck were drawn in, the eyes were closed, and the wings drooped along the sides.

When turning eggs, hens crouched by flexing the intertarsal joints; they did not stand erect. Several eggs were usually rearranged with a single motion of the head, but the activity seemed to be directed at only a single egg at a time. The motion of the head not only turned the eggs but also repositioned them in the nest so that no egg remained in the same part of the nest for more than a few hours at a time. Hens often arose and gazed down at their eggs for a few seconds, and sometimes settled back without turning them. They usually gazed intently before turning an egg—the gazing behavior seemed to involve some cue that led to egg turning.

While standing in the nest, the bird's body posture was the same as when it stood at other times. Hens settled back on the nest after standing or crouching by moving the body forward with an upward, swinging motion that placed some of the breast feathers over the eggs in front of the hen, thereby covering all the eggs.

As air temperatures increased during late morning, incubating hens began to pant, with partly opened bills, and sometimes ventilated back feathers. Panting became faster and the bill opened wider as midday temperatures increased. The sequence reversed as temperatures decreased in the afternoon. Hens would move their heads or change positions to avoid spots of direct sunlight that penetrated the vegetation overhead.

Two incubating hens retrieved single eggs that had rolled from their nests; however, the retrieval process was not observed. Two hens deserted their nests when most of their eggs had been rolled out intact by the rooting of armadillos. One hen continued to incubate a clutch containing one broken egg; 12 hens deserted nests that contained one or two broken eggs. It could not be determined whether desertion was due to the broken eggs or to the disturbance by which they were broken.

Nest Attendance During the Incubation Period

Incubating hens recessed for 98 minutes at a mean interval of 1.9 days (table 3.3). Some hens remained continuously on their nests for three days; the longest period of uninterrupted sitting was four days. A few hens recessed twice on

Table 3.3 Summary of nest attendance by eight hens monitored daily during the period of continuous incubating behavior

Band number	Number of full days monitored	Times recessed	Recesses per day	Recess interval (days)	Length of recess (minutes) $\bar{x}$	Range	SD	Fate of nest
255R	20	13	0.65	1.5	80	55–111	17.6	Hatched
2875	24	13	0.54	1.8	116	64–305	57.8	Hatched
476R	23	9	0.39	2.5	277	53–1445	460.3	Abandoned
484R	24	15	0.63	1.6	70	34–177	33.3	Hatched
485R	24	13	0.54	1.8	80	3–186	47.2	Hatched
487R	27	13	0.48	2.1	132	36–487	113.7	Hatched
489R	26	23	0.88	1.1	106	15–261	53.3	Abandoned
461R	16	7	0.44	2.3	109	75–231	55.6	Predator
MEANS[a]			0.55	1.9	98			

a. Means calculated only for the six nests that were not abandoned.

several days. The period of nest attendance immediately preceding hatching averaged 2.4 days (N = 5).

There was a tendency for a given hen to recess in morning or afternoon on several consecutive days (table 3.4). Consecutive daily recesses were during the same morning, noon, or afternoon period 32 times and during a different period 30 times. None of the five hens observed finished the entire incubation period without changing recess patterns from morning or noon to afternoon or vice versa at least once. Thus, hens do not recess at the same time of day throughout the duration of the incubating period.

Thirty-nine percent of 67 recesses by five hens began before noon and 61 percent began after noon (table 3.4), indicating a tendency for the hens to take more recesses in the afternoon. Only 16 percent of the recesses of these five hens included noontime (1200 hours).

Hens were observed while on recess from incubating on at least 9 occasions. They moved quickly from place to place and hurriedly consumed large amounts of green vegetation. They seemed to be much less particular about selecting vegetation to eat than they were at other times. They did not use the same route each time in returning to their nests and would have been impossible to track except by telemetry. They moved very rapidly for short distances and were observed running on several occasions.

Blakey (1937) reported that turkey hens tend to recess at midday after the first few days of incubating, and Hillestad (1970) stated that midday would be the best time for hens to recess because air temperatures then most nearly approach required incubation temperatures. The midday recess pattern was not predominant in this Florida population. Only 10 percent (27) of 271 recesses occurred between 1130 and 1230 hours. A similar tendency for hens to avoid recessing at

Table 3.4 Consecutive nest recesses ($N = 67$) of five hens monitored during the period of continuous incubating behavior

Period of recess	Length of recess (minutes)	Date	Day of incubating period	Period of recess	Length of recess (minutes)	Date	Day of incubating period
Band 255R				Band 485R			
Afternoon	94	18 May	7	Noon	58	26 April	9
Afternoon	76	20 May	9	Noon	87	28 April	11
Noon	111	22 May	11	Afternoon	96	28 April	11
Morning	90	24 May	13	Morning	68	28 April	11
Morning	85	26 May	15	Noon	186	29 April	12
Afternoon	60	27 May	16	Afternoon	55	29 April	12
Afternoon	106	28 May	17	Afternoon	82	1 May	14
Afternoon	76	29 May	18	Morning	49	2 May	15
Noon	55	31 May	20	Afternoon	3	3 May	16
Afternoon	80	2 June	22	Afternoon	46	3 May	16
Morning	78	4 June	24	Afternoon	73	4 May	17
Morning	58	5 June	25	Afternoon	80	5 May	18
Morning	66	6 June	26	Morning	34	7 May	20
				Afternoon	54	7 May	20
Band 2875				Morning	80	9 May	22
Afternoon	395	22 April	1	Afternoon	82	10 May	23
Afternoon	96	23 April	2	Afternoon	116	11 May	24
Morning	90	26 April	5	Afternoon	59	12 May	25
Morning	103	27 April	6				
Noon	164	28 April	7	Band 487R			
Morning	105	29 April	8	Noon	487	23 May	2
Afternoon	103	1 May	10	Afternoon	137	24 May	3
Afternoon	64	3 May	12	Afternoon	66	28 May	7
Afternoon	99	3 May	12	Afternoon	36	28 May	7
Afternoon	91	7 May	16	Afternoon	66	31 May	10
Afternoon	78	9 May	18	Afternoon	115	1 June	11
Afternoon	117	11 May	20	Afternoon	119	4 June	14
Noon	95	13 May	22	Afternoon	56	5 June	15
				Afternoon	175	7 June	17
Band 484R				Afternoon	136	11 June	21
Afternoon	59	12 April	2	Afternoon	129	13 June	23
Afternoon	79	12 April	2	Afternoon	78	14 June	24
Afternoon	34	13 April	3	Noon	125	16 June	26
Morning	26	13 April	3				
Noon	56	21 April	4				
Morning	73	22 April	5				
Afternoon	130	22 April	5				
Noon	177	23 April	6				
Afternoon	81	24 April	7				
Morning	62	25 April	8				

noon was noted in a recent study in Michigan (Green 1982). Recesses were less frequent in early afternoon than during late afternoon (fig. 3.8). The traditional closure in Florida of spring gobbler hunting each day in early afternoon probably lessens the risk of incubating hens being shot by careless hunters.

The period of absence from the nest for hens that recessed at noon averaged 137 minutes, whereas hens on re-

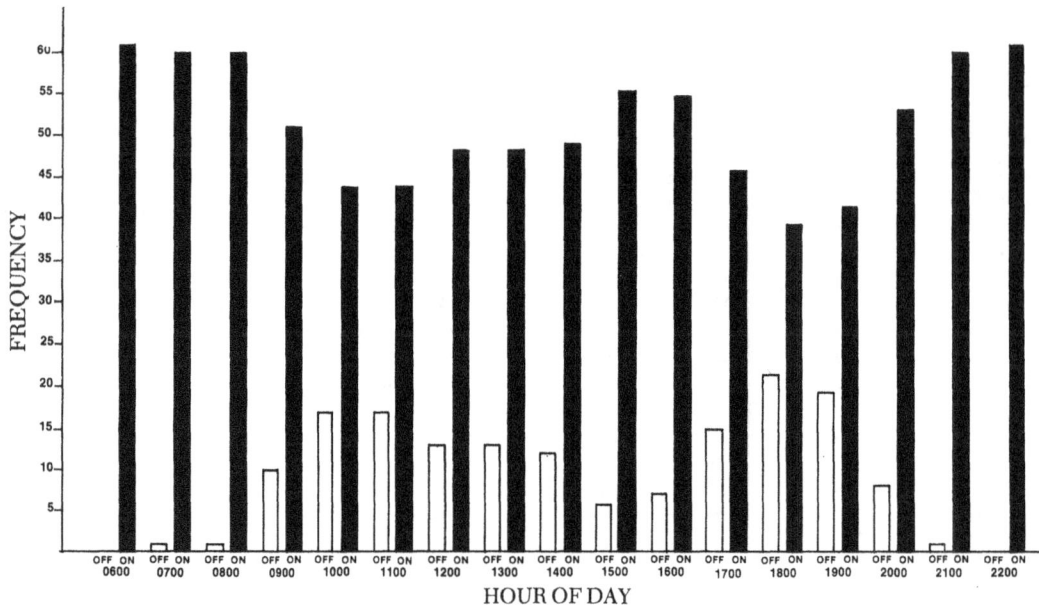

3.8 Mean daily recess pattern of 22 incubating hens during 162 recess days monitored.

cess in the morning stayed away 129 minutes; the difference is not statistically significant ($p = 0.05$). A mean midday recess period of 137 minutes was greater than the afternoon period of 91 minutes ($Z = 2.03$, $p = .021$). The mean length of recesses for 128 adult and 32 yearling hens was 106 and 103 minutes, respectively, and did not differ significantly ($t = 0.097$, $p = 0.50$). Recesses averaged 109, 95, 84, and 140 minutes during the first through fourth weeks of continuous incubating behavior, respectively (table 3.5). The percentage of time hens spent off their nests was greatest (10 percent) during the final week of incubation.

Green (1982) reported a mean recess time of 53 minutes for four hens in Michigan ($N = 41$). The mean for 67 recesses in five Florida hens was 95 minutes. The difference between the length of recesses in Florida and Michigan was highly significant ($t = 4.24$, $df = 113$, $p = 0.001$). The Michigan study was conducted on a stocked population more than

Table 3.5 Mean length of recesses during the period of continuous incubating behavior

Interval during period (days)	Mean length of recesses (minutes)	Mean percentage of time off nest	Sample size
1–7	109	8	38
8–14	95	7	35
15–21	84[a]	6	48
22+	140[a]	10	37

a. The difference between these means is significant (Fisher's least significant difference test—$df = 154$, $t = 1.98$, $LSD = 55.66$, $p = 0.05$).

100 km north of the northern limit of the turkey's range in Michigan; the present study was at the southern limit of the wild turkey's range in the eastern United States. The longer recesses in Florida may be an adaptation to warmer air and soil temperatures; the eggs might not cool as rapidly in the hen's absence in Florida as they might in Michigan. The difference may be a reflection of genetic differences between wild and semiwild turkeys.

The Incubation Period

The periods from the beginning of continuous incubating behavior until the first poult hatched and until the brood left the nest averaged 26 days ($N = 7$) and 27 days ($N = 8$), respectively (table 3.6).

Healy et al. (1975) reported a mean incubation period of 28.6 days for captive wild turkeys but did not define the period or note the occurrence of a gradual onset of incubating behavior. In artificial incubators, domestic turkey eggs require 26.92 days to hatch and another 0.33 day for the poults to dry, which totals 27.25 days (Abbott and Craig 1960). This latter figure does not provide for the several hours that are required for imprinting in wild broods, and, therefore, would be more comparable to the 26-day period required for the first poult to hatch in wild Florida turkey nests.

The period of continuous incubating behavior for Florida turkey hens measured in the present study was briefer than the 28 days reported for the wild turkey (Mosby and Handley 1943), or the 27.3 days (Abbott and Craig 1960), or 28 days (Marsden and Martin 1949) for domestic turkey eggs in incubators. The reason for the disparity in incubation periods is that Florida wild turkey eggs are incubated for approximately 25 hours during the laying period before continuous

Table 3.6 Time intervals between events observed during the incubating periods of nine hens

Band number	Date and hour incubating began	Days until first poult hatched	Days until brood left nest	Clutch size	Number of eggs hatched
436R	11 Apr 1000	25.9	27.0	10.0	9.0
398R	23 Apr 0900	25.3	26.3	10.0	10.0
287R	20 Apr 0900		27.0	13.0	13.0
485R	11 Apr 0900	27.0		10.0	10.0
506R	02 Apr 1000	25.3	30.0	12.0	12.0
367R	05 May 1100	26.4	27.0	13.0	13.0
276R	12 May 0900		26.0	11.0	11.0
342R	24 Apr 0900	25.2	26.2	6.0	5.0
374R	21 Apr 1100	26.6	27.0	4.0[a]	4.0
MEANS		26.0	27.0	9.9	9.7
SD		0.7	1.3	3.1	3.10

a. This clutch was reduced to only four eggs, probably by predation, after incubating behavior began.

Table 3.7 Elapsed time from first egg pipping until nest departure for three closely monitored broods

First egg pipping			First poults seen			Elapsed time to first poult seen (hours)	Brood left nest		Number of poults	Elapsed time from pipping eggs to departure (hours)
Date	Hour	No.	Date	Hour	No.		Date	Hour		
29 May	1025	1	30 May	1500	4	28.6	31 May	0955	8	47.5
29 May	1400	1	31 May	1830	2	52.5	1 Jun	0840	13	66.7
10 May	1430	1	10 May	1458	1	0.3	11 May	1340	9	23.2

incubating behavior begins. No incubation occurs during the laying period when artificial incubators are used because the eggs are removed from the nests and stored at cool temperatures until placed in the incubator.

Few published data exist concerning the time required for whole clutches of wild turkey eggs to hatch after the first egg has pipped. Most writers, such as Mosby and Handley (1943), state that the hatching of the entire clutch requires about "24 hours." Healy et al. (1975) reported that artificially incubated wild turkey eggs each hatch in an interval of four to 21 hours; that whole clutches hatch in 12 to 48 hours; and that eight hours is required for a poult to dry. Cook (1972) reported that two wild nests hatched in 23.3 and 26.2 hours.

In the present study, the interval between the time the first egg of a clutch was observed pipping and the time at least one poult was seen hatched ranged from less than one hour to over 52 hours (table 3.7).

Hatching Behavior Hatching behavior was monitored in 14 nests: 7 by direct observation and 7 by electronic nest recorders. Eight of the 14 nests were inspected during the hen's last recess prior to hatching. In two nests, one egg was pipped; in another, two eggs were pipped; none was pipped in the other five nests. None of the 14 hens recessed later than the pipping stage.

Vocalizations of hens and poults in three nests were recorded through microphones during the hatching process. Brood hens made a number of calls that are used by turkeys at other times and two calls that are restricted to the hatching period. One hatching call is a "yelp" (Williams 1984) that begins with single notes at 400 Hz spaced about 0.5 to 1.0 second apart (fig. 3.9), sometimes accelerating to more than four notes per second. Images of sonograms resemble quarter notes in standard musical notation. This hatching yelp is uttered by the hen immediately after a poult peeps. Another previously undescribed call peculiar to the hatching period, termed the "hatching hoot" (fig 3.10), consists of a pro-

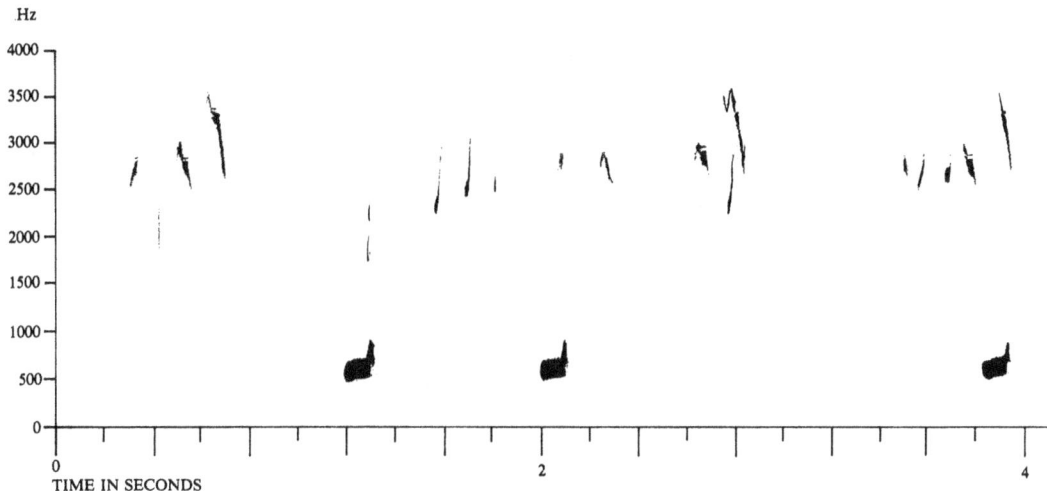

3.9 Sound spectrogram of the calling of the poults and the responding hatching yelps of the hen, recorded simultaneously during hatching.

3.10 Sound spectrogram of the "hatching hoot" of a brood hen. Typical examples may have three syllables, as shown here, or only one or two syllables.

longed, 600 Hz note given irregularly throughout the hatching process.

While in the nest, poults give peeping calls of three types (fig. 3.11): (1) a single note that is usually repeated; (2) a two-part ascending and descending note; and (3) a multisyllable call resembling the lost whistling call that poults use when they become separated from the hen.

These five calls, which were heard from all seven nests monitored by microphone, appear to be the basic vocal communications between the hen and her poults. This vocabulary enables the poults to identify the voice of their mother by the second day of life (Ramsay 1951).

As the poults hatched and the nest became crowded, the hen moved farther back, surrendering the front of the nest to the young. Poults napped, mainly under the sides, tail, and drooped wings of the hen; they sometimes ventured outside the nest during periods of activity. When a poult ventured as far as 1 m from the nest, the hen would yelp for it to return.

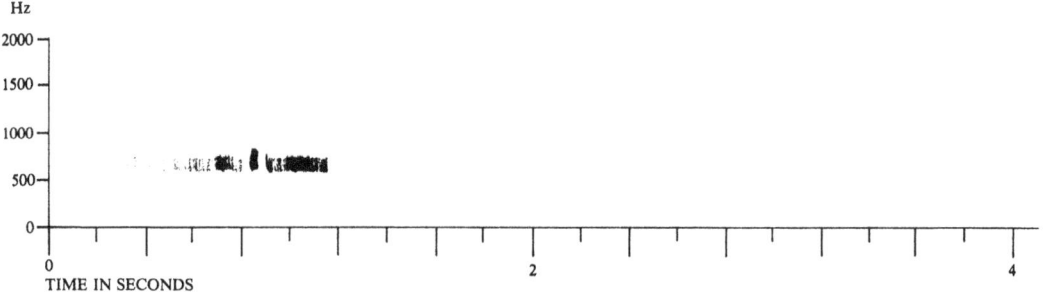

Hens did not leave the nest or respond in any way other than vocally when poults ventured out of the nest.

Egg Hatchability Hatchability was 89 percent (SD = 0.143) of 839 eggs in 85 undisturbed nests. McDowell (1956) reported a "hatching rate" of 96.8 percent in 13 nests in Virginia in 1953. Everett et al. (1980) reported a rate of 95 percent in 14 nests in a study in Alabama. Green (1982) reported only 71.5 percent hatchability in a Michigan study in which the stock was descended from pen-reared turkeys.

The Imprinting Period Parental imprinting is a learning process by which young birds of many species become socially attached to their parents and gain self-identity as members of their own species (Lorenz 1937). Imprinting takes place during the first few hours of life and is crucial for wild nidifugous birds. Imprinting is said to be irreversible in the turkey (Schein 1963). Although there is some dispute about the irreversibility of imprinting (Salzen and Meyer 1968), it is at least persistent and very difficult to reverse (Fabricius 1962).

Much of the research on imprinting has been with the mallard (*Anas platyrhynchos*). Ducklings remain in the nest for 24 to 62 hours after hatching (Hess 1972), which is 10 to 12 hours after the last-hatched duckling is dry (Kear 1965). Imprinting is complete (Bjarvell 1967), or nearly so (Fabricius and Boyd 1954), by the time of nest departure. Both auditory and visual cues are involved in imprinting (Ramsay 1951). Auditory cues are stronger and reach a peak effect several hours after visual cues. This is probably because of the greater need for audible communication between the hen and ducklings after they leave the nest and travel in vegetation where visibility is obscured (Fabricius 1964). Visual

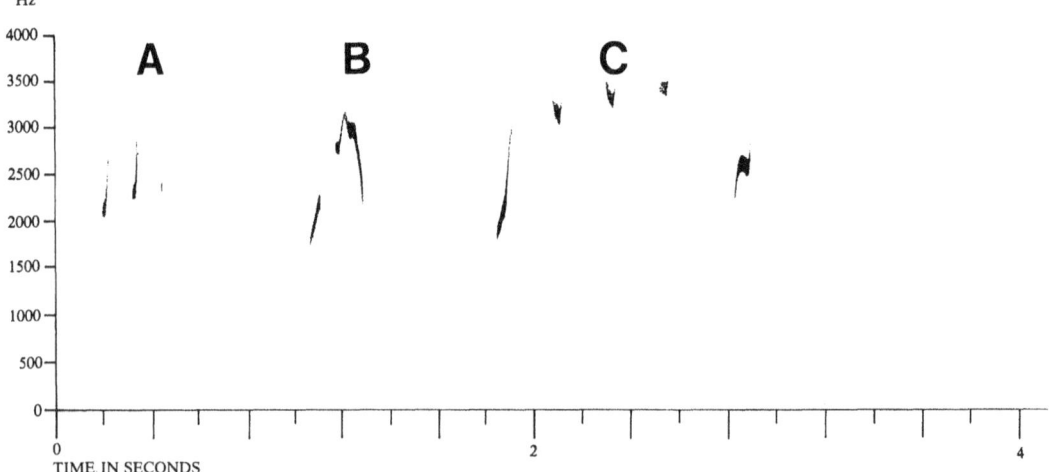

3.11 Sound spectrogram of the vocalizations of poults during the hatching period. A. Peeping notes, uttered singly or in groups of two to six. B. A two-part call with rising and falling pitch. C. A call similar to lost whistling— probably a distress call.

cues for imprinting are enhanced and following behavior is strengthened when ducklings make short excursions from the nest and can see the hen while she is calling (Bjarvell 1967). Ducklings without visual reinforcement probably would not follow as strongly upon nest departure. Our observations suggest that the imprinting process is similar in the wild turkey.

Seven turkey broods were observed from blinds. Broods remained in the nest for a variable interval of time after the last-hatched poult was dry and active. Hens vocalized softly during this time and the poults made short excursions out of the nest and returned at the command of the hen. Twelve to 14 hours after hatching, the poults became restless. During the 10-minute period prior to nest departure, hens called more frequently than before. Hens then arose abruptly, stepped out of the nest without hesitating, and moved slowly away while continuing to yelp softly to the poults.

In each of the seven brood departures, there was a gradient in the strength of the following response among poults—some followed at the hen's side, whereas others straggled behind. In three cases, a few poults failed to follow the hen farther than about one m from the nest, which caused the hen to stop and call. In two cases, a few poults remained in the nest, apparently more strongly attracted to it than to the hen. They followed the hen only after she returned to the nest and coaxed them.

Once we erected an observation blind too near a nest, causing the brood to depart prematurely about six hours after the last poult had hatched. Three of the poults remained in the nest for five minutes during which time the hen called to them from a distance of about two m. The hen had to return to within one m of the nest repeatedly before the poults finally followed her.

Another brood hatched on 30 May and, due to investigative disturbance, left the nest about 12 hours later. Four poults did not follow the hen, despite her continuous yelping. The observers left the area so that the brood could reassemble; however, the next morning one poult was found alone near the nest. Radio signals indicated that the hen was still near. The observers again left the area. The following morning, the four stray poults were found near the nest—the hen had left the area without them. Three of the poults were captured eventually by playing back the sounds of hatching that had been recorded at the nest three days earlier. The poults later became parent-imprinted on humans, which indicated they had not imprinted on the brood hen. These probably were some of the younger poults that had not associated with the hen long enough to follow her and that had a stronger attachment to the voices of their siblings and the sounds heard in the nest during the hatching process. The foregoing observations suggest that one of the reasons poults remain in the nest as long as they do after hatching is to become adequately imprinted on the hen.

Time of Nest Departure by Broods

None of 28 broods departed the nest before sunrise or after sunset (fig. 3.12). Nineteen (68 percent) departed during morning hours. Brood departure at midday was infrequent, corresponding to the reluctance of incubating hens to recess at that time. Only one brood departed after 1800 hours, and it traveled only 10 m before roosting that night. No brood returned to its nest after departing.

Hatching Synchrony

Some birds with large clutches have adaptations that hasten the hatching of the last-laid eggs so that all eggs hatch at nearly the same time. Synchronized hatching is advantageous for nidifugous birds with large clutches because it facilitates nearly simultaneous parental imprinting and early nest departure of the brood. Hatching synchronization is so well developed in the northern bobwhite that the entire clutch usually hatches in less than two hours (Vince 1969).

If hatching is synchronized, the time required for hatching should be less than the total incubating time experienced by the first egg before the last egg is laid. The regression equation for the onset of incubating behavior in the turkey (fig. 3.4) shows that, on an average, the first eggs received approximately 25 hours of incubation by the time the twelfth egg was laid. It would appear, then, that in taking more than

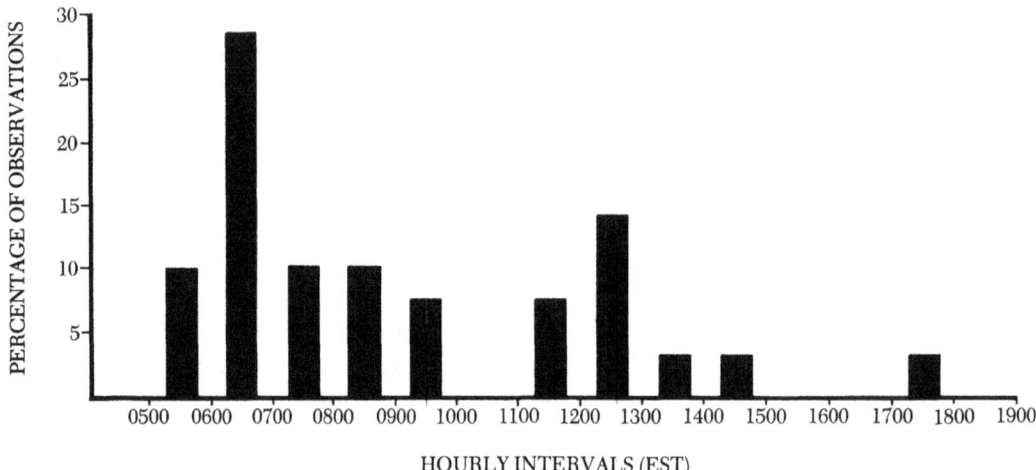

3.12 Hourly intervals that broods left their nests after hatching show a strong tendency to depart in the morning.

24 hours to hatch the clutch, the turkey exhibits poorly developed synchronizing mechanisms.

Attendance of Infertile Eggs

Two incubating hens attended infertile clutches for 35 and 64 days. The hen that incubated continuously for 64 days exceeded the normal incubation period by 38 days, incubating about 2.5 times the normal period. The northern bobwhite has been reported to sit on unhatched eggs as long as 56 days or 2.4 times its 23-day incubation period (Stoddard 1931).

Nesting Habitat

Of 236 nests, 58 percent were in the palmetto ecotone, 31 percent were in cypress woods, and 11 percent were in miscellaneous types of habitat (table 3.8). The proportions of the three habitats in the study area were 5, 51, and 44 percent for palmetto ecotone, cypress woods, and miscellaneous types, respectively. Hens selected nesting habitats in different proportions than the habitats occurred in the area ($X^2 = 1328$, $df = 2$, $p < 0.001$). Saw palmetto was favored for first, second, or third seasonal nesting attempts (table 3.8). Nesting habitat was used in similar proportions by adults and yearlings ($N = 223$, $X_2 = 0.68$, $df = 2$, $p = 0.018$).

Cypress woods and palmetto habitats differed notably in plant species composition (table 3.9) and structure. There was a tree canopy in the cypress woods (fig. 3.13) but none in the palmetto ecotone (fig. 3.14). Low vegetation in the cypress woods habitat was fast growing in contrast to the relatively unchanging composition and structure of the woody vegetation that predominated in the palmetto habitat.

Saw palmetto and wire grass occurred at all 44 nest sites in the palmetto ecotone (table 3.9), occupying more than 50 percent of the area within 1.5 m of 80 percent of the nests and no less than 20 percent of the area near any nest site in that habitat type. *Lyonia lucida* was the second most prevalent shrub at palmetto nests, occurring at 32 sites (73 per-

Table 3.8 Proportions of first, second, and third nests established in a single season, by habitat type

	Percentage of nests			
	All nests ($N = 236$)	First[a] nests ($N = 191$)	Second[a] nests ($N = 38$)	Third[a] nests ($N = 7$)
Palmetto	58	60	47	57
Cypress woods	31	30	37	14
Other	11	10	16	28
	100	100	100	100

a. These were the first, second, or third nests observed for the respective hens. A few nests were probably depredated during early laying stages and not detected or counted; therefore, some nests listed as first were probably the second, etc.

Table 3.9 Major plants occurring within 1.5 m of 63 nest sites, Fisheating Creek study area, 1968–72

	Percent occurrence		
Plant name	Palmetto (N = 44)	Cypress woods (N = 15)	Miscellaneous (N = 4)
Trees			
Taxodium distichum		100	
Shrubs			
Baccharis halimifolia			25
Callicarpa americana	20		25
Ilex glabra			25
Lyonia ferruginea	36		
Lyonia lucida	73		25
Myrica cerifera			25
Quercus chapmanii	32		
Querus geminata	18		
Serenoa repens	100		25
Vines			
Smilax spp.	25		25
Rubus sp.			25
Vitis sp.			25
Herbs			
Aristida stricta	100		25
Quercus minima	64		
Andropogon sp.	32		
Vaccinium myrsinites	25		
Panicum sp.	36		25
Axonopus compressus		95	25
Hydrocotyle umbellata		33	
Centella asiatica		47	
Saururus cernuus		20	
Polygonum sp.		40	
Rhus radicans		47	
Hypericum sp.			25
Iris savannarum			25
Eupatorium coelestinum		73	
Eichhornia crassipes		33	25

NOTE: Nineteen additional plants, mostly immature seedlings, which occurred at no more than two nest sites, are not listed.

cent). Nine other plant species occurred near more than 18 percent of the nests in the palmetto habitat type.

In cypress woods, cypress trees occurred within 1.5 m of all 15 nests and the grass, *Axonopus compressus*, occurred near 13 nests. Nests in the cypress woods usually were in the densest ground cover available, which was often in semi-aquatic vegetation such as *Centella asiatica*, *Saururus cernuus*, and *Polygonum* sp. (table 3.9).

Each of the four nest sites in the miscellaneous habitat category was in distinctly different vegetation: a narrow, dry ditch; a flood control dike; a high, isolated saw palmetto clump; and a wax myrtle thicket along a fence row.

Ninety-five percent of the 20 cypress woods nests and

3.13 Investigator standing beside a turkey nest site in cypress woods.

94 percent of the 62 nests in palmetto had 30 percent or more overhead cover (table 3.10). Only one nest (5 percent) in the cypress woods and two (3 percent) in the palmetto ecotone had less than 10 percent overhead cover. Thirty-eight percent of the nests in palmetto had 70 percent cover and 24 percent had more than 90 percent cover. None of the nests in cypress woods had more than 90 percent cover overhead.

Forty-two percent of 36 hens that were first observed nesting in the palmetto ecotone renested in another habitat; 33 percent first observed nesting in the "other" habitat type renested elsewhere; and 22 percent first observed nesting in cypress woods renested in another habitat (table 3.11). There was considerable variability in nesting habitat used in different years (table 3.12). The tendency to change freely from

Table 3.10 Overhead cover of 82 nests in cypress woods and palmetto nesting habitats

Percentage overhead cover[a]	Number and percentage of nests	
	Cypress woods	Palmetto
<30	1 (5%)	4 (6%)
30–40	2 (10%)	10 (17%)
51–70	6 (30%)	10 (17%)
>70	11 (55%)	38 (61%)
TOTALS	20 (100%)	62 (100%)

a. Visually estimated.

Table 3.11 Percentages of successive nests in the same or different habitat types

	Second in cypress	Second in palmetto	Second in "other"	Total switching
First nest in "cypress woods" (N = 9)	78	22	0	22
First nest in "palmetto" (N = 24)	29	58	13	42
First nest in "other" (N = 3)	0	33	67	33

one habitat to another for renesting in the same year and between years suggests that habitat preferences are weak and habitat imprinting may not be an important factor in nesting habitat selection by the Florida turkey.

3.14 Investigator standing beside a turkey nest site in palmetto-scrub ecotone.

Table 3.12 Number and percent of 236 turkey nests in three habitat types, Fisheating Creek and Lochloosa study areas, 1968–82

Year	Nesting habitat type						All nests	
	Palmetto		Cypress woods		Other			
	No.	%	No.	%	No.	%	No.	%
1968	16	84	3	16		0	19	8
1969	12	86	2	14		0	18	6
1970	15	79	4	21		0	17	8
1971	10	71	1	7	3	21	11	6
1972	7	50	7	50		0	14	6
1973	12	67	5	28	1	6	18	8
1974	12	55	6	27	4	18	22	9
1975	11	65	5	29	1	6	17	7
1976	7	58	5	42		0	12	5
1977	9	75		0	3	25	12	5
1978	5	50	3	30	2	20	10	4
1979	8	29	15	54	5	18	28	12
1980	12	38	14	44	6	19	32	14
1981	1	20	3	60	1	20	5	2
1982	137	58	72	31	27	11	236	100

Nesting Seasonality The earliest egg found in the study was laid on 6 March; the last egg was laid on 6 June. The last clutch hatched on 2 July. The median date of laying the first egg was 23 March ($\bar{x}$ = 25 March) and the median date that the last nest hatched was 8 June ($\bar{x}$ = 10 June) (fig. 3.15). Nests initiated after 1 May were probably the second or third nests of the respective hens that season. The molting pattern of at least 3000 juve-

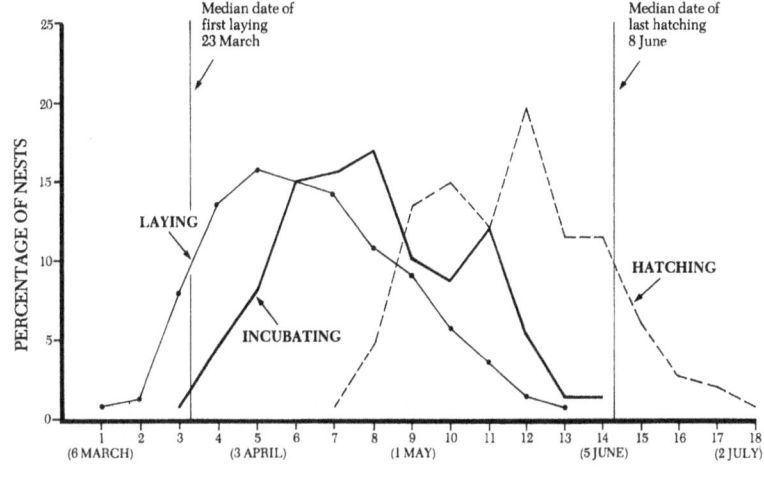

3.15 The nesting season of 121 Florida turkey hens on Fisheating Creek and Lochloosa study areas.

Reproductive Behavior and Performance

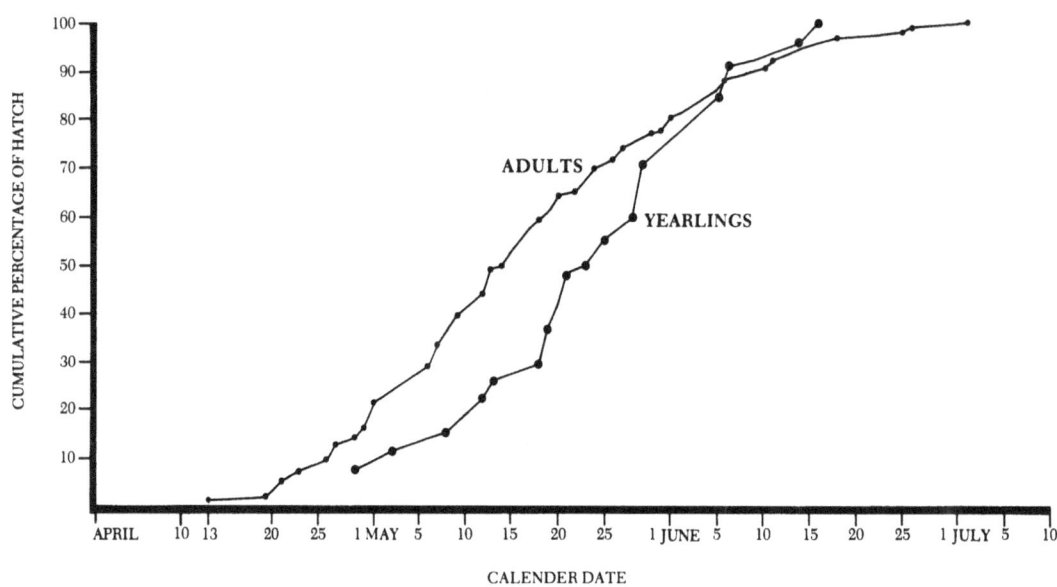

3.16 Cumulative percentage of hatching by calendar date comparing adult and yearling hens.

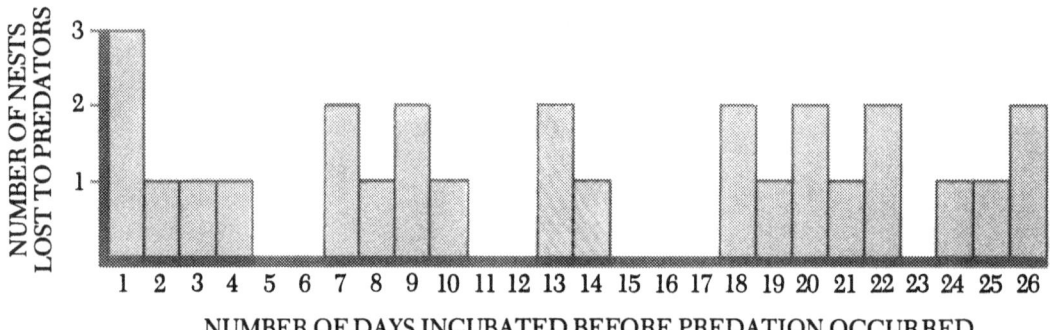

3.17 Distribution of predation incidents (N=27) with respect to the stage of incubation.

nile turkeys examined during summer and fall on the Lochloosa and Fisheating Creek WMAs substantiated the fact that very few poults were hatched after early July.

Yearling hens began nesting about two weeks later and finished two weeks earlier than adults (fig. 3.16 and 3.17). The difference was significant ($N^1 = 88$, $N^2 = 25$, Kolmogorov-Smirnov Z = 1923, maximum difference = 0.436, two-tailed p = 0.001). Later initiation of nesting by yearlings apparently occurs also in the Rio Grande turkey. Smith (1977) reported that adult hens in Texas began copulating before leaving their winter range, whereas yearlings did not begin copulating until after reaching their spring range.

Nesting Success and Predation

Sixty percent of the 171 nests that were not disturbed by the investigation were successful (table 3.13). This is not necessarily an accurate estimate of nesting success, however, because not all the nests were observed from the time of clutch initiation, a factor that would tend to bias nest discovery in favor of successful nests. The Mayfield (1961) method, which provides an appropriate adjustment for nests observed during only a portion of their full terms, was used to calculate nesting success. During the study, eight nests were lost to predators during the laying period (table 3.14). During the same 14-year period, "nest days" under observation totaled 218. Thus, 0.0367 (8/218) nests were lost per day during the

Table 3.13 Fates of nests under observation

	All nests (N = 237)		Nests not disturbed by investigators (N = 171)	
Fate	Number	Percent	Number	Percent
Hatched	103	43	102	60
Predator	59	25	59	35
Flushed	42[a]	18		
Deserted	31[b]	13	8	5
Flooded	2	1	2	1
TOTALS	237	100	171	100

a. Includes 15 from which the hens were flushed intentionally.
b. Includes 23 that may have been accidentally disturbed by the investigators.

Table 3.14 Nest survival data used to calculate the probability of successful nesting (Mayfield 1961)

	Laying period		Incubating period	
Year	No. depredated	Days exposed	No. depredated	Total days exposed
1968	1	5	7	260
1969	0	0	2	108
1970	0	29	1	298
1971	1	25	1	196
1972	1	8	2	187
1973	1	17	2	297
1974	1	34	7	337
1975	0	14	2	195
1976	0	7	2	183
1977	0	0	0	0
1978	2	21	1	153
1979	1	22	1	174
1980	0	10	5	259
1981	0	26	3	377
1982	0	0	2	63
TOTAL	8	218	38	3,087

Reproductive Behavior and Performance

laying period. The daily probability of survival for any nest would be 0.963 (1 − 0.0367). Since approximately 12 days are required for a clutch of 10 eggs to be laid (one egg per day plus two skipped days in a typical clutch), the entire laying period would be 12 days. The probability of a nest surviving the 12-day laying period would be 0.963^{12} or 0.638. Survival during the incubating period was calculated similarly using 27 as the number of days in the incubation period yielding 0.716 ([38/3087] − 1.0 = 0.98769; 98767^{27} = 0.716) as the probability of survival to hatching for each nest during the incubating period. The probability of a nest hatching would be 0.638 × 0.716 = 0.457. Thus the proportion of nests surviving the laying period was 63.8 percent, those surviving the incubating period was 71.6 percent, and those surviving the entire nesting period was 45.7 percent. As expected, the latter figure is lower than the 60 percent hatching success recorded for all nests under observation (table 3.13).

It is possible to take renesting into account to estimate the success of the nesting hen population by using the probabilities calculated previously:

0.566 = the probability that a hen will renest if the nest is lost during the laying period;
0.280 = the probability that a hen will renest if the nest is lost during the incubating period;
0.638 = the probability that the nest of a laying hen will reach the incubating stage;
0.716 = the probability that a clutch that reaches the incubating stage will hatch;
0.362 = (1 − 0.638) = the probability that any nest will be lost during the laying period; and
0.284 = (1 − 0.716) = the probability that any nest will be lost during the incubating period.

In applying these calculations to nesting success of the population, it would have to be assumed that all hens will attempt to nest and will renest once if the nest is disrupted during the incubating period and twice if disrupted during the laying period. These calculations yield:

(0.638) × (0.716) = 0.457 as the proportion of first-time nesters that will be successful;
(0.362) × (0.566) × (0.638) × (0.716) = 0.094, the proportion of hens losing their nests during the laying period that will successfully renest;

(0.638)(0.284)(0.280)(0.638)(0.716) = 0.023, the proportion of hens losing their nests during the incubating period that will successfully renest;

(0.362)(0.566)(0.362)(0.566)(0.638)(0.716) = 0.019, the proportion of hens losing their nests twice during the laying period that will hatch a clutch.

Overall nesting success would be the sum of the products: 0.457 + 0.094 + 0.023 + 0.019 = 0.593, or 59.3 percent.

The calculated rate of overall nesting success may not accurately reflect nesting success of the entire population because hens that do not nest are not accounted for in the calculations. If some hens did not attempt to nest, which is likely, the overall nesting success rate would be lower. Despite this nesting success of only 59.3 percent, turkey populations on the study areas were believed to be increasing slightly during the period of this study.

Predation on 27 nests was distributed evenly throughout the incubation period (fig. 3.14). Predatory species responsible for nest losses could not be ascertained in every case, but evidence at nest sites indicated that raccoons (*Procyon lotor*) were prominent predators in the cypress woods, and the striped skunk (*Mephitis mephitis*) and spotted skunk (*Spilogale putorius*) were the major predators in and around oak scrub and palmetto. Other predators included the opossum (*Didelphis virginiana*), gray fox (*Urocyon cinereoargenteus*), bobcat (*Felis rufus*), and domestic dog. In only a single instance was an American crow (*Corvus brachyrhynchos*) believed to have destroyed a nest.

Potential nest predators that were not known to take turkey eggs included the feral hog (*Sus scrofa*), which has been reported to depredate turkey nests (Barkalow 1942, Blakey 1937), and the armadillo (*Dasypus novemcinctus*), which many laymen suspect of taking turkey eggs. Although armadillos did not eat any turkey eggs, they rooted through two nests, rolling out some of the eggs and causing the hens to abandon the nests.

A higher proportion of nests was depredated in the cypress woods (55 percent) than in saw palmetto (32 percent) or in the "other" (21 percent) habitats ($N = 148$, $X^2 = 8.043$, $df = 2$, $p = 0.018$). The "other" habitat category was heterogeneous in plant species composition and structure, whereas the cypress woods and palmetto were relatively homogeneous. The lower predation rate in the heterogeneous "other" habitats supports the experimental findings of Bowman and

Harris (1980), who predicted that nest predation rates would be higher in homogeneous habitats.

Predator success is reportedly high when prey is abundant and increases with hunting experience of the predators (Tinbergen et al. 1967). If these factors were important in the present study, nest losses should have been higher in mid- or late-season nests than in early nests because nests are more abundant in midseason and predators by that time have had an opportunity to enhance their search image. However, predation rates did not differ among early-season (hatching before 1 May), midseason (hatching 1 May through 20 May) or late-season (hatching after 20 May) nests ($N = 117$, $X^2 = 2.6$, $df = 2$, $p = 0.26$). This may be because relatively few turkey nests were involved. It seems unlikely that individual predatory animals would gain sufficient experience in finding turkey nests to enhance that skill.

Defensive Behavior Predation is an important factor in the life and evolution of the wild turkey. Nest losses to predators were 54.8 percent, as previously calculated, and poult losses during the first two weeks were about 70 percent. The annual population turnover rate has been estimated to range from 30 percent (Logan 1973) to 50 percent (Smith 1977). The brood's defensive behavior has an important bearing on countering this predation.

The major behavioral adaptations of the turkey hen to avoid nest predation are: (1) selecting a well-hidden nest site; (2) laying eggs in midday when common nest predators are inactive; (3) covering the nest with debris before leaving it during the laying period; (4) minimizing activity near the nest; (5) remaining on the nest when predators approach; (6) sometimes flying to and from the nest rather than walking; and (7) not defecating near the nest.

The plumage of the hen is cryptically marked with brown and black. Natural colors of the ground litter at nesting sites tend to optimize the camouflage effect. Nests are covered lightly with a few dead leaves while unattended during the laying period. Overhead cover at nests is at least 40 percent. Sunlight through the vegetation creates a broken pattern of irregular light and dark spots, which accentuate the cryptic effect of the hen's speckled back pattern and the camouflage of dried litter covering the eggs.

Hens lay in midday at which time the major nest predators (raccoon, opossum, and skunk) are inactive. It is unlikely that predators would see the hen approaching her nest at midday or would track her by scent when they emerge to hunt several hours later.

Hens do not linger near their nests. During the normal laying routine, they roost at least 0.5 km away and spend their inactive daylight hours away from the nest. When approaching the nest to lay, hens move steadily and enter the nest quickly. If a hen sees a person as she returns to the nest, she delays her approach but returns quickly to the nest when the person leaves the area.

Eight hens were monitored from observation blinds and by radiotelemetry as they left their nests during the laying period. They did not dust, rest, or feed until they had moved farther than 200 m. Only two of the eight hens were known to visit their nests for activities other than to lay or incubate, and each did so only once.

Hens chose dense cover for nesting and sat still when investigators walked near their nests. The turkey's defense strategy of holding tightly to the nest is a general defense strategy of many prey animals (Edmunds 1974). An observer approached within 6 m of 13 nests located in palmetto habitat a total of 19 times; in no case did the hen flush when the investigator passed at a distance greater than 2 m.

Hens on recesses during continuous incubating behavior waited until they were at least 50 m from the nest before defecating. At such times the droppings were approximately 20 times as large as normal hen droppings and two that were weighed exceeded 50 g (2 oz). Evidently, feces collect in the cloaca and nearby large intestine during incubating sessions. Hens on recesses have been noted to defecate several times but only the first defecation is so massive.

In seven cases, hens returning to their nests were frightened away by an investigator who was within 5 m of their nests; none abandoned.

In approximately 30 000 man-hours of field work, only one active nest was found accidentally. This, coupled with the observations on nest-holding behavior, suggest that disturbance of hens on their nests by humans in cover conditions such as those on the study areas is minimal.

Turkey hens in Alabama (Wheeler 1948) and in the Rocky Mountains (Ligon 1946) have been observed flying to and from their nests. In the present study, 20 percent ($N = 140$) of the hens flew from or to the nest site. In flying to their nests, turkeys usually landed 3 to 15 m away and walked the remaining distance; when flying from the nest, they took two to five steps before flying, often taking wing within 3 m of the nest.

Much has been written about nest abandonment as a result of human disturbance of nesting hens (see Schorger 1966:265–266 for a review). Logan (1973) reported that seven

Table 3.15 Number and percentage of hens returning to their nests after being deliberately flushed by an observer

Nesting period	Number of hens flushed	Hens returning	
		N	Percent
Laying period	8	3	38
First week of incubation	19	8	42
After first week of incubation	10	6	60
Incubation period	30	18	60
Entire nesting period	38	21	55

Table 3.16 Number and percentage of hens by age class and habitat type that returned to their nests after being flushed by an observer during the laying and incubation periods combined

Habitat type or age class	Number of hens flushed	Hens returning	
		N	Percent
Palmetto	22	13	59
Cypress woods	18	7	39
Adult	32	18	56
Yearling	11	3	27

of nine hens in Oklahoma were flushed repeatedly from their nests without abandoning. The two hens that abandoned were flushed during the laying period—the other seven were incubating when flushed. In the present study, several hens that were flushed two to five times returned to their nests. Of the 38 hens flushed from their nests a single time in the present study, 55 percent did not return (table 3.15). Hens apparently have differing tolerances to being flushed from the nest.

It is widely believed that nesting hens are more likely to abandon their nests if flushed during the laying period than if flushed during the period of continuous incubating behavior (Schorger 1966). In this study, 60 percent of the hens that were flushed during the continuous incubating behavior period returned to their nests in contrast to 38 percent flushed during the laying period (table 3.15). Although the observed behavior supports the consensus view on the subject (Schorger 1966), the difference was not significant ($X^2 = 0.84$, df = 2, $p = 0.359$).

Habitat type appeared not to influence nest abandonment significantly. Thirty-nine percent of the hens flushed from nests in the cypress woods returned, compared to 59 percent returning to nests in palmetto ($X^2 = 1.61$, df = 1, $p = 0.446$) (table 3.16). However, a higher proportion of yearling hens (73 percent) abandoned their nests after being flushed than did adults (44 percent) and the difference was statistically significant ($X^2 = 2.751$, df = 1, $p = 0.097$).

4

Life History and Other Observations

Roosting of Young Broods

Early accounts of turkeys' roosting behavior were reviewed by Schorger (1966:161–172). Three studies since Schorger's review concern winter roosts (Kothmann and Litton 1975, Haucke 1975, and Smith 1975). Two others (Beoker and Scott 1969 and Hoffman 1968) are about summer and winter roosting of the Merriam's turkey (*M. g. merriami*), presumably adult and older juvenile turkeys. Roosting of the younger age classes has not been studied before.

The following account is based on a 1969 study of radio instrumented broods, observed from the time of hatching through about 12 weeks of age (Barwick et al. 1971) on Lykes Fisheating Creek and Lochloosa wildlife management areas.

Hens were radio instrumented in early spring. Roosting information was collected on their broods later. Tree heights, limb diameters, and overstory cover percentages were estimated visually. Surface distances were paced or measured on maps. Tree diameters (dbh) were measured with tapes or estimated in a few cases.

Position radio fixes on roosting broods were made at least once each night during the first two to three weeks after hatching and less frequently thereafter for about three more weeks. Most preflight roosts were found by approaching in predawn darkness and hiding close to the roost until the brood awoke and left. When broods reached approximately 10 days of age, they were closely monitored each morning to determine with certainty when they began roosting in trees.

Preflight Roosts Most roosting spots on the ground were under a forest canopy of either cypress (Fisheating Creek study area) or slash pine (Lochloosa study area) in ground cover that did not always completely conceal the brooding hen laterally. Broods often roosted beside a tree, cypress knee, large bush or tree stump. Lizard tail (*Saururus cernuus*), smartweed (*Polygonum* sp.), iris (*Iris* sp.), grasses, and sedges were typically present.

Broods roosted outside the forest canopy only when high-water conditions in Fisheating Creek flooded them out of the cypress woods, at such times using mainly saw palmetto cover, which lies at elevations immediately above the high water zone. Broods sometimes roosted in openings in the cypress woods where no canopy was directly overhead (fig. 4.1), usually near stands of cypress trees. The only brood regularly

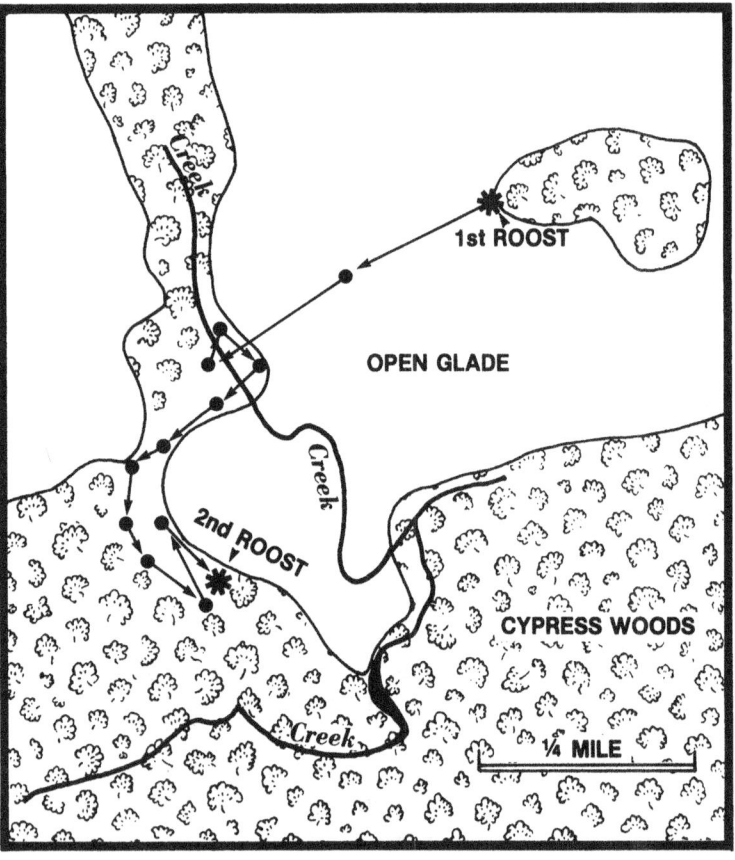

4.1 Movement pattern of a one-day-old brood from the first night roosting place, to the woods, and to the second night's roost. Solid dots are positions of the brood each hour on the hour. The most rapid movement was across the open glade.

observed during the preflight period on the Lochloosa study area roosted several times in an open swamp of a type Laessle (1942) called a "flat-woods bog," but most of the time roosted under a slash pine canopy.

When roosting on the ground, broods were completely covered by the body, drooped wings, and partly spread tail of the hen. (The nighttime positions of the poults were obvious when the spread of the poult droppings was seen in the roost spot after the brood had left.) The roosting spot was easily detected by the body depression of the hen left in the vegetation. Normally, one or two very large droppings were deposited by the hen from six to about 20 feet (1.8 to 6 m) from the roost when the hen departed in the morning. Only one of approximately 40 hens was known to defecate in the ground roost spot in more than 70 observations made.

On the Fisheating Creek study area, five cover situations rarely used by ground roosting broods were: (1) open glades; (2) shrubby thickets; (3) low, overhanging vegetation; (4) heavily grazed live oak hammocks; and (5) saw palmetto prairies (except the edges during high water). Too few broods were monitored on the Lochloosa area to justify generalizations about cover types that were avoided there.

Roosts in Trees   Although turkeys can fly well at 10 days of age, they do not begin roosting in trees until 12 to 19 days old (table 4.1); more than half of the 14 broods monitored were roosting in trees by the time they were 14 days old. None roosted again on the ground after once roosting in trees.

Table 4.1 Dates and ages of 14 broods when first roosting in trees

Band number of hen	Nest departure date	Date of first roost in tree	Age of brood in days[a]
267R	8 May 1969	20 May 1969	13
289R	13 May 1969	24 May 1969	12
6R	19 May 1969	31 May 1969	13
288R	5 June 1969	17 June 1969	13
255R	23 May 1970	4 June 1970	13
335R	6 June 1970	20 June 1970	15
226R	6 June 1970	20 June 1970	15
321R	24 May 1970	4 June 1970	12
314R	19 May 1970	30 May 1970	12
342R	20 May 1970	3 June 1970	14
3020M	7 May 1970	22 May 1970	16
6R	13 May 1970	25 May 1970	13
330R	6 June 1970	22 June 1970	17
4966M	10 June 1970	28 June 1970	19

a. The number of whole or partial days after the newly hatched brood left its nest. Since more than one day is required for a complete clutch to hatch, some of the older poults in each brood were at least one day older than the youngest in the brood.

There is wide disparity in the literature about the age when turkey poults begin to roost in trees, probably because it has been difficult to determine the age of wild broods accurately or to observe them at will. Latham (1956) said that broods first roost in trees after four or five weeks. Mosby and Handley (1943) reported it was four weeks. Some other writers (Ligon 1946, Wheeler 1948) were in closer agreement with our findings in reporting tree roosting between 10 and 14 days of age. Audubon's (from Bent 1932:332) estimate of a "fortnight" (14 days) agrees very closely with our observations.

The 13 broods monitored on the Fisheating Creek study area roosted in cypress trees exclusively. The single brood observed on the Lochloosa study area used only pine trees. These were the most abundant trees in the home range of the broods. The choice of tree types, however, was not strictly in proportion to availability.

The first night off the ground was typically spent on a horizontal limb a few feet lower than limbs used by older broods but of about the same diameter (two to three inches, or about 7 cm). The average height above the ground for first night tree roosts was 22 feet (6.7 m) (extremes 14 to 35 feet). Three nights later, the average roost height was 31 feet (9.5 m) (extremes 15 to 55 feet). Broods did not appear to roost any higher after about the fifth night of tree roosting, but this may have been related to the characteristics of the trees present and might vary under different circumstances.

During the first week of roosting in trees, the poults roosted close beside the hen. Unobstructed observations could rarely be made, but it appeared that all the poults were under the hen's outspread wings for the first few days, after which some roosted nearby on the same limb but not necessarily under her wings. At three or four weeks, the brood was usually on the same limb or at least closely grouped at about the same level in the tree. By midsummer, at eight weeks of age, the brood often occupied more than one tree. When two or more broods roosted together the poults of the different broods sometimes mingled.

Roosting places used by young broods (table 4.2) were similar in general character to the places used by adult turkeys. Most were over water, or, if over dry ground, they were in low areas that were usually flooded. Broods did not roost in dry, open pine flatwoods or in bare or especially leafy trees. Neither did they crouch next to the tree's trunk nor seek concealment in the moss or thick foliage that was sometimes present.

According to Wheeler (1948) young broods in Alabama roosted in thickets on low limbs. Hillestad (1970), also refer-

Table 4.2 Characteristics of brood tree roosts used by turkeys in summer

Date of observations	Number of flocks	Number of hens	Number of poults	Height in tree (feet)	Number of trees	DBH of trees used (inches)[a]
1969						
May 1–15	5	5	16	45	5	15
May 16–31	1	1	5		1	14
June 16–30	9	19	49	53	17	13
July 1–15	4	7	14	57	6	14
July 16–31	4	10	38	50	11	12
Aug. 1–15	5	11	46	53	12	12
Aug. 16–31	6	14	48	62	14	12
1970						
May 16–31	1	1	2	55	1	14
June 1–15	7	10	25	43	10	11
June 16–30	8	13	17	50	10	
July 1–15	4	6	16	62	5	15
June 16–30	2	3	10	30	3	7
July 1–15	4	11	[b]	39	11	9

a. Mean of all trees used by broods during date interval.
b. Undetermined number of poults.

ring to Alabama, reported that two young broods he observed were roosting in grape vines (*Vitis rotundifolia*). The contrast between early roosting sites used in southern Florida and in Alabama cannot be attributed to differences in availability of vegetation types because grape vines and thickets were available on our study areas and could have been used by the Florida turkeys. Additional information is needed to clarify this.

In southern Florida, turkeys show a strong preference for roosting in cypress ponds. A typical roosting pond has a variety of tree size classes and contains water during most of the year. Any future study of preferred roosting cover in Florida should attempt to determine minimum sizes of timber stands used, particularly when isolated cypress ponds are involved. The information could be useful in habitat management decisions in the future.

Movement Between Roosts

The average distance from nests to first night roosting places was 212 yards (194 m), with extremes of seven yards (6 m) to 600 yards (548 m), for 10 monitored broods (table 4.3). The shorter first-day movements were by broods that left the nest late in the afternoon and simply stopped for the night before moving very far. One-day-old broods typically moved rapidly across open areas when necessary to reach forest cover and remained in the woods for most of the summer. Figure 4.1 shows characteristic movement of a brood from the first night's roost, which was very near the nest site, to the cy-

Table 4.3 First day travel of 11 turkey broods

Band number	Age-class of hen	Number of poults	Time of leaving nest	Distance to first roost (yards)	Distance moved first day (yards)
237R	Yearling	9	0745	7	7
222R	Adult	5	Unknown	100	Unknown
233R	Adult	10	After 1211	250	Unknown
2831R	Adult	10	After 1500	300	Unknown
213R	Adult	10	After 1000	200	Unknown
215R	Adult	10	After 1045	200	Unknown
229R	Adult	9	After 1330	70	Unknown
006R	Adult	6	Before 0845	600	675
289R	Adult	10	About 0830	475	925
265R	Yearling	9	About 1830	100	100
288R	Yearling	10	After 1330	Unknown	Unknown

NOTE: Measured by distances between successive fixes throughout the first day or portion thereof after leaving the nest. This is an underestimate of the distance actually traveled.

Table 4.4 Distances between successive nightly roosts of four broods

Hen band number	Distance before roosting in trees (miles)		Distance while roosting in trees (miles)		Overall miles
	Range	$\bar{x}$	Range	$\bar{x}$	$\bar{x}$
276R	.04–.43	.21	0.04–0.54	.25	.24
289R	.09–.48	.25	0.06–0.72	.31	.29
006R	.06–.58	.23	0.04–0.78	.18	.21
4966M	.07–.79	.24	0.13–1.31	.55	.35

press woods. When the brood reached the edge of wooded cover, it would turn back into the woods.

Late summer, fall, and winter flocks have favorite roosting places and will return to them often, sometimes using the same trees for several consecutive nights. Summer broods in this study mostly used different places to roost each night and did not return to exactly the same stand of trees repeatedly.

The minimum, maximum, and average distances that four broods traveled between successive ground roosts were measured (table 4.4). This gives a conservative estimate of the distances traveled. The broods moved an average of 0.27 miles (0.43 km) between nightly roosts. Distances varied from 0.04 miles (0.06 km) to 1.31 miles (2.11 km). One brood on the Lochloosa study area moved greater distances between several roosts before the poults could fly than after. This brood averaged at least 0.24 miles (0.39 km) farther between roosts each night than did the other three broods. The three others moved greater distances each day between successive roosts after they began roosting in trees.

The rate of daytime movement for two broods was roughly calculated by the time and distance between successive fixes. When undisturbed, one brood traveled 0.09 miles per hour during parts of its first day. Another day-old brood, after being disturbed by an observer, moved 0.45 miles per hour for 40 minutes.

Early Morning Behavior on the Roost

Three broods were watched closely one morning in June as they were roosting together, accompanied by two hens without broods. The radio instrumented brood in the group was five weeks old. The other poults were estimated by their size to be six and seven weeks old.

As the observer approached the roosting turkeys in the darkness, several of the poults and a hen acted as though they had heard him, but after he was hidden and still, the turkeys showed no further concern. The broods were spaced 30 to 80 feet (9 m to 24 m) apart on the lower limbs of cypress trees, 30 feet (9 m) above the water of a shallow slough. The five hens were in different trees.

At 0616 hours, the only hen in clear view was still squatting on a limb in the sleeping posture, but her poults were hopping from limb to limb in the same tree and in one nearby. At 0630 hours, one poult spotted the observer and gave an alarm putt (Williams 1984), then resumed its restless behavior and paid no further attention to the observer. At 0632, one hen glided silently to the ground in the cypress woods about 400 feet (120 m) from her roost and was followed at about 5-second intervals by four poults from the same tree. Sunrise was at 0639. At 0640, a second hen flew down in the same general direction and distance as the first, and was followed immediately by eight poults. The poults flew approximately as far as the hens did. Neither hen was heard to yelp. The radio instrumented hen flew down at 0642, followed immediately by three poults.

At 0645, a hen on the ground gave a brood assembly yelp and several more poults immediately flew in her direction from the trees, indicating that all of her poults had not flown down with her earlier. The quick reaction to her calling suggested that the poults recognized her voice. One of the poults glided to a landing in the calm water of the slough, which it evidently mistook for land, and flopped its way to the bank. At 0700, the five hens and the poults were seen at a distance feeding along the edge of a small opening in the cypress woods.

To summarize the roosting pattern of young broods: the turkeys roosted on the ground until they were two to three weeks old, after which they roosted in trees. Height of roosting was slightly lower for the first few nights than it was about a week later. Broods did not seek heavy cover while roosting in trees. Young broods did not roost in the same places repeatedly. There was little difference in the distance between nightly ground roosts and nightly tree roosts.

The broods had no peculiar roosting requirements either while roosting on the ground or in trees and special provisions for brood roosting habitat are probably not warranted in habitat similar to the study areas. There may be important relationships between brood ground roosting conditions and poult predation rates during the extremely vulnerable ground roosting period, as will be discussed later.

Flight Attainment

Written statements about the age at which wild turkeys and some other gallinaceous birds begin to fly have sometimes been given in terms of a "flightless" period. For example, in reference to turkeys, Lewis (1967, pp. 45–72) says, "Poults are unable to fly during the first two weeks after hatching" and Wheeler (1948) states, "The hen remains on the ground with her brood for the first two weeks. During this period the young are not able to fly." These writers probably realized that flying ability is attained gradually by turkeys, but their statements give the impression that the young suddenly acquire that ability.

The tendency in the published literature has been to report "age of first flight" based on observations of flying poults that were thought to be younger than any reported before. Earlier writers, such as Mosby and Handley (1943), reported early flying ability in four-week-old poults that we now know had probably been flying for about two weeks. Two others, Nixon (1962) and Hillestad (1970), reported flight in seven-day-old poults. As reports of "age of first flight" approach the date of hatching, the question becomes more one of defining the term "flying" than of discovering the chronology of the behavior. Actually, there is hardly a definable point during this learning process that poults can be said to "fly for the first time."

We have watched more than 30 wild turkey broods engaged in various activities from hatching to several weeks of age. After hatching, poults improve steadily in agility and muscular strength. At one and two days of age, they stay close to the hen as the brood travels. By the third and fourth day, the same poults dart away chasing insects and may be left a short distance behind the brood. When a four-day-old straggler discovers that it is being left, it runs, hops, and flaps its wings while catching up. At four days of age a poult's stride may be shorter than one foot (0.3 m) as it catches up with the brood. By the sixth day, the young bird touches the ground ever more lightly and fewer times in covering the distance. When it springs over elevated roots or dead limbs, it may move three feet (1 m) or more through the air, assisted by its wings. Their strength and agility is such that poults could probably fly quite well except that they do not at this age have the wing feathers for it. By the eighth day of life, the feathers are larger and the poults can move through the air as high as five feet (1.5 m); most observers would agree that at this age weak flight has been attained. It would be as logical, however, to say that a bird is "flying" as soon as it can travel through the air farther than it can jump. That would be as early as six days after turkey poults leave their nests.

Thus flying ability is attained in small degrees, and, while it is true that there is a period when "poults cannot fly," that time is briefer than is generally supposed. The "flightless" condition in young turkeys disappears gradually between four and about eight days of age. Although they can fly well at 10 days of age, poults continue to roost on the ground at night until they are about two weeks old.

Foods

Most food studies of the wild turkey have dealt with grown young or adult turkeys during fall and spring when crops and stomachs were available from legal hunting. The only food habits research done heretofore in Florida was based on the crops of 32 fall and winter specimens and a large number of droppings from throughout the state (Schemnitz 1956). In that study, no distinction was made as to the age of the turkeys or season of the year. Such studies have given a general picture of the foods eaten by turkeys in fall and winter.

In the present study (Barwick et al. 1973), we took advantage of an opportunity to identify the foods eaten by young poults and by a few summer adults that were shot for studies of parasites and diseases, molt and plumage development, and growth rates. While this is not a definitive report of poults' food habits, it is evidently only the second study of foods of young poults. The first report was a paper by Hamrick and Davis (1971) in Alabama. Three other recent studies (Martin and McGinnes 1975, Hurst and Stringer 1975, and Blackburn et al. 1975) are in the Proceedings of the Third National Wild Turkey Symposium (Halls 1975). Additional food habits studies have been conducted recently in Mississippi (Owen 1976) and in Pennsylvania (Nenno and Lindzey 1979). Hurst (1973) compared the foods eaten by pen-raised turkey poults that had fed on burned and unburned study plots, and Healy (1978) studied human-imprinted poults' feeding behavior.

The present study was done on Fisheating Creek and Lochloosa wildlife management areas. Eighty-three wild turkeys (75 poults, 8 adults) were hand-caught (when too young to fly), cannon netted, or shot between 22 April and 31 October 1969 and through 1972. Crop and gizzard contents were preserved in buffered 10 percent formalin and later air-dried, sorted, and identified. Items measuring less than 0.05 ml were recorded as traces. A few specimens that were collected near baited areas had eaten small amounts of corn bait, which is tabulated but not used in assessing food preferences. Grit occurred in all samples but is not included in the tables.

Of the 75 poults collected, 14 that had been toe-clipped soon after hatching were of known age. The others were aged by comparing their plumage development with known-age specimens. The ages of the poults were well distributed between one and 164 days.

Scientific names of the grasses are from Hitchcock (1950). Other plant names are from Fernald (1950) or Small (1933).

Table 4.5 lists the food items of 21 poults from one to 14 days old. Plant foods were found in 85.7 percent of the poults and accounted for 75.0 percent of the total food volume. Stargrass, the most important single plant food for this age group, occurred in 61.9 percent of the samples and accounted for 21.8 percent of the total food volume. It was closely followed by mixed vegetation (volume percent 17.5) and a small-fruited huckleberry (volume percent 14.1).

Animal parts occurred in 61.9 percent of the one- to 14-day-old poults and made up 25.0 percent of the total volume. Insects accounted for all of the measurable animal foods. Spider parts were found in one poult in trace amounts. Beetles were the single most important insect order, accounting for 19.6 percent of the insect volume.

The volume percent of animal foods (25.0) found in the one- to 14-day-old group was in close agreement with the findings of Hamrick and Davis (1971) but considerably less than reported for some other gallinaceous birds. In a study of the northern bobwhite, small insects were the most frequently eaten food of chicks two to 20 days old (Hurst 1972). Insects were reported to make up 70 percent of the diet of

Table 4.5 Plant and animal foods of 21 wild turkey poults, one to 14 days old, Glades County, Florida, listed in order of importance

Food item	Occurrence		Volume	
	Times	Percent	ml	Percent
Plant foods (total)	18	85.7	3.45	75.0
Stargrass seeds, *Hypoxis leptocarpa*	13	61.9	1.00	21.8
Misc. mixed vegetation, leaves, stems (partly Spanish moss)	2	9.5	0.80	17.5
Huckleberry fruit, *Gaylussacia* sp.	3	14.3	0.65	14.1
Tear thumb seeds, *Polygonum sagittatum*	6	28.6	0.20	4.4
Arrowhead tuber, *Sagittaria* sp.	2	9.5	0.20	4.4
Grass seeds, *Paspalum conjugatum*	3	14.3	0.15	3.3
Wax myrtle fruit, *Myrica cerifera*	3	14.3	0.15	3.3
Blueberry fruit, *Vaccinium* sp.	1	4.8	0.10	2.2
Bahia grass seeds, *Paspalum notatum*	3	14.3	0.10	1.6
Dayflower, *Commelina elegans*	2	9.5	0.05	1.1
Unidentified seeds	1	4.8	0.05	1.1
Unidentified grass leaves	1	4.8	trace	
Black haw seeds, *Viburnum* sp.	1	4.8	trace	
Animal foods (total)	13	61.9	1.15	25.0
Insecta, Insects (total)	13	61.9	1.15	25.0
Coleoptera, beetles	12	57.1	0.90	19.6
Hemiptera, bugs	1	4.7	0.05	1.1
Orthoptera, grasshoppers	2	9.5	0.05	1.1
Curculionidae—adults	14	25.9	3.85	2.0
Carabidae—adults	4	7.4	1.10	0.6
Cantharidae—adults	2	3.7	1.10	0.6
Elateridae—adults	4	7.4	0.50	0.3
Tenebrionidae—adults	4	7.4	0.50	0.3
Histeridae—adults	3	5.6	0.65	0.3
Scarabaeidae—adults	3	5.6	0.50	0.3
Hydrophilidae—adults	1	1.9	0.20	0.1
Anthribidae—adults	1	1.9	0.10	trace
Hemiptera bugs				
Pentatomidae—adults	12	22.2	2.60	1.4
Belostomatidae—adults	1	1.9	2.00	1.1
Cydnidae—adults	7	13.0	1.10	0.6
Coreimelaenidae—adults	3	5.6	0.90	0.5
Lygaeidae				
Nymphs	5	9.3	0.80	0.4
Adults	6	11.1	0.70	0.4
Reduviidae—adults	4	7.4	0.55	0.3
Coreidae—adults	4	7.4	0.50	0.3
Saldidae—adults	1	1.9	0.10	trace
Odonata dragonflies and damselflies				
Libellulidae				
Nymphs	1	1.9	2.00	1.1
Adults	2	3.7	0.40	0.2
Coenagrionidae—adults	2	3.7	0.40	0.2
Diptera flies				
Tabanidae—adults	1	1.9	2.00	1.1
Tipulidae—adults	3	5.6	0.30	0.2
Caliphoridae—adults	1	1.9	0.10	trace
Syrphidae—adults	1	1.9	0.05	trace
Homoptera leafhoppers and spittle bugs				
Cicadellidae—adults	9	16.7	1.05	0.6
Cercopidae—adults	3	5.6	0.40	0.2

(continued)

Table 4.5 (continued)

Food item	Occurrence		Volume	
	Times	Percent	ml	Percent
Dermaptera earwigs				
Labiduridae	2	3.7	0.20	0.1
Hymenoptera braconids, ichneumons, sawflies				
Ichneumonidae—adults	3	5.6	0.10	trace
Tenthridinidae—cocoons	1	1.9	0.05	trace
Braconidae—adults	1	1.9	0.05	trace
Neuroptera antlions				
Myrmeleonidae—adults	1	1.9	0.20	0.1
Arachnida, spiders	14	25.9	3.90	2.1
Oligochaeta, earthworms	2	3.7	1.40	0.7
Gastropoda, mollusk, snails	1	1.9	0.40	0.2
Reptilia, bone fragments	1	1.9	0.20	0.1
Myriapoda, millipedes	1	1.9	0.10	trace

ruffed grouse (*Bonasa umbellus*) during the first two weeks of life (Bump et al. 1947).

Table 4.6 lists the plant foods of 54 poults from 2 to 24 weeks old. Seeds of the grass *Paspalum conjugatum* occurred in 16.7 percent of the samples and amounted to 17.4 percent of the food by volume, the highest volume for any single wild food item. Three grasses together made up 25.1 percent of the total food volume. Live oak acorns accounted for 8.8 percent, stargrass 6.1 percent, arrowhead 5.0 percent and laurel oak acorns 4.2 percent of the plant food by volume. Swamp cabbage berries occurred in more samples (19) than any other plant food, but accounted for only 2.2 percent of the total volume.

Table 4.7 lists the animal foods of the same group of 54 poults 2 to 24 weeks old. Butterflies and moths (caterpillars) were the most important animal foods for this age group. Two insect families accounted for most of the animal foods by volume: Geometridae made up 49.5 percent and Noctuidae 19.8 percent.

Table 4.8 lists the plant foods of eight adult wild turkeys collected in the same areas during the same months as the poults. Wild grapes made up 44.9 percent of the plant food volume but occurred in only two of the samples. Seed of *Paspalum conjugatum* was next in volume percent and accounted for 25.8 percent. Black gum seed occurred in more samples (three of the eight samples) than any other plant food but comprised only 0.8 percent of the volume. Table 4.9 lists the animal foods of the same eight adult turkeys. As in the 15- to 164-day-old poults, caterpillars were the most important animal food items. Larvae of Geometridae accounted for 66.8 percent of the total. Both age classes of poults (one

Table 4.6 Plant foods of 54 wild turkey poults 2 to 24 weeks old, Alachua and Glades Counties, Florida

Food item	Occurrence		Volume	
	Times	Percent	ml	Percent
Zea mays, corn seeds	15	27.8	187.30	37.0
Paspalum conjugatum, seeds	9	16.7	88.00	17.4
Quercus virginiana, live oak acorns	6	11.1	44.50	8.8
Hypoxis leptocarpa, stargrass seeds, pods	15	27.8	30.70	6.1
Sagittaria sp., arrowhead tubers	13	24.1	25.15	5.0
Quercus laurifolia, laurel oak acorns	4	7.4	21.30	4.2
Panicum sp., panic grass leaves	2	3.7	20.00	4.0
Panicum, sp., panic grass seeds	11	20.4	15.40	3.0
Nyssa sylvatica, blackgum seeds	12	22.2	13.45	2.7
Unidentified leaves	2	3.7	13.00	2.6
Sabal palmetto, swamp cabbage berries, seeds	19	35.2	11.35	2.2
Rhus radicans, poison ivy seeds	8	14.8	6.20	1.2
Commelina elegans, dayflower seeds, pods, stems	10	18.5	6.00	1.2
Parthenocissus quinquefolia, Virginia creeper seeds	4	7.4	4.40	0.9
Paspalum notatum, bahia grass seeds	7	13.0	3.60	0.7
Ampelopsis arborea, pepper vine seeds	2	3.7	3.20	0.6
Myrica cerifera, wax myrtle seeds	12	22.2	3.00	0.6
Muscadinia munsonaria, grape seeds, fruit	4	7.4	2.45	0.5
Hydrocotyle sp., pennywort leaves	1	1.9	2.00	0.4
Taxodium sp., cypress twigs	1	1.9	2.00	0.4
Smilax sp., greenbriar seeds	7	13.0	0.85	0.2
Callicarpa americana, beautyberry seeds	1	1.9	0.40	0.1
Celtis laevigata, hackberry seeds	3	5.6	0.30	0.1
Diodia teres, buttonweed seeds	2	3.7	0.30	0.1
Ipomoea sp., morning glory seeds	1	1.9	0.20	trace
Desmodium tortuosum, seeds	1	1.9	0.20	trace
Triticum aestivum, wheat seeds	2	3.7	0.15	trace
Aneilema nudiflorum, seeds, pods	2	3.7	0.15	trace
Polygonum sagittatum, tear thumb seeds	7	13.0	0.15	trace
Viola sp., violet seeds, pods	1	1.9	0.10	trace
Unidentified seeds	1	1.9	0.10	trace
Zanthoxylum sp., prickly ash seeds	1	1.9	0.10	trace
Rubus sp., blackberry seeds	1	1.9	0.05	trace

to 14 days and over 14 days) and summer adults all ate animal and plant foods in the ratio of about 1:3 (table 4.10). This is similar to the ratio found in Alabama (Hamrick and Davis 1971) for poults over 45 days old, but it is at variance with a study in Mississippi, where Hurst and Stringer (1975) found younger poults eating a higher proportion of animal items until they were about three weeks old. The discrepancies between these studies may be due in part to the way the poults were grouped by age.

The turkey's diet is so broad that a very large sample would be necessary to fully reveal regional and temporal variation. Certainly, the 21 poults less than two weeks old in

Table 4.7 Animal foods of 54 Florida wild turkey poults, 2 to 24 weeks old, listed by common names of the orders and scientific names of insect families within each order

Food item	Occurrence		Volume	
	Times	Percent	ml	Percent
Lepidoptera butterflies and moths				
Geometridae				
Larvae	9	16.7	93.30	49.5
Pupae	1	1.9	0.30	0.2
Adults	1	1.9	0.20	0.1
Noctuidae				
Larvae	18	33.3	37.25	18.8
Adults	5	9.3	0.80	0.4
Citheroniidae—adults	1	1.9	1.50	0.8
Pyralidae—adults	5	9.3	0.80	0.4
Hesperiidae—larvae	3	5.6	0.25	0.1
Arctiidae—larvae	2	3.7	0.10	trace
Nymphalidae—adults	2	3.7	0.10	trace
Pieridae				
Larvae	2	3.7	0.10	trace
Pupae	1	1.9	0.05	trace
Orthoptera crickets, short-horned, long-horned, and pygmy grasshoppers				
Tetrigidae—adults	13	24.1	8.80	4.7
Acrididae				
Adults	8	14.8	6.20	3.3
Nymphs	2	3.7	0.40	0.2
Tettigoniidae				
Adults	7	13.0	1.10	0.6
Nymphs	2	3.7	0.40	0.2
Gryllidae				
Adults	5	9.3	0.55	0.3
Nymphs	3	5.6	0.30	0.2
Coleoptera beetles				
Chrysomelidae adults	12	22.2	4.50	2.4
Lepidoptera, moths, butterflies	2	9.5	0.05	1.1
Diptera, flies	1	4.7	0.05	1.1
Hymenoptera, ants, wasps, bees	1	4.7	0.05	1.1
Dermaptera, earwigs	1	4.7	trace	—
Arachnida, spiders	1	4.7	trace	—

this study are not a sufficient sample. We doubt that stargrass (22.8 percent of the plant volume) would be so prominent in a much larger sample or in another place or time.

It would be useful to know more than simply the names and quantities of foods that turkeys eat. To be of greater management value, food availability, its nutritional value, the ultimate success of reproduction, and general health of the population should be ascertained. To study the foods eaten without determining whether the study population is productive defeats the idea that knowledge of what the turkeys are eating is important—after all, in declining and unhealthy populations turkeys are eating something, even if it is of low nutritional value.

Table 4.8 Plant foods of 8 adult wild turkeys, 22 August to 1 November, Alachua and Glades Counties, Florida

Food item	Occurrence		Volume	
	Times	Percent	ml	Percent
Vitis rotundifolia, fruits, seeds	2	25.0	149.70	44.9
Paspalum conjugatum, seeds	3	37.5	86.10	25.8
Zea mays, corn seeds	3	37.5	86.10	25.8
Centrosema sp., butterfly peas, leaves, flowers	1	12.5	15.00	4.5
Serenoa repens, saw palmetto seeds	1	12.5	9.00	2.7
Myrica cerifera, wax myrtle seeds	2	25.5	8.00	2.4
Gramineae, grass leaves	2	25.0	8.00	2.4
Rhus radicans, poison ivy seeds	2	25.0	3.65	1.1
Desmodium tortuosum, beggarweed seeds	1	12.5	3.00	0.9
Nyssa sylvatica, blackgum seeds	3	37.5	2.75	0.8
Callicarpa americana, beautyberry seeds	1	12.5	2.00	0.6
Paspalum notatum, bahia grass seeds	1	12.5	1.50	0.5
Quercus laurifolia, laurel oak acorns	2	25.0	1.20	0.4
Ampelopsis arborea, pepper vine seeds	1	12.5	1.00	0.3
Panicum sp., panic grass seeds	2	25.5	0.70	0.2
Rhus copallina, seeds	1	12.5	0.30	0.1
Zanthoxylum sp., prickly ash seeds	1	12.5	0.30	0.1
Hydrocotyle sp., pennywort leaves	1	12.5	0.20	0.1
Celtis laevigata, hackberry seeds	2	25.5	0.20	0.1
Sabal palmetto, swamp cabbage berries, seeds	1	12.5	0.20	0.1
Parthenocissus quinquefolia, Virginia creeper seeds	1	12.5	0.20	0.1
Commelina elegans, dayflower seeds	1	12.5	0.10	trace
Serinea oppositifolia, seeds	1	12.5	0.10	trace
Carex sp., sedges seeds	1	12.5	0.05	trace

The magnitude and nature of turkey movements in relation to food availability and quality need clarification. How closely are high food availability and quality correlated with small home range, reduced movement, and high population density? Do turkeys compensate for low-quality food by eating more? Do they compensate for low food availability by spending more time feeding? If they have to compensate by spending more time feeding, are their home ranges larger? At what point will turkeys desert a range with inadequate quantities or quality of food? Does greater movement due to low food quality lead to greater vulnerability to predation? It would seem that predation rates, especially of poults, would be linked to the abundance and quality of foods through the lesser risk-taking that would be required of poults to feed when food is very nutritious, very abundant, and distributed in such a way that the turkeys have numerous options about where and when to feed.

Research on turkey movement to date has concentrated on estimating the surface area encompassed by the ranging of turkeys over various periods of time. Such information is of interest, but there is much uncontrolled variability in the

Table 4.9 Animal foods of 8 adult wild turkeys between 22 August and 1 November, Alachua and Glades Counties, Florida

Food item	Occurrence		Volume	
	Times	Percent	ml	Percent
Lepidoptera butterflies and moths				
Geometridae—larvae	2	25.0	73.00	66.8
adults	1	12.5	1.00	0.9
Citheroniidae—adults	2	25.0	1.30	1.2
Noctuidae—larvae	3	37.5	1.00	0.9
pupae	2	25.0	0.80	0.7
Nymphalidae—adults	1	12.5	0.50	0.5
Hesperiidae—larvae	1	12.5	0.20	0.2
Orthoptera, crickets, mantids, shorthorned, longhorned & pygmy grasshoppers				
Acrididae—adults	2	25.0	6.10	5.6
nymphs	1	12.5	0.20	0.2
Tetrigidae—adults		12.5	2.00	1.8
Tettigoniidae—adults	1	12.5	2.00	1.8
Blattidae—adults	1	12.5	0.40	0.4
Mantidae—adults	1	12.5	0.20	0.2
Homoptera, leafhoppers & spittle bugs				
Cicadidae—adults	1	12.5	5.00	4.6
Cercopidae—adults	1	12.5	0.50	0.5
Fulgoridae—adults	1	12.5	0.10	0.1
Cicadellidae—adults	1	12.5	0.10	0.1
Coleoptera, beetles				
Scarabaeidae—adults	3	37.5	1.40	1.3
Chrysomelidae—adults	2	25.0	1.10	1.0
Curculionidae—adults	1	12.5	1.00	0.9
Carabidae—adults	1	12.5	1.00	0.9
Cerambycidae—adults	2	25.0	0.50	0.5
Buprestidae—adults	1	12.5	0.20	0.2
Hemiptera, bugs				
Pentatomidae—adults	2	25.0	2.20	2.0
nymphs	1	12.5	0.15	0.1
Coreidae—adults	2	25.0	1.20	1.1
Lygaeidae—adults	1	12.5	0.20	0.2
Scutelleridae—adults	1	12.5	0.10	0.1
Reduviidae—adults	1	12.5	0.10	0.1
Diptera, flies				
Tabanidae	1	12.5	0.20	0.2
Stratiomyidae	1	12.5	0.20	0.2
Amblyomma americanum—adults	1	12.5	0.10	0.1
Odonata, skimmers				
Libellulidae—adults	1	12.5	0.40	0.4
Hymenoptera, vespid wasp, ants and brachonids				
Braconidae—adults	1	12.5	0.20	0.2
Vespidae—adults	1	12.5	0.10	0.1
Formicidae—adults	1	12.5	trace	trace
Dermaptera, earwigs				
Labiduridae—adults	1	12.5	0.10	0.1
Pulmonata, slug—adults	1	12.5	2.00	1.8
Gastropoda, snail—adults	1	12.5	1.00	0.9
Arachnida, spiders	3	37.5	1.00	0.9
Nematamorpha, worms	1	12.5	0.20	0.2

Table 4.10 Comparison of food types by age groups

	Age group					
	1–14 Days (N = 21) Percent		15–164 Days (N = 54) Percent		Adult (N = 8) Percent	
	occurrence	volume	occurrence	volume	occurrence	volume
VEGETABLE[a]	85.7	75.0	93.9	72.8	100.0	75.3
Grass (leaves and seeds)	33.3	7.2	61.1	25.1	75.0	29.0
Herbs (leaves and seeds)	66.6	42.0	46.3	12.7	37.5	5.5
Trees, shrubs, vines (fruits and seeds)	28.6	26.1	77.8	22.6	100.0	53.6
ANIMAL	61.9	25.0	63.6	27.2	62.5	24.7

a. All plant material including unidentified particles, bait corn, and wheat is tabulated for total vegetable matter to reveal the true proportion of vegetation vs. animal matter in the diet; however, unidentified material and bait grain are not tabulated for the vegetable subdivisions listed as grass, herb, or trees.

data. The statistics are not very useful for making comparisons among studies due to differences in methods of measurement, definitions employed, field techniques, and other factors (Brown 1980). Anyone familiar with turkey feeding and movement behavior knows that turkeys do not actually use all the acreage that is within the outermost points of their travel, but published comparisons seem to assume that. Measurements are needed on the distances that turkeys actually travel over whatever routes they use. Such measurements would provide a common basis for comparisons of data between studies and would yield accurate estimates of the time and energy spent in movement as well as distance traveled and range covered. Such data would also reveal more clearly whether turkeys have definite home ranges over long periods of time, as is presently assumed, and would indicate daily and seasonal shifts in habitat utilization in a meaningful way.

Summer Movement of Hens with Broods

In 1971, two hens with broods were tracked during June, another was tracked during June and July, and three others were tracked from June to August or September. The tracking was done in connection with other objectives of the study and was not intended for elaborate analysis. Figures 4.2 through 4.7 roughly depict summer ranges of hens and broods on the study area.

Considerable individual variation can be seen in the size of summer ranges. One hen with poults (fig. 4.4) moved more than twice as far during June as another (fig. 4.6). One hen

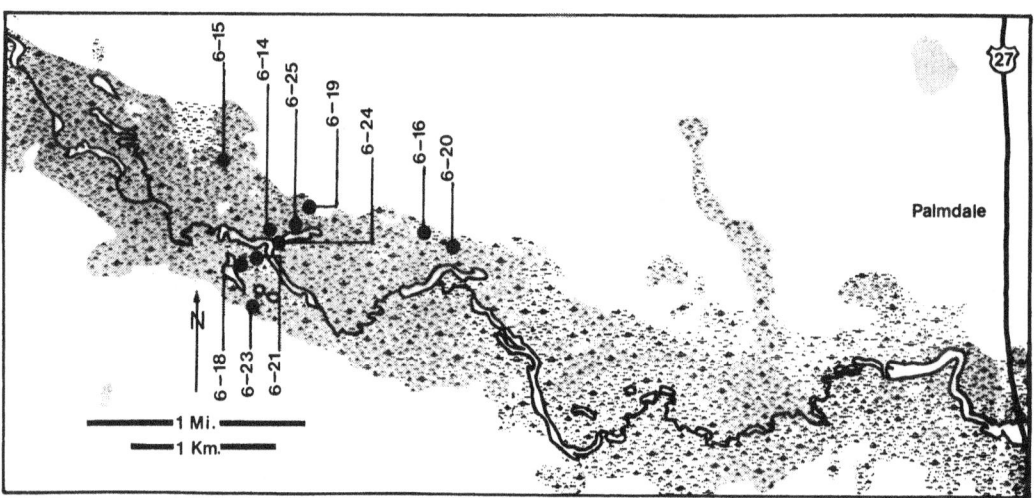

4.2 June range of a hen and brood.

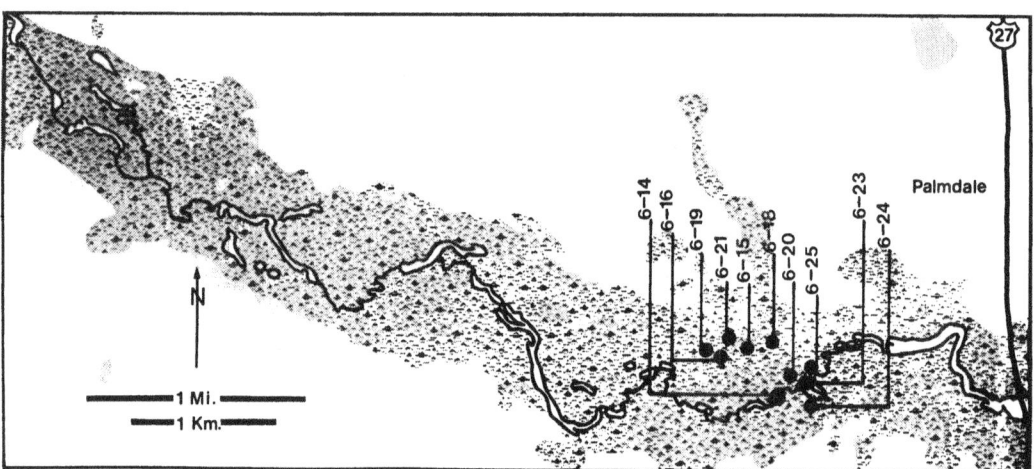

4.3 June range of a hen and brood.

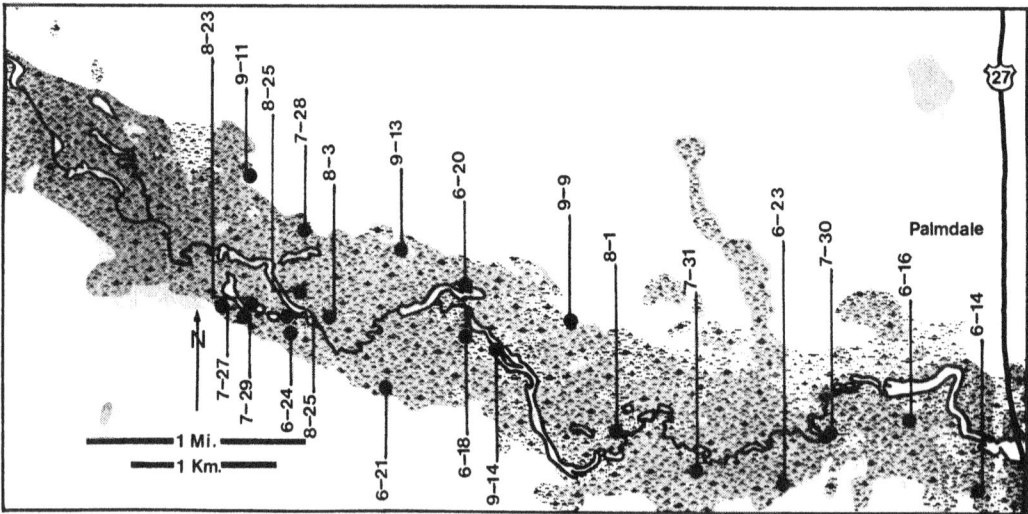

4.4 Summer range of a hen and brood.

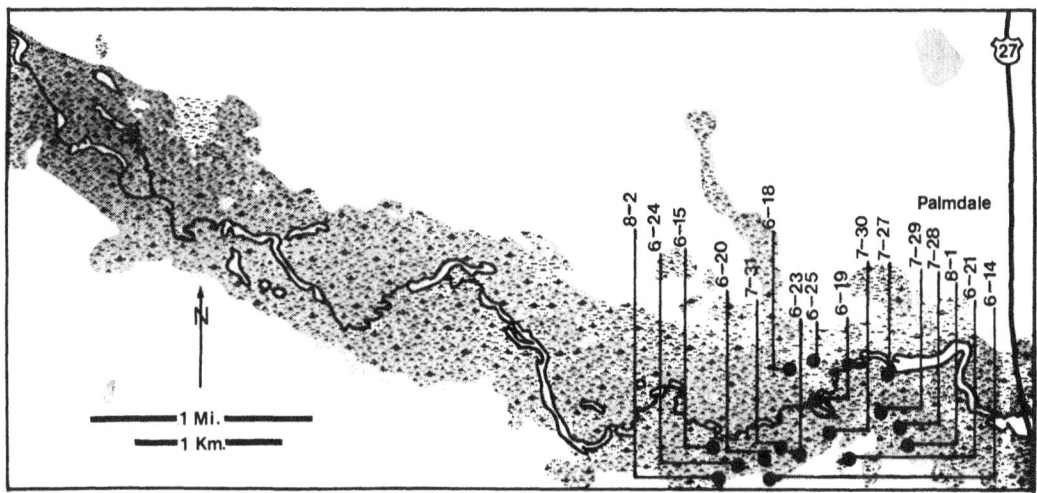

4.5 Summer range of a hen and brood.

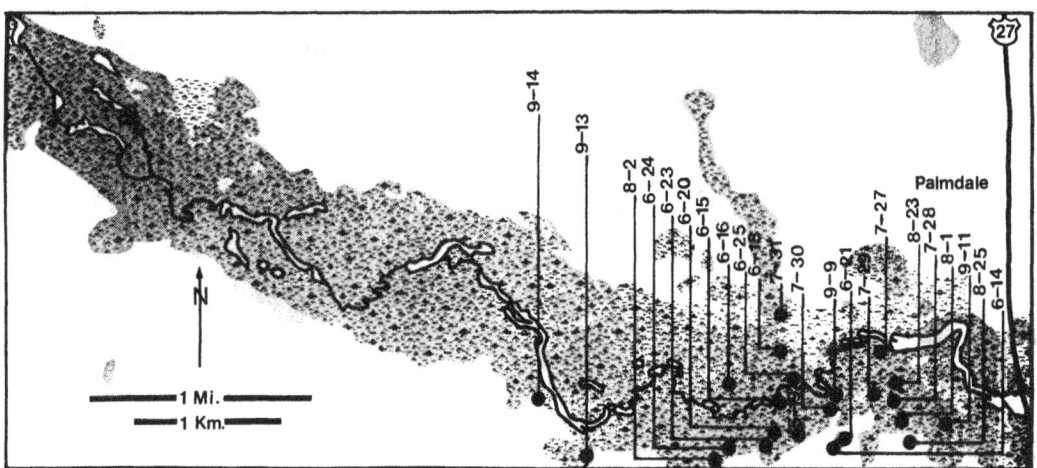

4.6 Summer range of a hen and brood.

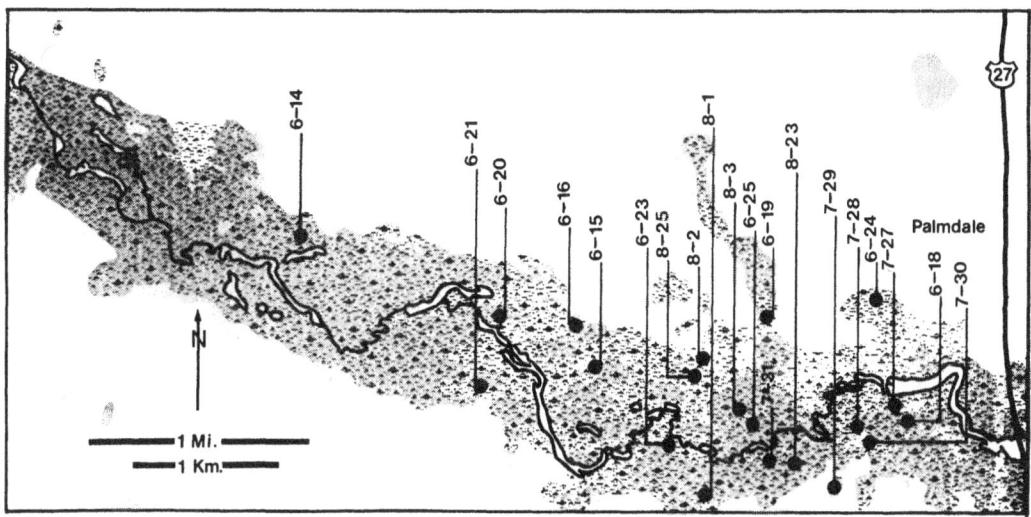

4.7 June range of a hen and brood.

with nine poults (fig. 4.5) moved much less than another with eight poults (fig. 4.2). No effort was made to determine the makeup of the flocks with which these broods associated or to discover any other factors that may have caused the differences in their movement.

Defensive Behavior of Young Broods

We have not observed a flightless brood while it was being attacked by a wild mammalian or avian predator, but we have approached broods closely and disturbed them; we assume that broods react to an intruding man as if he were a predator.

The defensive behavior of the hen with very young poults when approached by a man consists of: (1) huddling with the brood in a "frozen" posture when disturbance threatens and remaining immobile until detected or until the intruder leaves; (2) giving vocal commands for the brood to freeze upon being detected; (3) feigning attack on the intruder; and (4) remaining in the vicinity of the brood and "putting" loudly to quiet the poults. When hens leave their broods in response to an intrusion, most do so by running rather than flying—they fly only if startled at very close range. The hen may return for the brood within 10 minutes if the brood is very young but may take as long as 40 minutes if the brood is older.

The defensive behavior of the poults is in concert with the hen and consists of (1) huddling with her during the frozen posture routine; (2) creeping and hiding as she commands when the brood has been detected by an intruder; (3) remaining still, even if not well hidden; and (4) refraining from calling. We will use the nomenclature of vocalizations as reported by Williams (1984).

Huddling On several occasions while radiotracking turkeys, we have been aware of the approximate location of a hen and her one- to three-day-old brood before we visually spotted them. In such cases, the hen did not attempt evasive tactics as we approached but tended to squat and remain still until we spotted them. At the instant the hen was spotted, she would usually rise, make alarm calls to the brood, and begin running in circles around the intruder while sounding threatening calls. The hens showed remarkable ability to know when they had been spotted by an observer and equally remarkable stamina in remaining absolutely still even when approached within 50 feet (15 m) before being spotted.

Freezing Posture of the Poults

When the intruder spotted a hen, she arose, and the poults usually scattered at her command by running and creeping in an irregular circle. We did not carefully measure the time elements of this behavior, but we estimate that the time from scattering to freezing was about two to four seconds. After stopping, mostly under sprigs of vegetation, the poults did not usually move again. This is the typical defensive behavior of small, flightless, cryptically colored birds, such as grouses, quails, shorebirds, and many others.

When poults moved during such an intrusion, they were conspicuous to an investigator (and presumably would be also by a predator); those that remained still were found only by thorough searching. Since an efficient predator would probably take any poult that moved, the selective pressures to maintain and strengthen this behavior would seem to be high.

Regrouping

Most hens remained within hearing distance of their hiding poults and sounded alarm calls regularly. The continuous "putting" seemed to keep the poults from giving "lost whistles" (which might attract predators to them). But even when the hen was not putting nearby, poults usually remained still and silent for 20 to 30 minutes. This was tested by chasing hens far from the disturbed broods so that the hiding poults could not hear the putting. If the hen were kept away, one-day-old broods would begin to give lost whistles and would begin to move around in about 20 minutes. This could be stimulated sooner by our imitating the lost whistling calls of poults. When the hen was close enough to hear the poults (or us) calling, she would give harsh putting commands for silence which the poults would usually obey. When the hen returned for the brood, she would move quickly to the area of the disturbance and give an "assembly yelp." The brood would immediately come out of hiding and join her. The hen and brood would quickly and silently leave the area. The lost whistling of poults in distress is a signal to the hen that one or more of her young is not with her and is not a signal for the poults to gather among themselves (Williams 1984).

When a hen is frightened from her nest or young brood, she runs or flies. We have flushed hens from their nests or broods at least 50 times and have not seen one feign anything that we would consider a "crippled act." They do, however, perform threatening behavior by running in circles around the intruder and sometimes nearly attacking him. Brood hens will sometimes approach a human intruder within 2 m under such circumstances. A turkey hen would never approach an intruder so closely under any other circumstances. There is, however, great variation in this. Some brood hens will not undertake such behavior; one hen permanently deserted her young brood when it was disturbed by an investigator.

It seems likely that the nature of a turkey hen's defense of her brood would depend upon the type of predator and certainly would be different in response to a man than it would be toward a smaller predator. We observed a brood hen drive off a large snake by attacking it when it approached the nest during the hatching period.

One-day-old poults are completely dependent on the hen when faced with an intruder—their behavior consists simply of following the hen's command and freezing. This is a simplistic defensive strategy for an animal faced, as the turkey is, with a wide variety of predators having varied hunting strategies. Young poults are taken by most birds of prey and mammalian predators including dogs, screech owls (*Otus lineatus*), red-tailed hawks, raccoons, and bobcat. There can be little doubt that any other predator capable of eating a small bird would take a hatchling turkey. It would appear that freezing behavior would make the poults especially vulnerable to any predator that hunted by scent rather than by sight.

Fortunately, the poult's complete dependence on the hen, and the simplistic escape strategy, are short-lived. By the third day after hatching, the initial dispersal of a brood under attack has usually increased to at least 20 feet (6 m), and the poults hide under concealing cover when freezing. If approached, they will sometimes run farther away; while this could result in their being detected, they can run so fast and dodge so well that they would probably draw a predator away from the rest of the brood. By seven days of age the brood will actively evade a man on foot, rather than merely freeze, and the hen will sometimes run away, hiding the brood along the way. At nine days old, poults can fly into low vegetation and will usually do so when threatened. At this stage, they are not as vulnerable as they were before to mammalian predators. By three weeks of age, the hen will sometimes command the brood to fly into trees when she detects a man as far away as 200 m, after which she will depart as though she had no brood. By this time, the brood has begun to fly into trees to sleep at night and the poults are able to recognize danger and to react appropriately on their own.

Poult Losses During the Ground Roosting Period

One hundred sixteen observations were made on the poults surviving during the first two weeks of life in 61 broods of known initial size (table 4.11). The Mayfield (1961) method was used to calculate survival. The mean number of poults lost per poult-day was used as the probability of any single poult being lost in any single day during the period. Brood observations were largely unplanned and usually made in connection with some other study objective. In many cases the exact time of the brood count was not recorded in field notes, although the date was recorded in all cases. Since the observations were made at more or less random times during the daylight hours each day, the average time of the observations would be about 1200 hours standard time. In 26 broods that were closely observed, the mean hour of leaving the nest was 1030 hours. Therefore, the broods would be about 1.06 days old at noon of the second day because they had been out of the nest since 1030 hours the previous day, on the average. Counting days of survival from noon to noon each day, a poult began its fourteenth day of life out of the nest at noon of the thirteenth day after leaving the nest.

There were 204 poult losses during 2249 poult-days of exposure. The daily probability of any single poult being lost in any one day was 0.0907; or conversely, the probability of a poult surviving any single day was 0.9093 (1−0.0907). Assuming an equal probability of death for each of the first 14 days of life, the probability of a poult reaching age 14 days

Table 4.11 Summary of the number of poults counted in 61 known-age broods at different ages during the first 14 days of life

Age of brood when counted (days)	Number alive when counted	Original number in brood when departing nest	Poults dying since departing nest	
			Number	Percent
1	113	137	24	17.5
2	32	43	11	25.6
3	37	47	10	21.3
4	41	74	33	44.6
5	39	68	29	42.6
6	26	39	13	33.3
7	14	27	13	48.1
8[a]	7	24	17	70.8
9[a]	5	23	18	78.3
10[b]	0	0		
11[a]	4	19	15	78.9
12[b]	0	0		
13	20	48	28	58.3
14	16	45	29	64.4

a. Days 8, 9, and 11 not used.
b. No observations for days 10 and 12.

would be 0.9093^{14} or 0.264. Therefore the mortality rate for the entire period was about 73.6 percent (1−0.264).

The same poult counts (table 4.11) were used in a weighted least squares analysis with a geometric probability model that used a different probability of survival for the first day (0.81700) than for days 2 through 14 (0.93863). Days 8, 9 and 11 were deleted because of small sample sizes for those days. Only one count was used for any one brood so that the observations would be independent. The test for lack of fit was not significant ($p = 0.3758$), indicating that the fit was good. The predicted proportion surviving the 14-day period was 0.36 (fig. 4.8), somewhat higher than calculated by the Mayfield (1961) method (0.264). By this model, the mortality rate would be 0.64 (1−0.36), or 64 percent lost during the first two weeks after leaving the nest, as compared to 73.6 percent calculated by the Mayfield method.

Whenever an observer was not certain that he had counted every poult, the observation was discarded, but it is likely that at least a few poults were not seen, causing the mortality rate calculated to be slightly inflated. The error, however, would be very small. A small bias of this type will exist in counts of very young poults because of the tendency of broods to remain in cover during this early period of life.

Glidden and Austin (1975) attempted to measure mortality of poults of radio instrumented hens in New York and reported 57 percent mortality during the first two weeks.

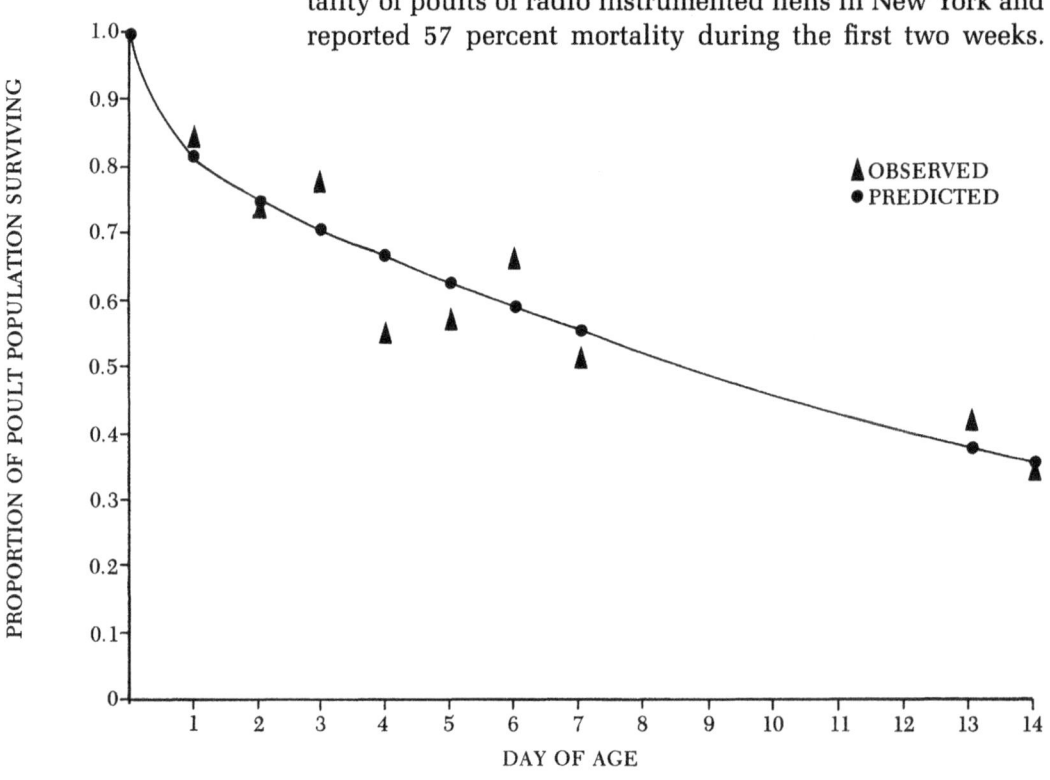

4.8 Weighted least squares prediction curve for poult mortality during the first 14 days of life.

152 Studies of the Wild Turkey in Florida

However, their sample sizes were small, and they combined observations made throughout the interval from 8 to 14 days rather than counting only survivors on the fourteenth day. Because survival would undoubtedly be higher on day 8 than by day 14, combining the observations as was done would result in an overestimate of survival. It is not possible to calculate the actual death or survival rate from the data presented in the New York study.

Everett et al. (1980), working in Alabama, reported poult mortality of 80 percent during the entire summer. In that study, 170 of 217 poults (78 percent) were lost during the first two weeks of life. Speake (1980), in another Alabama study, observed summer poult losses of 74.5 percent with 71.3 percent of the poults being lost during the first two weeks, and presented evidence that most of the poult mortality was due to predation. Akey (1981) reported losses of 33 of 52 (63 percent) radio instrumented poults during the first two weeks in a Florida study and found evidence that the losses were due to predation. If the data from the two Alabama studies and Akey's (1981) Florida study are combined, the resulting average mortality rate during the first two weeks would be 73.1 percent. This compares very closely with our estimate of 73.6 percent calculated by the Mayfield (1961) method from observations of 61 Florida broods. Obviously, there are a number of important variables affecting poult mortality rates in any given year or place, but present evidence suggests that the overall average mortality rate of the wild turkey is about 70 percent during the first two weeks of life.

Mortality so high during a brief interval of only two weeks would have a very pronounced effect on population production. Such losses would probably limit some populations. Accurate measurements of these losses and their causes, the role of various predators, cover types, and other factors are needed. Management procedures that would alleviate the high mortality would be of practical value in increasing population productivity. While we do not advocate killing predators in the light of present knowledge, it is likely that predation is the major cause of early poult losses. A number of environmental factors have their effects on predator populations and predator impacts on turkeys, and it does not necessarily follow that predators have to be killed in order for their effects to be controlled. Far too little is known about predator-prey relations in turkey management.

While the preflight predation rate seen in this study may seem alarmingly high (64–73 percent), it should be noted that these rates were observed in a turkey population that was increasing in numbers and that also was being hunted by the public. This suggests that poult mortality was much lower after the first two weeks.

Leopold (1944) hypothesized that the poor population replacement of stocked game farm turkey populations was due to poor poult survival caused by inappropriate defensive behavior during the preflying stages. He observed that the escape behavior of very young domestic and game farm turkeys was to run away, and that the behavior of the hen was to scold the predator and herd the brood. Such behavior may be appropriate in the relative security of captivity where the disturbance is likely to be by other domestic turkeys, farm animals, or human keepers, but such behavior would make a brood extremely vulnerable to most wild predators.

Leopold's hypothesis is probably correct. If completely wild turkeys can manage no more than 30 percent poult survival during the first two weeks of life, certainly maladapted game farm turkeys with domestic turkey behavior traits could not reproduce viable populations.

It may be that poult survival during the first two weeks of life determines the size of many wild turkey populations because mortality occurs very slowly after that. This aspect of wild turkey ecology warrants considerably more study. Behavioral differences between wild and game farm strains need to be determined. The survival of poults up to two weeks old should be measured in turkey populations of varying density with the objective of testing the hypothesis that productivity during this critical period limits the productivity of turkey populations.

Wariness and Fear of Man

The innate wildness of the wild turkey is the bird's strongest defense and was all that prevented its extinction in the eastern U.S. by overhunting by man in the early 1900s. There should be concern for the possible detrimental effects that semidomestic game farm turkeys can have on the genetic basis of wildness in populations of turkeys. Game farm turkeys are being raised and widely used in put-and-take hunting by hunting clubs on a private basis for stocking in Florida and elsewhere. Game farm turkeys are frequently released among established turkey populations.

A paper by Starker Leopold (1944) on "The Nature of Heritable Wildness in Turkeys" aptly directed attention to this problem, but there has been regrettably little research interest in the wildness of turkeys since then.

The process by which young turkeys learn to distinguish friends from enemies seems fairly clear as far as its major components are concerned. At the time of hatching, poults have no fear until they mentally "imprint" on the brood hen. This establishes the young bird's self-identity and is the basis for its association with the parent hen and other turkeys. After parental and sibling imprinting takes place, turkey poults are afraid of all other objects, especially large ones that move. Strange objects will be avoided by young poults until familiarity proves the objects to be harmless. This natural fear is the first sign of wariness in the turkey. This complex process has been thoroughly studied (Lorenz 1937, Hess 1964, Hess and Petrovich 1977) in the chicken, mallard duck, and other birds. Our observations suggest that the same general pattern applies to the young wild turkey.

In addition to the poult's increasing suspicion of objects other than its mother and siblings, there are a few animal forms that evoke fear and escape behavior in the young poult in the same way that other birds have been found to instinctively fear the image of an owl (Hartley 1950) and certain other distinct predator forms. Turkey poults show fear of large birds flying overhead from the very first time they are encountered. We have seen this in human-imprinted poults that were less than one week old, that had never been with an older turkey, had never been attacked by another animal, and, so far as we were aware, had never seen a large flying bird.

The role of parental guidance in the development of wariness and recognition of enemies begins during hatching. The obedient reactions of poults to the warning calls of the hen are innate. At first, the poults obey the commands of the hen in order to survive—poults are not alert to danger at a distance and do not themselves discern dangerous situations. The brood hen almost continuously utters vocal instructions. Although we have no direct evidence of it, we think that poults learn about many dangers by association among the vocal calls of the hen, the behavior of the hen, and the alarming situations that develop during predator attacks. Associative learning of this type is well known (Brower et al. 1970); such "cultural" transmission of enemy recognition has been demonstrated in other birds (Curio et al. 1978).

How could a turkey initially learn that man and certain other predators that it has never seen are deadly without actually being killed? We think it is primarily because turkeys are able to recognize predatory behavior. Large animals that consistently show interspecific attention are either territorial or predatory. Natural selection works against survival of turkeys that do not avoid animals that display such interest. Therefore, it is not necessary for a predator (or man) to initiate an actual attack to be perceived as potentially dangerous. In this way, the turkey is able to more or less ignore nonpredatory animals (and perhaps also predators that are not hunting) and, more importantly, is able to recognize almost instantly a new predator type regardless of the predator's appearance or the individual turkey's previous experience. That is why the turkey has a seemingly instinctive fear of man, despite the fact that it has probably not been subjected to human predation long enough to develop an innate avoidance reaction based on man's body conformation.

Therein also lies the explanation of the general aversion of so many other animals to man. Humans have great curiosity and reveal serious interest in other animals at almost every opportunity. A human attempt to be "friendly" to turkeys or other animals is so similar to a predator's preattack behavior that it is not perceived by a wild animal the way it is intended. Because of the persistence of this behavior in man, individual turkeys probably learn from experience to avoid man as a general type, with strong cultural reinforcement from the brood hen and other turkeys.

Turkeys show little or no alarm at seeing a dead predator or a man sitting completely still and will rapidly become habituated to virtually any motionless object placed in their environment. But turkeys show particular concern for sounds and motion, suggesting the importance of behavior, rather than form, in their recognition of enemies. From the adaptive standpoint, it is effective for a prey species to have generalized predator recognition based on predatory behavior; otherwise, exposure to a new predator form could be catastrophic to the population, or even to the species.

Thus there are four major components in the development of wariness in the young wild turkey: (1) the naturally increasing innate fear of strange objects after parent-imprinting; (2) the distinction between friends and potential enemies that is caused by habituation to harmless animals through experience; (3) the recognition of predatory behavior, which may be partly innate, and (4) associative learning involving the brood hen's behavior based on her personal experiences. Fear of man is probably due to man's predatorlike interest in turkeys as revealed to the turkey through his interest-revealing behavior and is probably passed on to the offspring from the turkey hen through associative learning.

Hazards of Rain and High Water

During our observations, heavy rains fell while several broods were hatching. Many broods under observation experienced one or more moderate to heavy rains before they were two weeks old; however, no brood was known to have been adversely affected by falling rain directly.

Three broods lost poults when they crossed water-filled ditches or streams within a few hours after leaving their nests. One hen hatched a brood of nine during a heavy downpour and crossed a swollen creek within the next two days. Five poults were missing when the brood was found a day later on the other side of the creek. Another brood was believed to have lost five poults when it crossed a six-foot-wide ditch of water the same day it left the nest.

Only two of 248 nests under observation were destroyed by rising water, but a few others would have been had they not been destroyed by predators before the Fisheating Creek rose after heavy late-spring rains. On the study areas, and in Florida generally, flooding is probably not a cause of serious nest losses because turkeys do not frequently use especially low places to nest. Much of the year's nesting has been completed by the time of heavy summer rains.

It is widely believed that heavy rains during spring are detrimental to turkey reproduction by the direct chilling effect of rain on the poults. There may be a correlation between wet spring weather and low fall turkey harvests (Powell 1965), but we have found no evidence that young poults become wet and debilitated during spring rains in Florida. On the contrary, the ability of the hen to keep her brood dry during rainy weather is impressive. We suspect that spring rains would have their most serious impacts on turkey numbers when general water levels rise high enough to prevent nesting or to drown out nests in the middle to late part of the nesting season. Rising water could drive the broods out of their normal habitat during a period when the young poults would be especially vulnerable to predation. There is also a possible connection between water-dependent disease vectors and turkey diseases. The effects of cold rain on small turkey poults should be tested by direct observations of drenched broods to answer the question about chilling.

The effects of spring rains may be different in the cooler climates of the northern part of the turkey's range. General flooding would certainly be a serious factor in the flood plains of larger river systems.

It has long been known that adult turkeys and poults can

swim (Martin and Atkeson 1954, Taber 1955). Our observations indicate that flightless broods in Florida may frequently find swimming to be necessary. We have not been able to observe whether the hens swim, wade, or fly when crossing water with flightless broods, but, in one case, the fact that the water was several feet deep indicated that she either had to fly or swim.

Homing Tendency

Many animals will return to their former home range if they are transported away. Some birds can do this spectacularly, traveling thousands of miles in a short period of time, as, for example, the manx shearwater (*Procellarius puffinus*) that returned from Boston to its point of capture in Wales in 12½ days (Mazzeo 1953). The homing capacity of turkeys, however, seems to be poorly developed or nonexistent. Experiments have shown that a number of other birds also lack homing ability (Welty 1975).

In studies by Eichholz (1974) and others it has been found that relocated wild turkeys soon settle into a new home range pattern. In our turkey restocking work we have noticed that relocated turkeys will usually orient themselves in relation to the release site and can be found near the point of release for several weeks before finally establishing a new home range there.

To test the strength of turkeys' homing abilities, 13 trapped turkeys were transported to various release points in the Fisheating Creek study area during the winters of 1971 and 1972. Three others were released at the point of capture in 1972 as controls, for a total of 16 turkeys (table 4.12). The birds were radio instrumented and monitored regularly.

The three turkeys that were released at the trap site all remained in the vicinity of the trap site (which was in their home range) as expected. Of the six that were transported 3 miles (4.8 km) or less, four returned home and two did not. All seven turkeys that were transported more than 3 miles (4.8 km) failed to return home. Fisher's Exact Test indicated that the homing performance of the turkeys that were moved more than three miles was significantly different from that of those that were moved less than 3 miles ($p = 0.04$). The turkeys that were moved only 0.5 and 0.9 miles (0.8 and 1.5 km) were probably released within their former home ranges and immediately resumed normal use of their range.

Table 4.12 Distance to release site and direction of subsequent travel of 16 turkeys tracked to test homing tendency

Age and sex	Trap site to release site miles (km)	Movement direction in relation to trap site	Did turkey return to vicinity of trap site?
Adult hen	0 (control)	Toward	Yes
Adult hen	0 (control)	Toward	Yes
Juvenile hen	0 (control)	Toward	Yes
Adult hen	0.5 (0.8)	Toward	Yes
Juvenile hen	0.9 (1.4)	Toward	Yes
Juvenile hen	2.0 (2.1)	Toward	Yes
Adult hen	3.0 (3.2)	Toward	Yes
Adult hen	1.5 (2.4)	Away	No
Juvenile hen	2.5 (4.0)	Away	No
Juvenile hen	4.2 (6.8)	Away	No
Adult gobbler	4.2 (6.8)	Toward	No
Adult hen	4.6 (7.4)	Away	No
Adult hen	4.6 (7.4)	Toward	No
Adult hen	4.7 (7.6)	Away	No
Juvenile hen	5.2 (8.4)	Away	No
Juvenile hen	5.2 (8.4)	Toward	No

If the turkey has no tendency to home, it would be necessary to move one only into range where it had never been in order for it to establish a new home range. It would not matter how close the release point was to the former home range except that a certain proportion of the birds would be expected through chance alone to enter a familiar part of their former range after being released and possibly resume the use of their former range. The two turkeys that returned home after being transported two and three miles were in that category—either they were familiar with the release site (perhaps it was part of a former home range), or they happened by chance to move a short distance into their old home ranges. The turkeys that were moved more than three miles were released in places that they had never been and did not happen across a familiar place in their routine travels before they had established a new home range.

The poorly developed homing instinct of the turkey has contributed to the successful restocking of uninhabited range with relatively small numbers of liberated birds. Successful transplants have been accomplished in Florida with as few as four hens and two gobblers.

Since the wild turkey has little or no homing tendency, one way to estimate average home range size would be to release trapped turkeys at various distances from the trap sites and measure the distances at which they failed to return home.

Maximum Longevity Observed

A hen trapped at Fisheating Creek in the winter of 1964 and shipped to Texas lived longer than any banded Florida turkey yet recorded. The Texas Parks and Wildlife Department, which was attempting to establish an eastern "strain" of wild turkey, was unable to obtain wild-trapped *M. g. silvestris* and was using *M. g. osceola* instead. The transplanted hen was at least one year old when trapped in the spring of 1965 and was retrapped in Texas during the winter of 1976. She was in her thirteenth year, at least, when retrapped in Texas.

Maximum Movement Observed

Measuring distances traveled was not an objective of the turkey studies, although movement is reflected in many topics discussed. Maximum movement may be of interest to some readers.

The greatest one-way air line distance that any of 1036 banded or 483 radiotracked turkeys was known to travel in its life was 18 miles (29 km). This was a juvenile hen banded in March 1969 and killed during the fall hunting season of 1970 in the next county south of the study area. The next greatest known distance traveled was by a banded adult hen that was trapped at points in Fisheating Creek Wildlife Management Area 15 miles (24 km) apart. Three radiotracked hens were known to move air line distances of 5 miles (8 km). Movement of 3 miles (4.8 km) during a single year was not unusual and movement of 2 miles (3.2 km) was routine.

Imprinting Studies

We attempted on several occasions before 1968 to rear poults from eggs taken from wild nests but the results were consistently disappointing—the young birds remained frightened by the sight of a man and were injured by flying around their pens. They would spend most of their time in searching and lost behavior, pacing the perimeter of the pen, and neglecting feeding and other requirements. Similar responses were seen whether the eggs were hatched in incubators or under turkey or chicken hens. When hatched by tame chicken hens, turkey poults were more afraid of humans than the chicken hens were. Placing tame chickens, domestic turkeys, or other birds in the same pen with wild turkey poults improved their feeding behavior but did not appreciably reduce their fear of humans.

In 1979, a small supply of wild turkey eggs was available in connection with the field studies at Fisheating Creek. Following methods described by Healy and Goetz (1974), we hatched and parent-imprinted 40 poults on humans by talking to them while they were hatching and spending three to six hours per day with them for the first several days of life. After that, the poults were taken for one-hour walks to forage, usually twice per day. The poults would approach and follow almost anyone near them.

The general aspects of behavioral development reported for *M. g. silvestris* (Healy et al. 1975) seem to apply also to *M. g. osceola* poults. The imprinted poults captured insects, dusted in the sand, and otherwise behaved as normal poults. They reacted cautiously to dogs and strange objects near them and were instinctively afraid of snakes and large birds flying overhead.

After the first three to seven weeks at the Fisheating Creek field station, the birds were transferred to the senior author's home near Gainesville and released there on the small farm for further observation as they grew older. They roosted in trees the first night out of the pens, stripped grass of seeds, and chased insects daily. Contact with the unwary, imprinted turkeys afforded many opportunities to observe turkey behavior that would not be possible under normal wild conditions.

Upon being released on the farm, the 40 poults that were imprinted in 1979 formed two social groups for foraging but regrouped as a single unit from time to time. No adult turkey was present. Losses to predators were high at first and the flock was reduced to about 23 by midsummer. Social relations remained poorly developed among the young birds, suggesting a major role of the brood hen in social organization. They called to each other but seemed to have a poorly developed vocabulary (which is not surprising since the turkey's voice is primarily a social tool). Except for this, they seemed normal. They ranged off the farm and into the surrounding woods, where they interacted with the native wild turkeys, sometimes by fighting. By fall, wild and imprinted turkeys were often seen foraging together.

It was apparent that the presence of the imprinted turkeys attracted the native turkeys—wild turkeys from surrounding woods had not visited the farm in the five years before the imprinted turkeys came, nor have they returned during the four years since.

Although there was some shifting from one roost tree to

another during the summer, the human-imprinted turkeys roosted all summer in a discrete area, consisting of large laurel oak (*Quercus hemisphaerica*) and a number of sweetgum (*Liquidambar styraciflua*) trees, within 100 m of the place they were fed every day. The barnyard was a major activity center in their much condensed home range. The flocks imprinted in 1980 and 1981 had similar ranging habits. The imprinted flock in 1981 was much more vocal than the two earlier flocks had been.

Dispersal Although many young turkeys were lost to predators during the summers of 1979 through 1981, losses were few each year after midsummer. The flocks remained virtually the same size from about September until late February or March when they dispersed. Usually, several birds would leave the barnyard area together. They sometimes returned after an absence of only three or four days, but they invariably left again and, except for one hen, never returned.

This early spring movement away from the farm involved all the hens each year but not all of the young gobblers. This apparent dispersal was not a case of merely enlarged home ranges—the turkeys did not come back to the barnyard even to feed or water once they had stayed away for more than a week. The habitat adjacent to the farm, including the woods on the property, was good turkey habitat and, as mentioned, was inhabited by wild turkeys. The human-imprinted turkeys could easily have lived near the farm, as the wild birds did, and could have visited the farm from time to time to feed. But they did not do so, despite the fact that they were seen from time to time less than one-half mile away. Since the ultimate fate of the dispersed turkeys remains unknown (except in the case of one hen that returned), it is possible that they were taken by predators, or met some other demise. But there is a suggestion in this behavior that the dispersal observed was caused by a strong urge to move away from the winter range and establish a different home range for the breeding season.

Nesting The hens did not mate while in the barnyard area or nest on the farm, although the five two-year-old gobblers strutted vigorously in their presence in 1981. In late June of 1981, a one-year-old hen returned to the barnyard with two two-week-old poults and remained until the following spring. The fact that the human-imprinted hen mated with a male turkey indicates that she had not sexually imprinted on humans.

During summer, the hen and two poults frequently left the barnyard for the night but were seen almost every day somewhere around the farm and were associating regularly with the new (1981) flock of imprinted poults by late summer. In early August, one of the wild poults disappeared and the other was lost about two weeks later, both probably to predation. After that, the hen associated more closely with the flock of imprinted young although they never "adopted" each other completely.

Precocious Strutting Male domestic turkeys strut much of the time from the day of hatching. This is also very common in imprinted wild turkeys as observed by Healy and Goetz (1974) and by us. But precocious strutting has not been reported in wild-living turkeys and in many hours of watching wild turkey broods, we have seen only one summer poult strutting. An incident involving the imprinted turkeys during the summer of 1981 provides a clue to a possible inhibiting mechanism of this behavior in normal wild poults.

As previously mentioned, a one-year-old imprinted hen returned from the woods in the summer of 1981 with two poults. Also on the farm at that time was a new group of 15 recently imprinted wild poults about the age of the hen's small brood. The free-ranging imprinted poults did not follow the hen as they would their mother, but did not avoid her or her two poults. One day in July, a 12-week-old human-imprinted male turkey was strutting. As we watched, the adult hen rushed across the yard as if to attack the strutting poult, causing him to stop strutting after which she resumed normal foraging. The hen's antagonism toward the male poult was repeated on several occasions, but only when he was strutting. At these times the hen made the harsh vocal sounds of "rattling" to indicate her intense displeasure and assumed threatening postures as she moved closely in front of the young strutting gobbler. When he stopped strutting, as he always did when the hen challenged, the hen would immediately resume other activities. No actual fighting occurred. There were, however, occasions when the hen tolerated the young male's strutting at a distance.

The human-imprinted adult gobblers that were present did not display antagonism toward young gobblers when they strutted in their presence and the adult hen paid no attention to the strutting adults.

There is a common belief that the failure of juvenile wild gobblers to strut and gobble is due to inhibition caused by the presence of dominant adult males in the population, but there is no empirical evidence for this that we know of. Since young gobblers associate with their mothers and other brood hens in summer, and not with adult males in the population, it is more plausible that the brood hens, rather than the adult gobblers, would inhibit the young males—at least until the young males leave the family flocks in winter. The antagonistic behavior of the hen we observed suggests that strutting by young males may be inhibited by the mother hen under natural conditions. The increasing antagonism between young males and their mothers may have much to do with the habit of young males to separate from the family flock in late fall.

Other Observations on Human-imprinted Turkeys

The two wild-hatched poults of the human-imprinted hen were wary of people, refusing to follow the hen closely when she approached a person and never allowing us to approach them even when the hen and human-imprinted young flock were within inches of us. Their failure to become tame suggests that the hen has only limited influence over the unwariness of her poults and that the poults do not learn to trust large, moving objects simply because their mother does. And there is the question of why the wild poults did not habituate to humans during their two-month stay at the farm since nobody ever attempted to frighten or harm them in any way. Perhaps the poults sensed our interest in them, and interest is a component of predatory behavior.

Three imprinted juvenile males did not disperse from the farm during the spring of 1981. During 1982 they became more aggressive and often attacked people in the area, including the authors. They were especially prone to attack small children. They strutted and gobbled almost continuously, year-round (with an increase in this behavior as spring approached). One of the few serious fights among them occurred in early February 1982 after which two of the three dispersed and the remaining gobbler, which was thought to be the victor, strutted vigorously for two days in a localized part of the farm. The hens were not present, having already dispersed. The victor may have been claiming a special territory within his winter range. Unfortunately, he was killed in an accident a few days later when he attacked one of the resident humans.

During the three-year period, five of the imprinted gobblers developed malformed snoods, but none of the hens did. It appeared that the snoods had been snipped off near the base, perhaps by fighting when they were very young. The small residual snood tissue of these males enlarged substantially in the spring, but it was badly deformed and never regained its normal elongate shape. The enlargement of the residual snood tissue in spring would appear to indicate a glandular function associated with the mating season. We have never seen a gobbler from the wild that had such a deformed snood.

After our unsuccessful attempts to tame wild turkeys, it may seem puzzling that the Indians were able to domesticate the wild turkey in Mexico. But several generations of imprinted turkeys in captivity and the intense selection that would accompany life with humans is a plausible explanation. As suggested by Hale (1962), human imprinting may be the antecedent of domestication in many animals.

Movement in Relation to Habitat Quality

Turkey movement on the Fisheating Creek study area was minimized by the nearly ideal composition, size, and spatial relationships of the habitat types. There was no part of the study area except treeless prairies that was not inhabited by turkeys year-round and no large part of it that was not used for nesting as well as for winter range. The fall population in recent years has been one turkey per 15–20 acres (6–8 ha) in the 10 000 acres (4000 ha) of the area used for this study. We know of no denser turkey population anywhere, based on the entire annual range of the population.

In a study of the movement of hens from winter to spring range (Williams et al. 1974), net movement consisted of 0.20 mile (0.32 km) to the west for the seven hens that shifted westward; two hens did not shift at all, and three shifted to the east. Some of both groups that shifted range (eastward or westward) left habitat in which other hens remained to nest. The same pattern was observed in many other cases during the period of study. Movement from winter to spring range was not necessitated by the separation of suitable nesting habitat from winter habitat, but was a reflection of some innate minimal movement characteristic of the animal itself as was also suspected in the human-imprinted turkeys. It appears that most hens simply moved to a new home range to nest, although that was not dictated by habitat conditions.

Only minimal seasonal movement would be expected when all necessary habitat components are available in a very small area. If such an area of required resources is smaller than the adaptive movement tendency of individuals in the population, the magnitude of the population's movement will be determined primarily by innate factors, and the turkeys would move more than absolutely necessary to obtain the resources for survival and reproduction. In such cases, dispersal should be more or less random in direction. Some turkeys would breed where others wintered. This would amount to a mere shifting of range rather than a true migration. In such a case the entire area would be used at all times by at least some members of the population; net movement direction would be zero; and the maximum habitat-controlled population density would be attained. Furthermore, when food, cover, roosting places, and water were available in such a small area, turkeys would not be expected to move fast or far, which would further minimize their movement. Healy (1978) observed such movement behavior in human-imprinted poults.

When resources are sparse or widely distributed, the innate mobility of the species is exercised up to its adaptive maximum; consequently, overall population density would be low. If the separation of resources should exceed the mobility of the species, the locale would be uninhabitable for the species. When seasonal habitat resources are widely separated, net seasonal movement will be highly directional, rather than random, and will resemble true migration. The turkey's innate ability to move great distances is an adaptation to cope with widely spaced or sparse resources.

The foregoing can be reduced to the prediction that daily and seasonal turkey movement will be greater where habitat is poorer and less where habitat is better, and that small movement, high habitat quality, and high population density will be positively and closely correlated.

From the management standpoint, this concept offers a basis for a habitat management strategy. Habitat management should be (1) directed at increasing the density of all critical dissimilar habitat resources, and (2) designed to lessen distances between critical resource patches that are widely separated. That will promote more complete utilization of the entire landscape by turkeys; otherwise population density will remain low because there will be significant unused parts of the landscape—unused either because they are too far separated or are not suitable due to sparsity of the resources within them. Maximum turkey population densities will be achieved when all the landscape is used, more or less, year-round. The effect of successful application of this management strategy will be more animals per unit of area as calculated for the entire life cycle of the population.

The greatest obstacle to research on this concept is the lack of a suitable census method for the wild turkey.

Utilization of Forest Openings

Between fall and early summer, turkeys did not frequently use the grassy zone that lies outside of, and parallel to, Fisheating Creek and its associated cypress woods. This would appear to be at variance with other studies (i.e., Hillestad and Speake 1970), which assign considerable importance to "openings" in turkey habitat. However, there is no real contradiction—use of openings is a matter of scale.

The cypress woods in the Fisheating Creek study area exist in varying stand ages and densities, some of which permit substantial sunlight penetration through a sparse overstory and allow good growth of ground-covering grasses and forbs. Ground cover is also enhanced by the mild winter climate at the time cypress trees are leafless. Thus at Fisheating Creek, the cypress woods contain seasonal openings of varying size. There are small openings between widely spaced trees, larger openings in small, treeless areas and nowhere does the cypress completely shade out the understory and ground covering vegetation. Large openings on the Fisheating Creek area would offer little to the turkeys that is not available within the woods. Consequently, turkeys do not make frequent use of the large natural, open glades outside of the woods during summer.

Throughout most of the range of *M. g. silvestris*, however, ground cover is sparse inside the woods in summer due to overstory shading, and very little food or low cover for very small poults exists there. Openings, when they occur in such places, contribute vastly different habitat situations that are vital, scarce, and therefore heavily used by turkeys. We have observed that turkeys will remain in or very near forest cover anytime they can find enough preferred foods there.

It would be difficult to improve on the placement of forest openings as they naturally occur in the cypress woods at Fisheating Creek. To simulate such conditions elsewhere would call for creating wooded stands of various age and density gradients and not merely the creation of open clearings here and there in otherwise homogeneous stands of trees.

5

Harvest Management

Game management strategy in Florida has concentrated on maximum population utilization despite the fact that turkey, quail, and gray squirrel harvests are declining (fig. 5.1), because populations of these species are declining. Increased utilization, in the sense of increased harvest levels, is no longer a wise policy. An appropriate goal would be to make better use of the present turkey population and its habitat by maintaining population levels high enough for optimum productivity and implementing hunting regulations that protect the breeding population while allowing maximum hunting enjoyment.

Overhunting may be widespread in the Florida turkey range that is accessible to the general public, such as the wildlife management areas and unposted land. Suspected overharvesting was the stimulus for a study of harvest patterns at Fisheating Creek from 1968 through 1974, which found that serious overharvesting was taking place. This chapter contains a revised and updated version of the report on harvest patterns resulting from that study (Williams et al. 1978). A summary of observations on turkey behavior under heavy hunting pressure, a pilot study for a public spring gobbler hunting system to remedy an overhunting problem at Fisheating Creek, and other information on harvest management are also presented in this chapter.

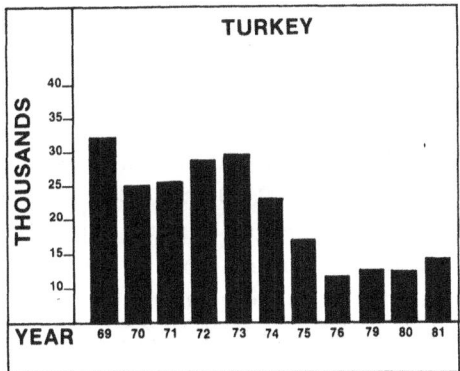
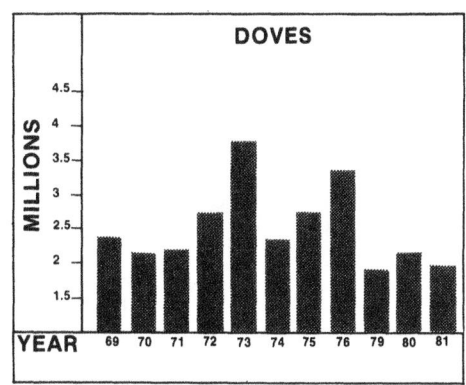
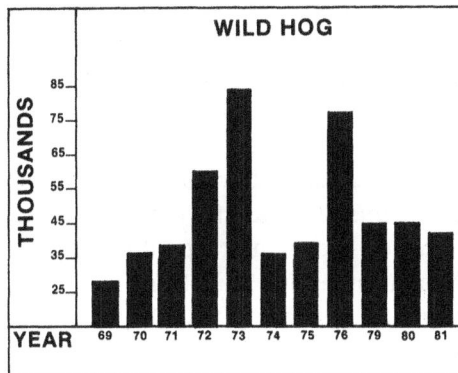
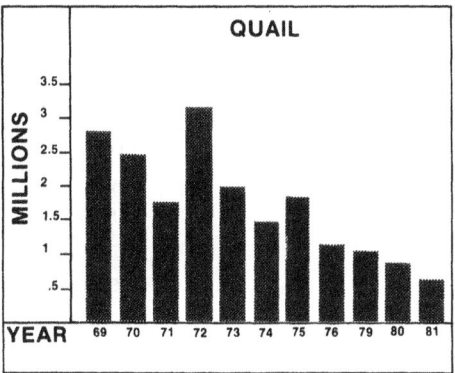
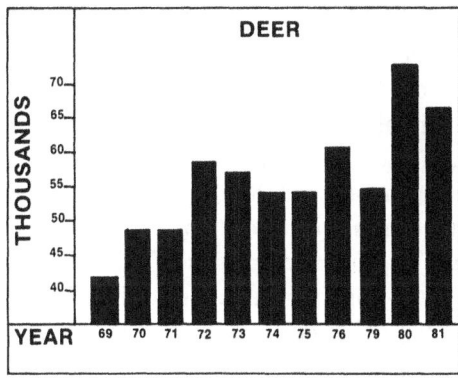
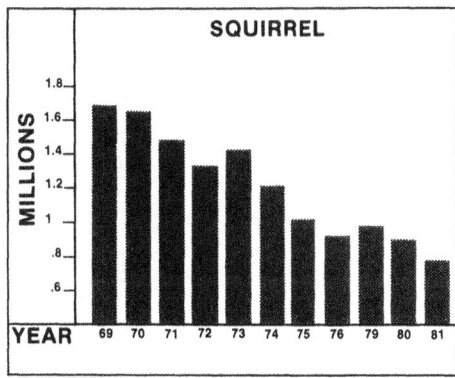

5.1 Harvest estimates for the turkey and other major game species in Florida since 1969. (Data are not available for 1977 and 1978.)

Harvest Patterns on a Heavily Hunted Area

Lykes Fisheating Creek Wildlife Management Area was once highly regarded as a public hunting area for fall turkey hunting. The fall either-sex harvest in some years was as high as 400 turkeys (Powell 1965), but a decline began in the 1960s; only 129 hens and gobblers were taken during the season of 1968–69. One factor in the declining harvest was the reduction in the size of the area from 125 000 acres (50 000 ha) in

Harvest Management 169

1951 to only 32 000 acres (13 000 ha) by 1965. It was also apparent that hunting pressure had reached excessive proportions and that turkey populations were not as high as they could be, despite annual restocking.

The area had a fall population of about 200 turkeys, or about one per 50 acres (20 ha), in the 10 000 acres (4000 ha) of turkey habitat in 1968. During the period of study, the area was stocked with 355 trapped wild turkeys from Lykes Fish-eating Creek Refuge (adjacent to the hunting area) before nesting season each year to augment the breeding population.

During the study, hunting consisted of seven weeks of daily hunting during November and December. Shooting hours were from one-half hour before sunrise until one-half hour after sunset. The bag limit was one turkey of either sex per day and two per season in 1968, 1969, and 1974, and one gobbler per day and two per season in 1971, 1972, and 1973. There was no tagging system. The regulations were similar to those in effect statewide in Florida. Other game was legal; hunters on the area were primarily after turkey, deer, and feral hog. Hunters who bagged radio instrumented turkeys were interviewed for information about their hunting.

There was no way to accurately measure turkey hunting pressure and to relate it meaningfully to harvest data because hunters entered and left the area at will at all hours. Many persons were there only for camping, fishing, or some other activity besides hunting. Some visitors hunted all species of game at the same time; others hunted turkeys only; and some did not hunt turkeys at all or shot turkeys only if the opportunity happened to present itself. Hunter visits to the management area were about 1500 during the opening and Thanksgiving weekends each year and about 6000 total hunter visits each season, without substantial variation from year to year. There was approximately one hunter per seven acres in the 10 000 acres of turkey-deer-hog habitat on opening weekends and on Thanksgiving weekend.

One hundred twenty-five radio instrumented turkeys were used as a sample of the turkey population for monitoring hunting effects. Each year's subsample (averaging 20 per year) was tracked daily and located while roosting on certain nights during the hunting season to determine whether any had been killed and to observe their behavior under hunting pressure. The proportional effects on the entire turkey population were inferred from the fate of the sample, using appropriate statistical procedures. Because of this approach, the possibility of biased vulnerability of the radio instrumented turkeys naturally arises. In this and other studies, we have tracked and closely observed nearly 500 turkeys that were radio instrumented. In only two cases did instrumented turkeys show any sign of injury from the radio package or harness. Both birds had callouses under the transmitter and on the wing muscle because they had been fitted too tightly with the surgical rubber loops. These injuries were minor and could be detected only when the birds were examined in hand. Special care was taken thereafter, and no similar problem was subsequently detected.

The maximum weight of transmitter packages was 90 grams, which is less than 2.5 percent of the body weight of an eight-pound (3.6 kg) hen; most transmitters were lighter, averaging around 70 grams or about the weight of a turkey egg. Nenno and Healy (1979) tested the effects of radio packages on turkey behavior and concluded that their transmitters (averaging 140 g and 3.7 percent of the weight of their hens) did not introduce serious behavioral biases. Their harness was more cumbersome than ours, involving a neck loop in addition to underwing loops. There was no reason to believe that the radio instrumented turkeys in these studies were encumbered by the transmitters.

Regression analysis was used to test for a relationship between daily hunting pressure, total kill, and hunter success rate. Fisher's Exact Test was used to test for a difference in harvest rates of adults versus juveniles and males versus females, and to test for a difference in overall harvest during periods when either-sex was legal versus periods when hens were protected. A correlation coefficient was calculated to test for a relationship between the harvest level each hunting day and the amount of gobbling reported. All confidence intervals or proportions followed the form

$$p \pm 1.96\sqrt{\frac{p(1-p)}{N}}$$

Overall Harvest The proportions of the radio instrumented subsamples taken by hunters during each of the six years of study are shown in table 5.1 and figure 5.2. The legal kill ranged from 81 to 94 percent of the population during either-sex seasons and 62 to 93 percent in years when only gobblers were legal. In three of the years of the study, a 95 percent confidence interval included 100 percent of the population. Even in the year of the lowest kill, the lower confidence limit was 43 percent, or nearly one-half of the population. The proportion of a turkey population that can be harvested without significant detriment to productivity has not been determined. In the pres-

Table 5.1 Survival of radio instrumented turkeys under heavy hunting pressure

	Number instrumented						Percent harvested (by sex & age)			
	Adult		Juvenile			Legal	Adult		Juvenile	
Year	F	M	F	M	Total	sex	F	M	F	M
1968	4	0	7	7	18	Both	100	—	86	100
1969	6	2	10	9	27	Both	100	100	70	78
1971	4	4	4	6	18	Male	75	50	50	83
1972	2	9	3	12	26	Male	0	67	67	67
1973	1	2	5	6	14	Male	100	100	80	100
1974	6	10	4	2	22	Both	100	70	100	100
TOTAL	23	27	33	42	125		87	70	76	86

NOTE: Percentages are not the same as in Fig. 5.2 because they reflect the total harvest which includes a few turkeys for which exact dates of kill are not known.

ent case, however, the level of harvest was high enough for us to confidently conclude that serious overhunting was occurring.

Harvest Rate of Relocated Turkeys

Harvest rates of wild-trapped turkeys that were released in the hunting area before hunting and those that were not relocated were approximately the same—80 percent and 82 percent, respectively, based on band returns of 43 relocated and 42 nonrelocated turkeys that were legal game.

Everett et al. (1980) found that turkeys that were trapped and relocated in Alabama required at least six weeks to establish new home ranges. About one-half of the stocked turkeys in the present study had less time than that in their new range and therefore may not have completely established new home ranges. It might be expected that a turkey's familiarity with its home range would influence its survival under hunting pressure, but the similarity in harvest levels of resident and introduced turkeys suggests otherwise. Radio-tracked turkeys avoided human intruders only when they could see them within approximately 200 m. The usual avoidance reaction was for the turkey to merely move into the cover of woods out of sight of the intruder. Nothing associated with this behavior suggested that knowledge of the surroundings was important to the turkey's escape. Home range familiarity is probably more important to feeding and intraspecific sociality than to defense.

Harvest Rate by Age Class

Fisher's Exact Test comparing adult and juvenile harvest rates (table 5.2) indicated that harvest rates were similar for adults and juveniles in years that either sex could be legally shot, but that adults were bagged at a lesser rate than juveniles in years when hens were protected ($p = 0.05$). DeGraff and Austin (1975) also found no difference in harvest rates of

Table 5.1 (continued)

Percent harvested (all turkeys)		Number survived season	Confidence interval on % harvested
First two days	Whole season		
50	94	1	1 + 0.11 — (83—100%)
63	81	5	5 + 0.15 — (66—95%)
11	67	6	6 + 0.22 — (45—89%)
15	62[a]	10	10 + 0.19 — (43—81%)
36	93[a]	1	1 + 0.14 — (79—100%)
64	86	3	3 + 0.15 — (71—100%)
		26	

Table 5.2 Proportions of 125 turkeys harvested/unharvested by age class in either-sex and gobbler-only years

Age class	Proportion harvested		
	Under either-sex hunting	Under gobbler-only hunting	Total harvested
Adult	$\frac{25}{28}$ = 89%	$\frac{14}{22}$ = 64%	$\frac{39}{50}$ = 78%
Juvenile	$\frac{33}{39}$ = 85%	$\frac{27}{36}$ = 75%	$\frac{60}{75}$ = 80%
TOTAL HARVESTED	$\frac{58}{67}$ = 87%	$\frac{41}{58}$ = 71%	

Table 5.3 Proportions of 125 turkeys harvested/unharvested by sex in either-sex and gobbler-only years

Sex	Proportion harvested		
	Under either-sex hunting	Under gobbler-only hunting	Total harvested
Male	$\frac{25}{30}$ = 83%	$\frac{29}{39}$ = 74%	$\frac{54}{69}$ = 78%
Female	$\frac{33}{37}$ = 89%	$\frac{12}{19}$ = 63%	$\frac{45}{56}$ = 80%
TOTAL HARVESTED	$\frac{58}{67}$ = 87%	$\frac{41}{58}$ = 71%	

adult and juvenile hens during either-sex fall hunting in New York.

Harvest Rate by Sex Fisher's Exact Test indicated no significant difference between harvest rates of hens and gobblers (table 5.3). A significantly ($p = 0.05$) smaller proportion of the hen population was killed in years when they were protected by regulations (only 63 percent killed) than in years when hens were legal game (89 percent killed). Although the safe limit of hen harvest is not known, 89 percent is clearly too high for sustained yield management and, if continued, would probably lead to early extinction of the population. Even the 63 percent illegal hen kill in gobbler-only years was probably too

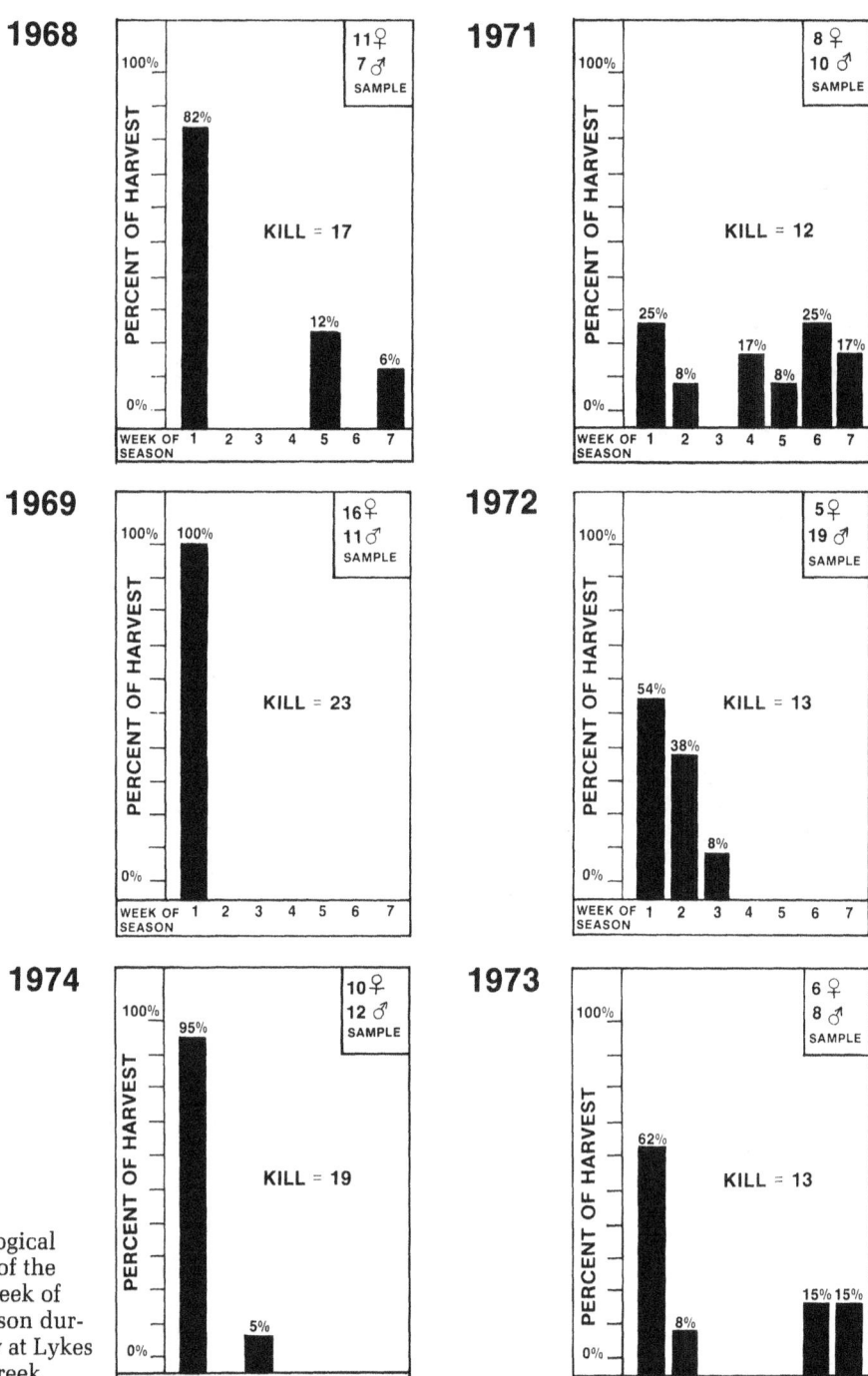

5.2 The chronological distribution of the harvest by week of the open season during the study at Lykes Fisheating Creek WMA.

high for maintenance of a high level of productivity and might also lead to eventual extinction of the population. Apparently, the annual restocking, and perhaps immigration from the nearby refuge, were all that had enabled turkeys to exist on the management area under the heavy either-sex hunting pressure after the mid–1960s.

The 63 percent illegal harvest rate of hens suggested a lack of hunting skills, serious disregard for the regulations, or both. This led to an attempt to measure turkey sex identification skills of the hunters during the 1972 hunting season.

Test of Hunting Skills A sample of 90 hunters was tested on turkey hunting knowledge at the main check station as hunters entered the management area the day before the 1972 fall hunting season. Hens were not legal game that year. Each hunter was taken aside and asked a few questions about how he would distinguish hens from gobblers. Because many said they depended on more than one anatomical feature, there was a total of 153 answers from the 90 hunters. The beard of the male was the most often cited feature and, while this is correct, the beard cannot usually be seen on a young gobbler in early November, which would force a large proportion of the hunters to rely on an alternative feature to identify young fall gobblers. This would be important in view of the fact that most of the gobblers in the population are young of the year. Upon analysis of the questionnaires, it was found that approximately 60.7 percent of the answers dealt with features that are useful in determining the sex of a turkey under hunting conditions, but 39.2 percent of the answers did not (table 5.4).

Table 5.4 Features used by hunters to distinguish hens from young gobblers

	Useful features			Not useful features		
	Beard	Head color and feathering	Body size	Body feather coloring	Leg or neck length	Other
Turkey hunters (N = 47)						a
Number	38	21	17	12	0	13
Percent	80.8	44.7	40.4	25.5		27.7
Nonturkey hunters (N = 43)						b
Number	28	11	8	5	1	2
Percent	65.1	25.6	18.6	11.6	2.3	4.7
Total answers by 90 hunters (N = 153)						
Number	61	32	27	17	1	15
Percent	67.7	35.6	19	18.9	1.1	16.7

Source: Results of check-in questionnaire, Fisheating Creek, WMA, 10 November 1972.
a. "Don't know."
b. "Yellow feet," 1; "big feet," 1.

This suggests that the hunters would make an "honest" error about 40 percent of the time.

Each hunter was asked whether he was primarily a turkey hunter and was shown live game farm turkeys in large enclosures and asked to identify them as to sex. The sample size was too small for elaborate analysis, but two observations about the outcome can be made: 40 percent of the hunters made incorrect sex determinations, and there was no significant difference in sex identification skills between those who considered themselves primarily turkey hunters and those who did not. The close agreement between the error rates on the questionnaire (39.2 percent) and errors on the practical test (40 percent) is evidence that hunters who use faulty methods for sex identification also perform poorly under field conditions. It is reasonable to expect hunters to perform similarly while actually hunting. With additional research, it may be possible to use testing procedures on hunters to predict the levels of hen harvest that will occur. This would be useful in setting and adjusting regulations to achieve prescribed levels of hen harvest and to maintain optimal population productivity.

In view of the large illegal hen kill in 1971 previously described and the results of the questionnaires and hunting skill tests, we anticipated that hens would continue to be harvested at a high rate despite any conceivable regulations to protect them. This assumption was borne out during the 1972 and 1973 seasons when seven of the 12 instrumented hens (58 percent) were killed illegally.

It is not surprising that many Florida hunters cannot, or will not, distinguish hens from gobblers. It has always been legal to shoot turkeys of either sex in Florida and there has been no motivation to learn to distinguish the sexes. The practice of shooting turkeys off the roost in near darkness, a long-standing hunting practice in Florida, leads to indiscriminate shooting. Posthunting questionnaires and general observations during the study indicated that most turkeys were taken on the roost in the early morning or evening. Since it is legal to take turkeys in the darkness one-half hour before sunrise and one-half hour after sunset, mistakes about the sex of the target are bound to occur and will continue as long as present hunting hours are in effect.

It is of interest that the self-proclaimed turkey hunters performed no better than the nonturkey hunters on the practical sex determination test. That may not be the case statewide in Florida because turkey hunting may be more widely practiced as a specialty in northern Florida where there is more turkey habitat and more public access to turkey hunting. A comparison of turkey hunter skills in various parts of the state would be instructive. There are many experienced and highly skilled turkey hunters in south Florida, many of whom hunted regularly at Fisheating Creek, but there may be average differences in skills of the overall hunting populations in different parts of Florida. Such differences could have a significant effect on the types of hunting regulations that would be appropriate in different areas.

Identification of the factors associated with poor compliance with hunting rules should have high research priority in the future. This will have an important bearing on the effectiveness of many of the more important hunting regulations, especially those for gobbler-only hunting in fall. There are probably differences in hunting skills, knowledge, and compliance with the regulations on private versus public lands. We believe that there is substantially more compliance with regulations on private lands, as compared to public hunting lands because an important hunting motivation on private land is stewardship, while the most prevalent motivation on public land is competition.

The "Caution Effect"

The harvest pattern in gobbler-only years was not concentrated during the first week of the season as it was in either-sex years (fig. 5.2). The longer period of harvest was due, we believe, to hunters having fewer opportunities to shoot when they were required to take time to make sex identification. This also influenced the proportion of adults versus juveniles shot, as previously mentioned (table 5.1), and the total eventual harvest each year (fig. 5.2).

The sex identification test previously discussed indicated that about 40 percent of the hunters in 1972 could not distinguish gobblers from hens, even when they had time to look closely at living birds. Interviews with successful hunters during the study revealed that many turkeys were being shot while they were running or flying. Under such conditions, even a split-second delay in shooting would permit a turkey to escape. The reason the caution effect resulted in fewer adults than juveniles being shot is probably a reflection of the greater wariness of adults that had prior experience with hunters and were quicker to fly or run when approached by hunters.

The caution effect thus limits shooting opportunities, reduces hunting success per unit of time, and tends to distribute the harvest more evenly among hunters over time. This can be expected also in hunting other species, such as deer, when hunters have to see antlers of a specified minimum size before shooting. In some cases, as with especially scarce or wary game, this will result in a reduction in the total harvest, as it did in the present study. It appears, then, that turkey harvest levels can be increased by eliminating restrictive rules that introduce the caution effect, or distributed more evenly among participants over a longer period of the hunting season if restrictions that make hunters more cautious are introduced.

A shortened hunting season in years when only gobblers were legal would have curtailed the total harvest, through the caution effect, while in years when both sexes were legal a shorter season would have had almost no effect on the total harvest. For example, shortening the season in 1968 to a single week would have reduced the harvest by only three birds (18 percent of the kill), would have had no effect in 1969, and had only a 5 percent effect in 1974. However, in 1971 through 1973, when only gobblers were legal, a one-week-long season would have reduced the harvest by 75 percent, 46 percent, and 38 percent, respectively (fig. 5.2). This is because the harvest was spread over a longer period of time in gobbler-only seasons.

The effect of caution before shooting would be expected to also reduce the total harvest of gobblers (in addition to its effect on the temporal distribution of the kill as previously discussed), but Fisher's Exact Test indicated that the difference in total harvest of males in gobbler-only seasons versus either-sex seasons (83 to 74 percent, table 5.2) was not statistically significant ($p > 0.05$). This may be a reflection of the small sample size.

The first week's harvest during gobbler-only seasons rose from 25 percent in 1971, to 54 percent in 1972, and to 62 percent in 1973, showing a trend each year toward the either-sex pattern. This was caused by a change in hunter attitudes during the study. Hunters were disregarding the sunrise-shooting rule that was in effect during the spring gobbler hunts and were making more errors in sex identification as they became less attentive each year. Shooting could be heard along the creek and in the favorite turkey roosts well before sunrise as hunters were shooting turkeys off the roosts.

Most hunters expected considerable law enforcement effort to accompany the new hunting rules in 1971, and, as a consequence, they complied with the regulations the first year. But they soon realized that the risk of being apprehended for early shooting or for shooting a hen was low. Not all hunters were shooting hens, but many were taking less care to determine the sex of the target.

Crippling Losses One of the initial objectives of the study was to measure crippling losses by finding injured or dead radio instrumented turkeys that were shot and not retrieved. No live cripples were found, but, upon routinely interviewing successful hunters, it was learned that they had often recovered turkeys that had been crippled by other hunters. In some cases, hunters admitted that they knew that their bird had first been shot at and hit by somebody else. This is probably a reflection of the high hunter densities, good visibility in the open cypress woods, and the tendency of hunters to congregate at favorite turkey roosting places to hunt. A few turkeys were found dead after the hunting season and may well have been crippled or killed by hunters during the open season, but we have no way of knowing that. Crippling levels were measured in a spring gobbler study on the Lochloosa study area as will be discussed later.

Escape and Dispersal Behavior Although movement of radio instrumented turkeys was sometimes increased by encounters with hunters, only when they were flushed several successive times did turkeys move far; this was the result of the distance involved in successive flights rather than an effort on the part of the turkeys to disperse from the area.

Throughout the study there were numerous opportunities to observe the escape behavior of radio instrumented turkeys that were disturbed while they were being radiotracked. Turkeys would typically avoid an investigator by moving away from him as soon as the investigator was seen by the turkey. Sounds had no effect on movement of turkeys—even the shooting of guns did not disturb them at distances of more than 200 meters. When a turkey saw an approaching investigator, it would rapidly move only far enough to be out of sight, after which it would continue to move away at a slower pace until it was about two or three times the distance that carried it out of sight. Concealing cover seemed to be the key to the turkeys' sense of escape. They would usually resume normal behavior within 10 minutes after being disturbed. However, when turkeys were flushed and alighted in trees, as they usually did, they would normally remain in the trees for nearly an hour before coming back to the ground and resuming normal activities.

Roosting locations of 24 radio instrumented hens (N=5) and gobblers (N=19) were plotted on the evening of 9 November 1972, two nights before opening of the fall hunting season on the Fisheating Creek study area. The survivors were located on the roost each night for the first four days of hunting and about once each week through the rest of the open season to observe their movement patterns under heavy hunting pressure and to measure their survival. The roosting pattern of the 24-turkey sample before hunters entered the area is shown in figure 5.3. Hunters were allowed to enter the area at noon on Friday, 10 November. They were not permitted to hunt that evening, but some hunters attempted to roost turkeys to gain an advantage in hunting the next morning. Past experience had shown that hunters would flush some of the roosting turkeys Friday night. This is reflected in the change in roosting patterns between Thursday and Friday nights (figs. 5.3 and 5.4), but dispersal was not very great before hunting began.

Hunting commenced on the morning of 11 November. Hens were not legal game. During opening weekend there were approximately 1500 hunters in the 10 000 acres (4000 ha) of woods where the turkeys were. As expected, noticeable dispersal occurred by roosting time Saturday night (fig. 5.5). About one-half of the hunters left the hunting area Sunday afternoon, but, as can be seen in figures 5.6 and 5.7, the widely dispersed roosting pattern persisted through at least Tuesday night, or through four days of hunting. The next roosting fixes were on Tuesday, 21 November, after 11 days of hunting (fig. 5.8) by which time most of the season's harvest had already occurred. Some regrouping may have occurred, but the sample size was too small to clearly reflect it.

Another week later, after 16 days of hunting (fig. 5.10), the surviving turkeys were still widely dispersed but no farther than the initial dispersal seen on opening day. The same

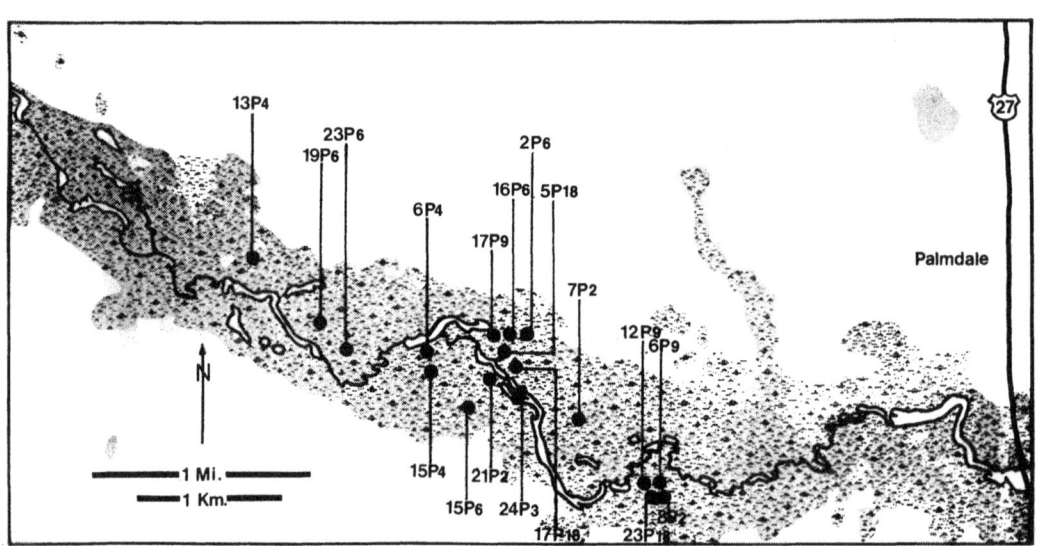

5.3 Roosting places of monitored turkeys on Thursday night, one day before hunters entered the management area.

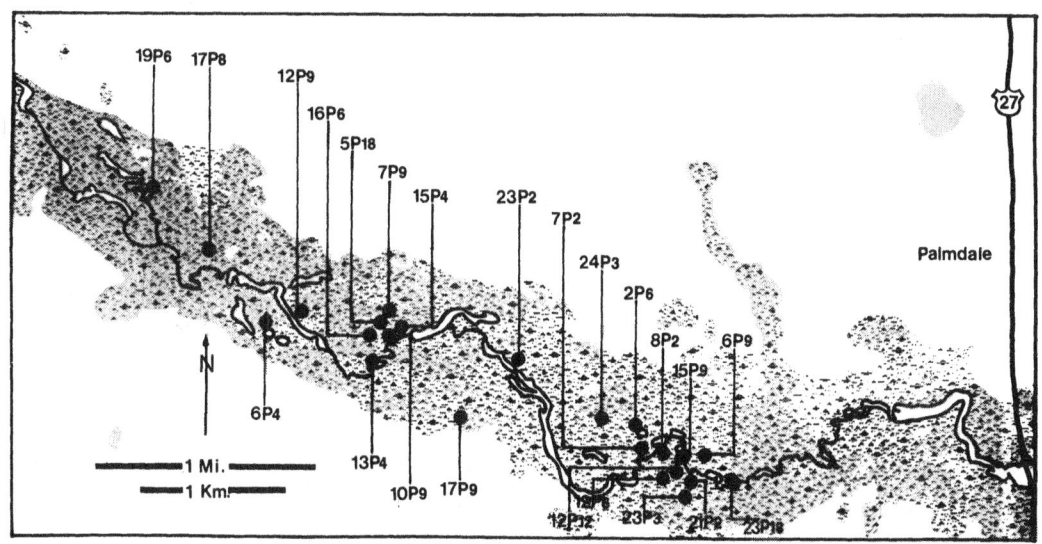

5.4 Roosting places used by monitored turkeys on Friday night after hunters were allowed in the management area. Hunting was not permitted until the next day.

5.5 Roosting places used by monitored turkeys on Saturday night, after one day of hunting.

pattern held for the remainder of the seven-week-long open season (figs. 5.11–5.14).

Only one of the 24 monitored turkeys left the hunting area. It remained in an unhunted area for one week and returned to the hunting area while hunting was still underway. Before the season was over, 63 percent of the legal males and 20 percent of the protected hens had been killed. Fifty-four percent of the harvest occurred during the first week of the open season.

Hunting activity sometimes curtailed turkey movement as when turkeys remained stationary in trees for several hours after being flushed and landing there. On three occa-

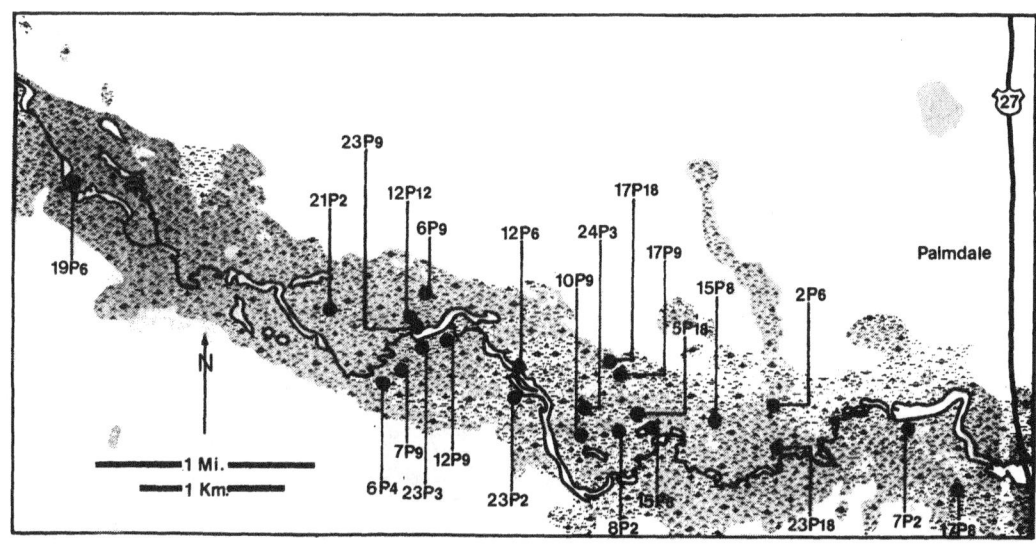

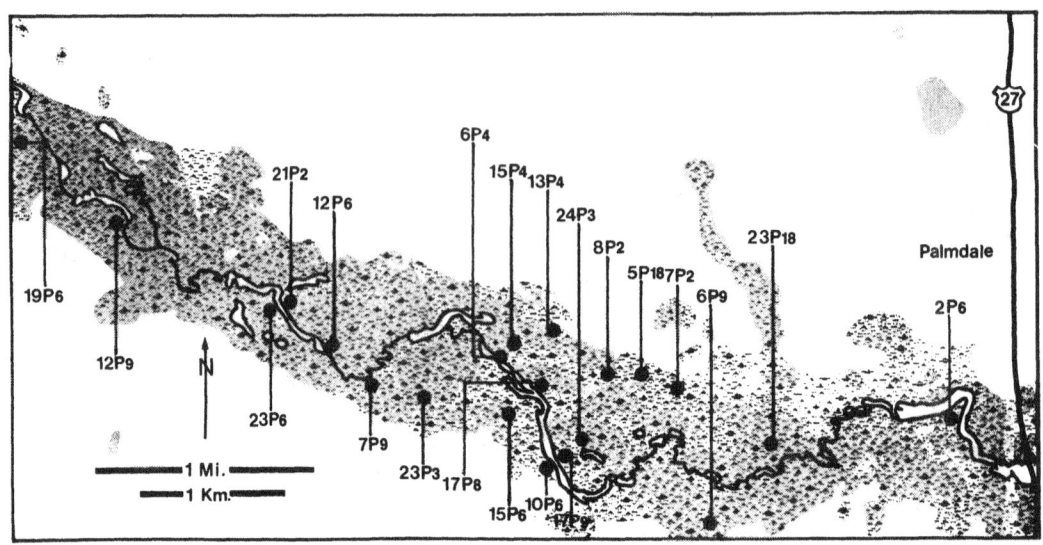

5.6 Roosting places used by monitored turkeys on Sunday nght, after two days of hunting.

5.7 Roosting places used by monitored turkeys on Monday night after 3 days of hunting. The turkeys are widely dispersed as compared to prehunting locations, but they have not left the hunting area.

sions, single turkeys (including both sexes) that were flushed repeatedly by hunters finally hid on the ground in thick cover while observers approached within 6 m. In two of these cases, observers were able to nearly touch adult gobblers before the birds ran away without flying.

One adult hen was flushed at least four times in less than two hours by different hunters while she was being radio-monitored closely. After the fourth flushing, the radio signal indicated that she was stationary in a small, dense thicket. Thinking that she may have been shot and crippled or killed, we approached closely, and found her standing still in the thicket, unharmed. She allowed us to approach within 10 m

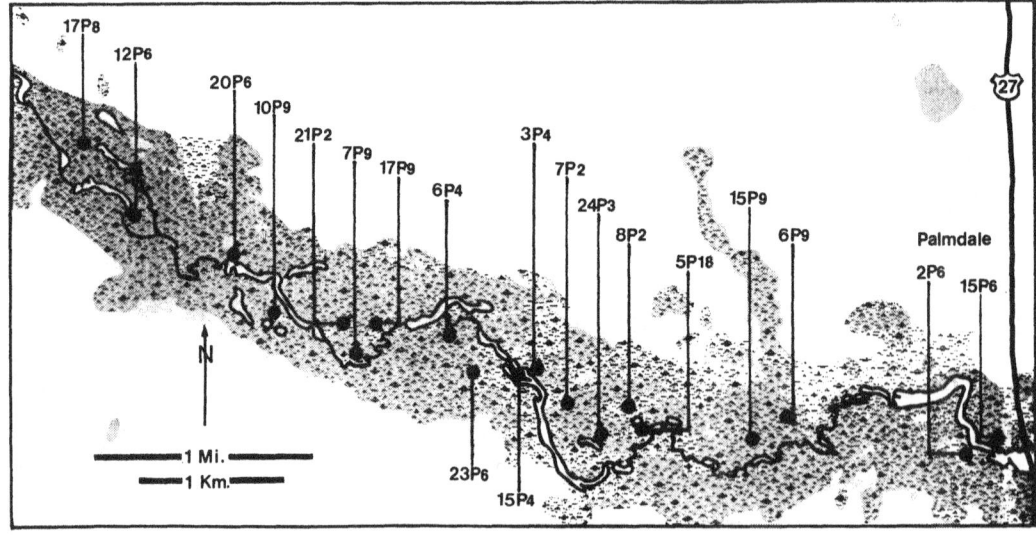

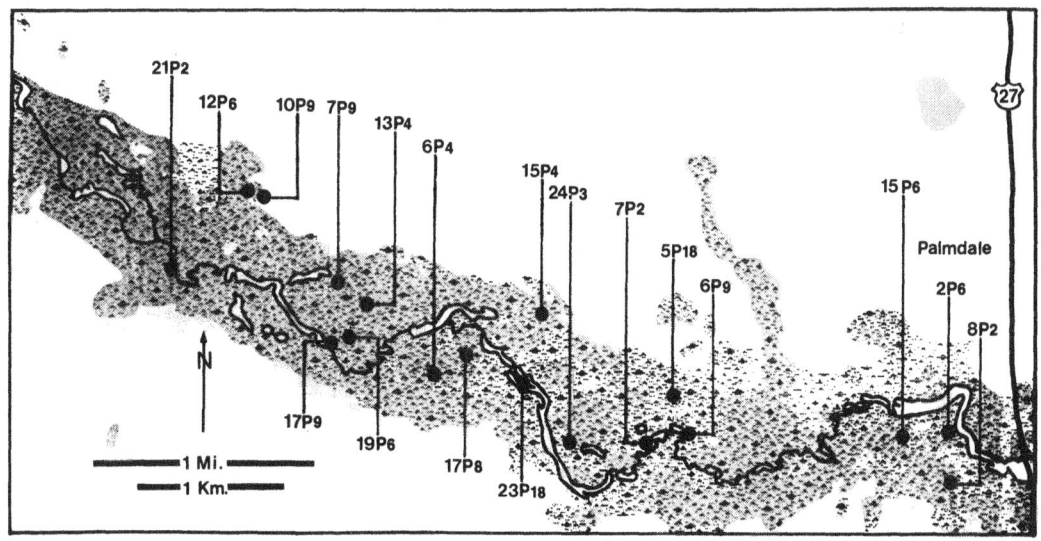

5.8 Roosting places used by monitored turkeys after 4 days of hunting.

5.9 Roosting places used by surviving monitored turkeys after 11 days of hunting. Many of the turkeys had been killed by this time, but not all survivors are plotted because of poor radio reception that evening.

and finally ran out of the thicket and across the palmetto prairie. She was observed behaving normally a few days later.

On five occasions, radio instrumented turkeys that had been closely pursued by hunters roosted at night on the ground rather than in trees. We know of no other example of adult turkeys roosting on the ground, except nesting and brooding hens. The hunted turkeys that roosted on the ground were later found roosting in trees, indicating that they were not crippled, or at least not seriously so, and that this behavior was temporary.

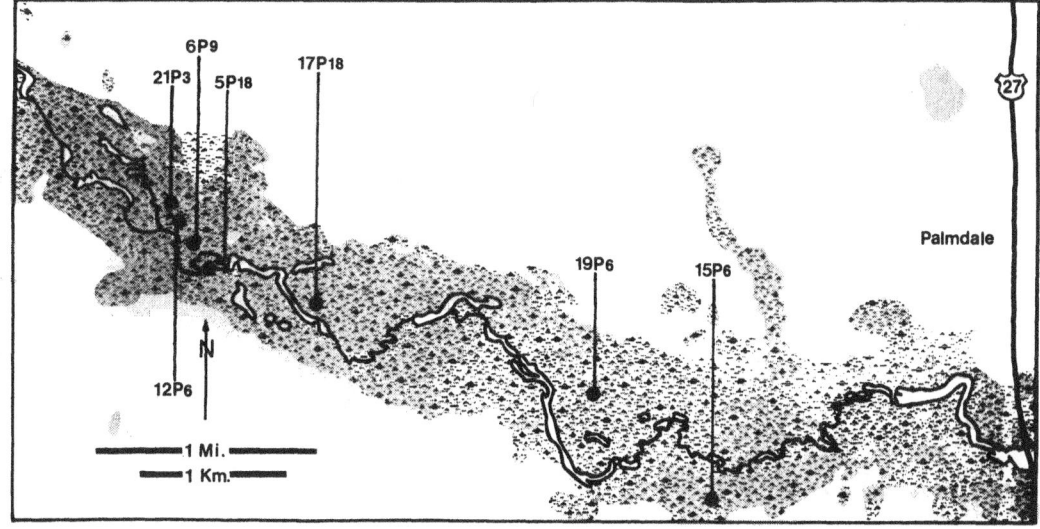

Harvest Management 183

Further Discussion on Hunting Pressure

Turkeys were seen regularly in early fall in the open glades away from the cover of cypress woods until hunting season opened and hunters entered the area. In the refuge portion of the Fisheating Creek Wildlife Management Area, which lies adjacent to the hunting area, turkeys continued to use the open areas during fall and winter. This apparent interaction between hunters and turkey habitat utilization suggests that the reactions of turkeys to human disturbance may depend partly upon the nature of the habitat. It appears that turkeys are relatively unaffected by human presence in heavy woods as compared to open woods and unforested openings.

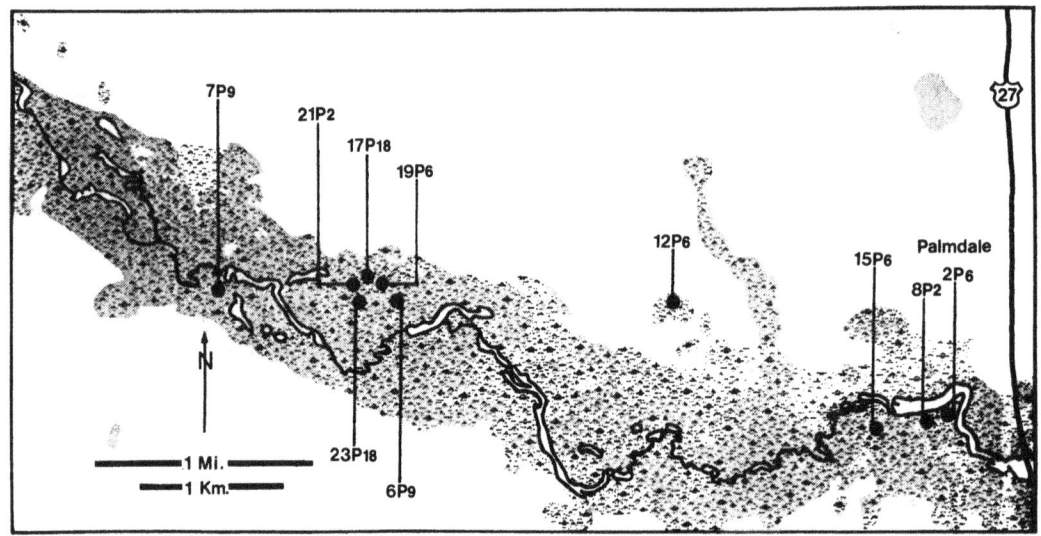

5.10 Roosting places of monitored turkeys after 16 days of hunting.

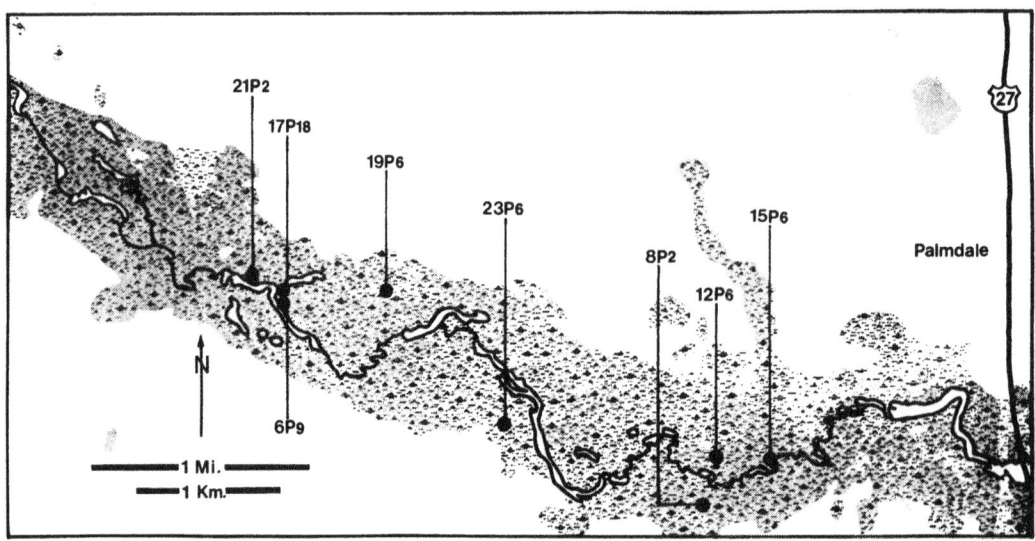

5.11 Roosting places of monitored turkeys after 23 days of hunting.

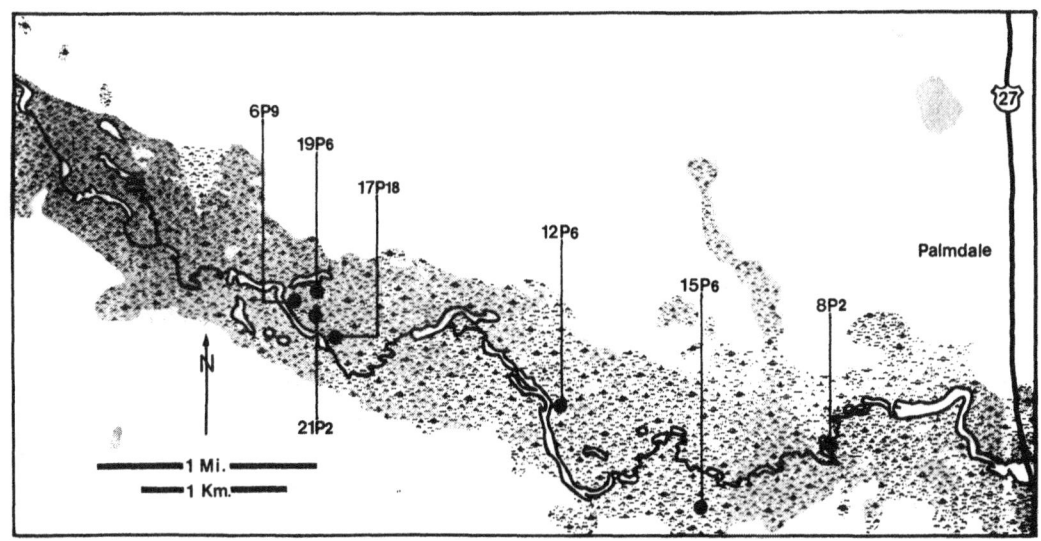

5.12 Roosting places of monitored turkeys after 31 days of hunting.

5.13 Roosting places of monitored turkeys after 38 days of hunting.

Some of the illegal hen shooting during this study was not due to mistaken identity. In several cases, transmitters were removed from hens and thrown into Fisheating Creek; in two cases transmitters were looped on tree limbs along with hen feathers, and at least three hen carcasses were skinned in the woods. But some hens had been mistaken for gobblers, as indicated by the fact that they were left where they had fallen after the hunter determined the sex.

In one case, a radio instrumented hen was being monitored by telemetry at the time she was shot and was found where she fell under the roost, a few seconds after being shot, with fresh human footprints in the mud leading directly to and away from the carcass. This indicated that the hunter

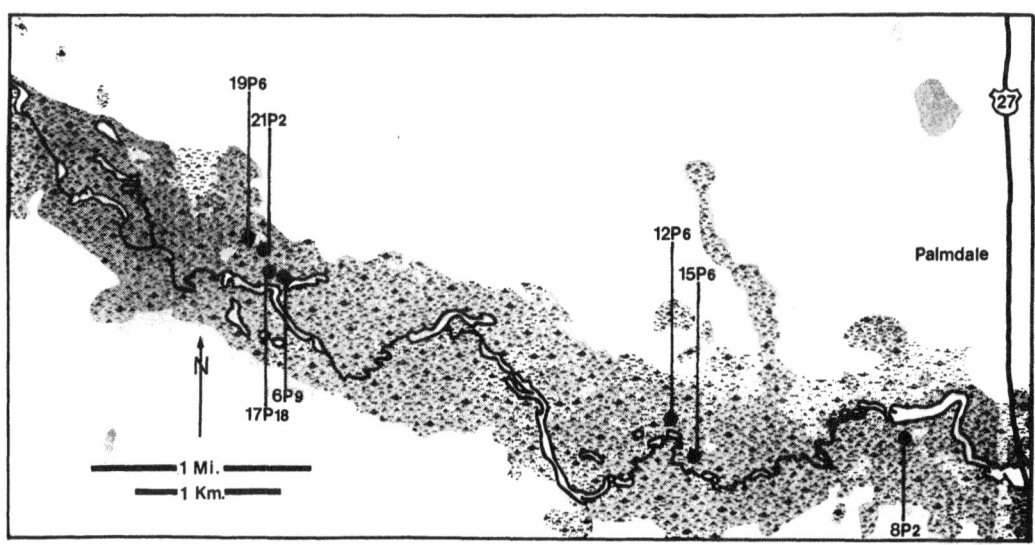

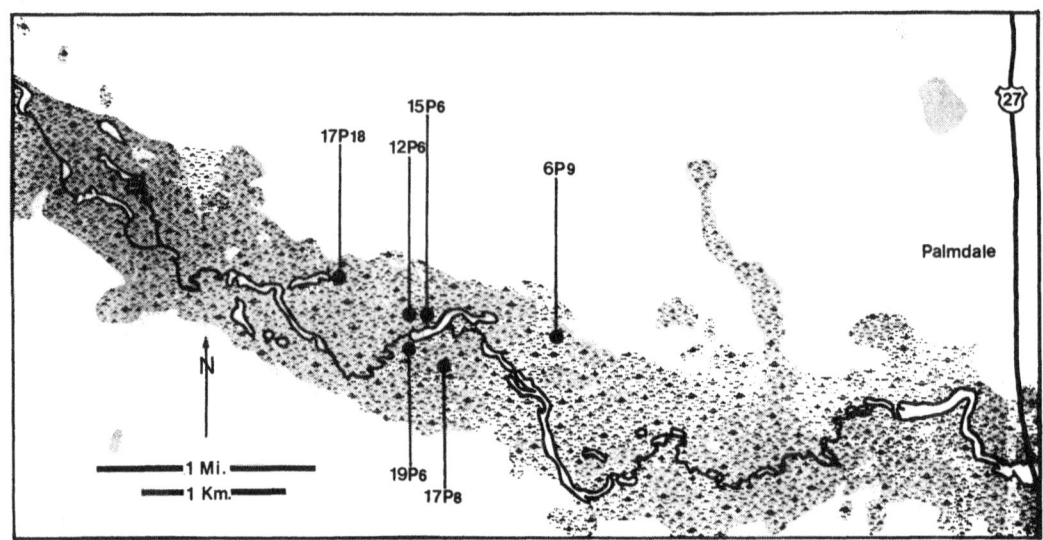

5.14 Roosting places of monitored turkeys after 52 days of hunting, at the end of the hunting season. Survivors are in the same general vicinity they had been in during the open season.

had left the scene when he found that he had shot a hen. Hunters brought in hens that they said they had found dead, and one hunter brought a hen to the checking station in the belief that he had killed a young gobbler. During one gobbler-only fall season, not even a single juvenile gobbler was brought through the checking station despite the fact that there should have been at least as many juveniles as adults killed. This suggests that no hunter who killed a juvenile gobbler that year had enough confidence in it being a male to take a chance on checking it out.

Sample sizes were too small to measure the chronology of the harvest with respect to age and sex. Young males or hens may have been killed sooner in the season, indicating that they were being taken with greater ease than were older hens or gobblers. Vulnerability of sexes and age classes would be more clearly expressed when a low proportion of the population is harvested. We know of no research that reveals differences in vulnerability of the sexes or different age classes of turkeys, but our personal hunting experience indicates that young of the year are more receptive to imitated calling by hunters in fall than are older turkeys.

Observation of the turkeys under heavy fall hunting pressure indicated that the only serious impact on the population caused by hunting was the effect of the harvest itself rather than disturbances associated with hunting. The turkeys did not disperse from the hunting area. The same thing was found in an Alabama study (Everett et al. 1978). This probably depends, to some extent, on the type of habitat, the size of the area, hunter density, and hunting pressure in the surrounding range. Since turkeys will sometimes avoid areas that are heavily used by people, even if hunting is not under way (Wright and Speake 1975), they should be expected to disperse in response to hunting pressure if the level of pressure were great enough. It appears, however, that at moderate hunter densities, disturbance associated with hunting is not of practical concern in Florida turkey habitat. We suspect that interference among hunters would become intolerable long before hunter density reached levels necessary to drive the turkeys from the hunted area.

It was found in this study that legal hunting could decimate a turkey population during the first few days of the open fall season. Even at lower harvest levels than those measured in the present study, an adverse effect on productivity would occur through the excessive shooting of hens.

It was also found that hens were shot even when they were protected by regulations. Too many of the hunters were unable or unwilling to shoot only gobblers during the fall open season. Complicating the problem is the fact that only a few young gobblers have visible beards by early November when the fall hunting season usually opens. If hens are to be protected, it will be necessary to prohibit roost shooting and delay the shooting hours until there is enough light to visually distinguish the sexes. It might be wise to delay fall turkey hunting until late in November so that the beards of more young gobblers would be visible. Objective data on the proportion of young gobblers with visible beards on various dates in the fall would be useful.

The study was undertaken not only to correct a problem at Fisheating Creek but also to begin to address the overhunting problem in a way that would be applicable to other wildlife management areas, when, due to rising hunting pressure, such measures would be needed on them as well. It is not known with certainty at this time the extent to which other areas, both in and out of the Florida management area system, are being overhunted.

Limited Quota Spring Gobbler Hunting Season

After overhunting was detected during the fall turkey season on Lykes Fisheating Creek WMA, a new study was initiated to find a way to continue turkey hunting on the area without overharvest. It was decided to test spring gobbler hunting. The initial step was to formulate hunting regulations. Little or no information on hunting regulations to meet specified turkey management objectives could be found in the literature, and although some state wildlife agencies monitored spring turkey hunting rates, their emphasis was on harvest levels and hunter success rates with particular attention to whether more hunting could be sustained. That was not of primary interest in the present study.

In South Carolina, Bevill (1973 and 1975) used field observation to determine the best seasonal timing of the spring gobbler season from the standpoint of hunting quality and the probable effects of hunting on nesting hens. In an essay dealing explicitly with turkey hunting quality (Madson 1975), hunter overcrowding was cited as the major factor that degrades spring turkey hunting on public areas. Also mentioned were the danger of hunters being shot while calling turkeys on crowded areas, the negative mental effects that hunters have on each other, and hunters that are "indifferent to proper hunting techniques and traditions."

Research on hunter attitudes and levels of satisfaction since the mid–1960s (Webb 1968, More 1973, Hendee 1971, Thomas et al. 1973, and Knopf et al. 1973) has identified a number of important ingredients of good hunting, including the importance of the beauty in the hunting environment, escape from the sounds of civilization, companionship, solitude, and a reasonable opportunity to kill game.

Potter et al. (1973) emphasized that hunters who are in pursuit of different species of game tend to have different expectations and different definitions of what is enjoyable about hunting. Our experience supports that view and we think it is especially appropriate to stress that in regard to turkey hunters.

Using available literature sources and our own personal insights into turkey hunting, we drafted spring gobbler hunting regulations for Lykes Fisheating Creek WMA to achieve the following objectives.

1. Permit hunting to be done safely in traditional ways, including imitated turkey calling.

2. Permit hunting to proceed without annoying interference among hunters.

3. Allow maximum hunting opportunity and harvest levels within the bounds of any constraints that might be needed to meet objectives 1 and 2.

4. Meet with the approval of a substantial majority of the participants.

5. Provide a sustained turkey harvest level for the management area from year to year without restocking.

The study plan called for closely monitoring hunter satisfaction and modifying the rules as necessary in 1977 through

1981. The regulations that evolved are summarized in the Appendix.

The study was on a public hunting area where constraints were imposed by various administrative levels within the agency and by the landowner. Procedures for issuing permits; making, printing, and distributing the regulations; deploying management and enforcement agents; releasing publicity about the hunts; and other important aspects were not under the control of the investigators. There was no opportunity for replications or experimental controls, and changes that occurred in the hunting rules and procedures from year to year to improve them made statistical comparisons all but impossible. The wisdom of attempting to do research under such circumstances was open to question, but we knew that no better opportunity was likely to ever arise and, in view of the urgent need to learn more about how to deal with excessive hunting pressure on turkeys, we undertook the study under these less than ideal circumstances.

Setting the Harvest Goal

The turkey population had increased considerably while the area was closed to turkey hunting in 1975 and 1976 (following the fall study previously discussed), and the population had been augmented with trapped turkeys in 1976. By 1977, the population was estimated to be one turkey per 25 acres (10 ha) of turkey habitat. Assuming an equal sex ratio, there would be approximately 200 gobblers in the management area for the first spring gobbler season in 1977.

We anticipated a harvest of 100 gobblers in 1977, but the harvest level was considered to be unimportant except as it related to hunter satisfaction. Our premise was that the product of hunting would be hunting recreation of high quality, and that would be indicated by the proportion of satisfied hunters rather than by the number of turkeys killed. Provisions were made to restock the area should overharvest occur. There would be no fall turkey season on the area, but fall hunting for deer and other game would proceed as before.

Finding Criteria for Hunter Density

No information was available about suitable hunter densities for spring gobbler hunting. Our own hunting experience supported Madson's (1975) belief that high hunter density during spring turkey hunting was both unsafe for calling turkeys and would lead to annoying encounters between hunters, but there was little basis for estimating the level at which hunter density became a problem. As a starting point, the daily quota was set at three hunters for each square mile, or 50 hunters in the entire study area per day. Only 50 permits were to be issued per hunt in 1977 and each applicant would be eligible for only one permit per year. We considered this to be somewhat arbitrary and planned to adjust the quota rules as suggested by the harvest rate, by interviews with quota hunt participants, and based on the results of a mail survey being mailed to selected turkey hunters (discussed below).

Determining Hunting Effects on Turkeys

Spring hunting may affect a turkey population adversely if too many hens are killed and by hunter interference with nesting. To check for these possible effects, immediately before the experimental hunts each year, 20 to 40 wild hens were trapped on the study area and radio instrumented for monitoring. The number of radio instrumented hens that were killed, or that disappeared from the population during hunting, would provide an estimate of the level of hen shooting. The surviving hens would be monitored to find their nests and to observe their nesting success. The results of that phase of the study were presented in Chapter 3.

Measuring Hunter Satisfaction

Hunter satisfaction was monitored each year by questionnaires mailed soon after the hunting season to each hunt participant and by oral interviews with hunters when opportunities arose.

Timing of the Open Season

The main considerations in the timing of the open spring season were the possibility of excessive harassment of the turkeys if hunters were in the area every day for a long period of time and the desirability of hunting during a period when the gobblers are receptive to imitated turkey calling. Since little was known about the effects of human disturbance on turkey mating activity, and since it is possible that continuous human presence in the woods could be harmful, it was decided to permit only Saturday-Sunday and Tuesday-Wednesday hunting. That would keep hunters out of the woods on Mondays, Thursdays, and Fridays.

Previous experience suggested that spontaneous morning gobbling from the roost could be expected any time from late January through mid-May, depending on the advance of spring and the local weather. Gobbling was usually heavy in February through April. A long gobbling season was also noted by Bevill (1973 and 1975) in studies over a period of three years in South Carolina. We thought it feasible to set the hunting season for 19 two-day hunts from 1 February through 5 April 1977. One constraint on the dates was a custom of the landowner to open the area to public fishing on Easter weekend.

Imitated turkey calling from time to time during the study confirmed the receptiveness of gobblers to calling (and therefore to hunting) from February to early May.

Quota Permit Procedures

Hunting permits were issued through an ongoing system administered by the Division of Wildlife Office in Tallahassee. Each fall preceding each spring hunting period, application forms for permits were made available to licensed hunters who also had wildlife management area permits. Applicants were required to mail applications to the Commission's office in Tallahassee, indicating their first through fifth choices of hunting dates. Permits were issued on a first-come, first-served basis. When the quota number was reached for a particular hunt, the next applicant preferring that date was assigned to the hunt of his second, third, fourth, or fifth choice, in that order. After the quota was filled for all hunts, the remaining applicants were notified that they would not receive a permit.

A provision was imposed by the agency's administrators to allow persons over 65 years old to hunt without a permit as often as they wished. We were able to measure, but not control, this additional hunter participation.

Summary of Hunting Regulations

The hunting regulations used in 1981 (Appendix) are those arrived at during the course of the study. Some provisions of the regulations warrant a brief explanation:

1. The prohibition on rifles was a requirement of the landowner.

2. Legal shooting hours began at sunrise (rather than one-half hour before as in the statewide rules) to discourage morning roost shooting. It is too dark one-half hour before sunrise to distinguish hens from gobblers. Hunting ended at 4 p.m. to discourage evening roost shooting.

3. Hunters were prohibited from operating vehicles during prime early morning hunting hours to minimize "road running" and the resultant annoyance to hunters on foot. The restriction of vehicles to designated roads and camping to semideveloped camp sites was for the same purpose.

4. Fishing was prohibited. If fishing were allowed, few turkey hunters would be able to get the limited number of permits because of the much larger demand for fishing.

5. Shot sizes larger than number four were prohibited to encourage close-range head-shooting and discourage long-range shooting and resultant crippling losses.

Modification of the regulations and hunting procedures was minor from year to year during the study. The number of permits issued was increased after 1977 from 50 to 60, and later to 75 per hunt, in an effort to offset the permittees who did not show up. Average daily participation showed an increasing trend each year from 21 hunters per day in 1977 to 42 per day in 1981. This was probably due in part to the increased quota, increased word-of-mouth publicity about the hunt, more repeat applicants, better participation in subsequent hunts, and an increasing number of overaged hunters who were allowed to hunt without permits.

Weekend Versus Weekday Hunting Success

When the number of turkeys killed per hunter was compared for weekdays and weekend days, the difference was not significant ($t = 0.326$, $p = 0.05$). Thus, for practical purposes, success rates on weekday and weekend hunts were the same.

Effect of Hunter Density

Regression analysis indicated a highly significant positive relationship between the number of hunters participating any one day and the number of turkeys killed that day—the more hunters who hunted, the more turkeys were killed, but there was no significant relationship between hunter density and average success per hunter. This was true of weekdays as well as weekend days. This means that the hunter success rate (mean number of turkeys harvested per hunter) was not related to the density of hunters. If hunter interference had caused lower average hunter success, there would have been a significant inverse relationship between higher density and hunter success. The result also suggests that hunting facilitation at the higher hunter densities (i.e., increases in hunter success due to the disturbance or a "driving" effect on the turkeys) did not occur. If it had, there would have been a positive association between higher hunter density and average success per hunter.

We cannot predict whether further increases in hunter density would result in better or poorer hunting success per hunter, but at some level either facilitation or interference will probably occur. Higher absolute harvest levels can be expected at higher hunter densities whether or not the average success rate is effected.

An important goal should be to determine the level at which increasing hunter density begins to degrade the quality of the hunting so that it can be avoided. It would be questionable logic to raise the hunter quota merely to increase the number of turkeys killed if by doing so hunter satisfaction were decreased.

Gobbling Activity During the Hunts

Hunters believe that gobblers are more receptive to imitated calling when they are gobbling. Gobbling also pinpoints the location of gobblers for the hunters. If vigorous gobbling enhances hunting success, there should be a positive correlation between them. We attempted to test this by asking hunters as they checked out after hunting whether they heard gobbling and by calculating a correlation coefficient for gobbling reported during each hunt with the number of turkeys killed during the same hunt. The correlation was very weak ($r = .131$). Bevill (1975) found that turkey gobbling patterns were more erratic on hunted areas than on nearby unhunted areas. The weak correlation we found would seem to support that. In all likelihood, turkeys that do considerable gobbling on a hunted area will be quickly silenced by hunters, in one way or another. If this was happening, it suggests that hunters were in contact with most of the gobblers that were gobbling, otherwise, enough undisturbed gobblers would have been gobbling to produce a stronger correlation.

It would be useful to have better information on the relationships between spontaneous roost gobbling, progress of the mating season, gobbler receptiveness to imitated calling, and average hunter success. Such information could be used to set the dates of the spring gobbler seasons to achieve specific harvest goals. A short season set at the optimum time would produce harvests comparable to longer seasons set at other times. From the standpoint of providing the maximum amount of quality spring turkey hunting, it would be better to set the season at a time when the gobbling level is satisfactory, and have a longer hunting period, than to have the season at a time when gobbling is greatest and having most of the harvest take place during a shorter interval, thereby degrading hunting conditions for participants at other times in the season. The question is whether to permit an optimal amount and quality of hunting or to have a large turkey harvest.

We attempted to analyze the seasonal differences in gobbling activity in northern, central, and southern Florida by using a large number of volunteers who reported gobbling activity heard afield by date, location, and time of day, but there was too much variability in the data for useful statistical analysis. This approach can probably be refined by selecting certain days in the different regions for listening simultaneously and ensuring a large enough number of listeners on each designated day. Regional gobbling patterns need to be characterized, especially in northern Florida.

Although we did not undertake a study of gobbling levels, we detected a decline in overall gobbling activity at the time of maximum copulation and a greatly increased level of gobbling at the time hens were incubating. This observation fits the general seasonal pattern of gobbling described by

Bevill (1973, 1975) wherein gobbling activity is high early in the season. The premating peak in gobbling comes in early March in south Florida. It might be desirable for the spring gobbler season to open there early enough to coincide with this early gobbling and terminate after the higher levels of gobbling have been resumed. This would necessitate an open season of at least six weeks.

Interviews with Successful Hunters

Hunters were asked a few questions as they checked out of the management area after hunting. Shot sizes used by successful hunters ranged from number 2 to 7½s with 66 percent of the hunters using number 4, 22 percent using number 6, and only 2 percent using 7½s. Seventy-eight percent of the turkeys were taken with a single shot, 15 percent with two shots, and 4 percent were with three shots. Turkeys were shot primarily while they were walking (40 percent), running (16 percent), or strutting (10 percent). In taking their turkeys, 64 percent of the hunters used a yelper. Thirty-five percent hunted from a temporary blind.

In any future monitoring of this kind, it would be instructive to interview unsuccessful as well as successful hunters for comparative purposes. If enough data were obtained on gauge and shot sizes over a period of years, it would reflect the best gauge and shot sizes for turkey hunting and reveal the gauges and shot sizes most likely to produce ineffective, crippling shots under hunting conditions.

Experienced Hunter Survey

Mail questionnaires were sent to 79 experienced and successful turkey hunters of mature age, who had at least four years of turkey hunting experience and considered turkey hunting to be their primary source of outdoor recreation. The list of hunters was obtained by asking a few hunters known personally to us, who met the criteria, to supply three or four additional names. The objective was to characterize the group and to obtain the hunters' views about standards for quality public turkey hunting. The information would be used to further refine the hunting regulations for the experimental hunts. Seventy-nine questionnaires were mailed. Sixty responded, but nine responses were discarded because it was found that respondents did not meet all of the criteria.

Of the 51 respondents tabulated, 88 percent had more than 15 years of turkey hunting experience, 39 percent had over 24 years. They had taken an average of 67 turkeys each. Thirty-three percent belonged to a hunting club. These characteristics indicated persons with considerable knowledge about turkey hunting whose views would be of value for our purposes.

A few prevalent habits of this group are of interest. One-third routinely weighed all turkeys they killed. Ninety-two percent wore camouflage clothing while turkey hunting. Ninety percent hunted turkeys with shotguns, 86 percent of which used 12-gauge, and 54 percent used number six shot; only one respondent used shot larger than four; 20 percent used size 7½ which was the smallest shot size reported. Eighty-one percent aimed at the head and neck of the turkey when shooting. Seventy-one percent preferred spring hunting over fall hunting. Most hunted in more than three states each year; 31 percent hunted in their home state only.

Their views about standards for quality turkey hunting were of particular interest. Over 74 percent considered relatively sparse hunter density to be very important for quality spring turkey hunting; only 3 percent did not think hunter density was important. On the question of how much space turkey hunters should have, 33 percent thought that each hunter should have more than 500 acres (200 ha) to himself, but a majority (67 percent) said that each hunter could get by with somewhat less room than that. (In this study we attempted to provide a minimum of 200 acres (80 ha) per hunter). Seventy-seven percent thought that spring gobbler hunters should be at least one quarter of a mile apart; only 4 percent thought that distance between hunters was not important.

The things most often cited as contributing to good turkey hunting experiences were: hearing a turkey's voice (80 percent); good weather (70 percent); and not seeing other hunters (63 percent). Other important ingredients cited were: simply being in the woods (28 percent); being able to call to turkeys (28 percent); "working" a gobbler (26 percent); seeing turkeys (24 percent); also cited were seeing a turkey sign; knowing that there was a good turkey population; and killing a gobbler.

To obtain their views of minimum yearly hunting success that would be considered acceptable, they were given a series of success level statements from the lower limit of merely being in nice woods without bagging a turkey to the opposite extreme of killing at least one adult gobbler. The intermediate options were: hearing or seeing a turkey on one-half of the hunts; hearing a gobbler on most hunting trips; calling up at least one gobbler; and killing one legal turkey (of either sex). Based on the responses, 25 percent said they would not have to kill a turkey to consider hunting successful and 23 percent said that calling up a turkey was sufficient success.

They were asked to list up to five things that degraded a turkey hunting experience. Seeing dogs in the woods was cited (67 percent), as was too many hunters in the woods (65 percent), and evidence of illegal hunting (54 percent). Baiting was the most often cited type of illegal hunting encountered. Other things cited by more than 17 percent of the respondents were: bad weather, poor hunter behavior, motor vehicle interference, and evidence of habitat destruction (with forest clear-cutting being most often cited). Other degrading factors listed were: overhunting, posted property, hunters shooting out of range, road hunting, presence of cattle, trespassers, and hunters doing the calling for others.

Many of the factors cited as contributing to a good hunting experience are directly related to the density of the turkey population while those factors most often cited as degrading to the hunting experience were things that can be directly attributed to human activities, many of which can be dealt with by regulations. A large standing population of turkeys may be as important as a large annual harvest. Management procedures (mainly hunting regulations and their enforcement) that permit hunters to enjoy their hunting, whether they kill a turkey or not, may be more important than management procedures that are designed for maximum harvests.

One bias in this survey was caused by the fact that experienced, serious turkey hunters usually hunt in places where there are enough turkeys to meet their expectations. One-third of the sample belonged to private hunting clubs, for example. We suspect that more casual turkey hunters, who hunt primarily on public lands, would consider the density of turkeys in their hunting area and their hunting success as more important factors contributing to their hunting satisfaction than would the respondents in this survey who would tend to take that for granted.

The responses of the expert turkey hunters generally confirmed the appropriateness of the hunting rules that had been made for the pilot study and helped guide us in their revision.

Hunter Satisfaction with the Hunts

In 1977 and 1980, a mail questionnaire was sent to each hunt participant soon after the spring hunts, to measure levels of satisfaction with hunting on the area. The same questions were asked both years. There was a 52 percent response rate in 1977 and a 44 percent response in 1980 with no outstanding differences in the nature of responses between years.

Most of the hunters had hunted at Lykes Fisheating Creek WMA the previous fall season, and a large majority had hunted there also at some other time in the past. More than

74 percent said that they enjoyed the spring hunt more than any previous fall hunt at Fisheating Creek. An even larger majority (79 percent) favored keeping the fall turkey season closed there. The things hunters most liked about the hunts were sparse hunter density and nice woods, in that order. Only 5 percent said that there were too many hunters. The high turkey population was the third most cited quality factor in 1977, but this ranked lower in 1980. Ninety-eight percent said they enjoyed their hunting there. Ninety-six percent said that they would like to see this type of spring gobbler hunting continued on the area.

In 1977, the number of turkeys on the area was judged adequate by 57 percent of the respondents but by only 47 percent in 1980. Fewer than 10 percent saw no turkeys while hunting in either year. A very large majority thought that the hunting dates were appropriate and that the shooting hours (sunrise to midafternoon) were correct.

A majority first heard about the public hunts from friends; only 18 percent learned about them through the news media. Seventy-nine percent knew that the fall turkey season had been closed the year before (which is probably a reflection on the large proportion of the spring hunters who regularly hunt the area in the fall). A small majority took advantage of the opportunity to scout the area during the afternoon of the day before the hunt. A substantial majority favored the idea of voluntary briefings about spring turkey hunting for hunt participants, and most said that they would attend such briefings if they were held before or during the spring hunting season at Lykes Fisheating Creek WMA.

When asked what they disliked or would like to see changed about the hunts, hunters most often replied that they would like to be able to go fishing after finishing turkey hunting for the day. A few hunters did not like having to camp only in designated areas. Curtailment of shooting hours at 1 P.M. was cited four times in 1977. (Shooting hours were later extended to 4 P.M.) Other complaints were that there should be three-day and four-day hunting periods (this was later done), that visitors should be able to accompany hunters (provisions already existed for that) and that larger shot sizes should be allowed (cited only six times). Mentioned only infrequently were the desires that permits be exchangeable and that unpermitted hunters be allowed to hunt when others with permits did not show up.

The rationale behind the items that a few hunters did not like was carefully explained when the occasion arose:

1. Camping in designated areas. This rule was intended

to keep hunters from camping in good turkey habitat which would create disturbance to the turkeys and degrade the hunting.

2. No fishing. Since the area was very popular for fishing in the spring, fishermen would apply for many, if not most, of the hunting permits only to go fishing. This would keep the spring turkey hunters out.

3. Shooting hours closed at 4 P.M. All-day hunting would encourage evening roost shooting which would result in hens being accidentally shot on the roost. This would be effectively precluded by ending hunting at 4 P.M. There is no known reason to close earlier in the afternoon.

4. Larger shot sizes prohibited. There is reason to believe that the greater mass and smaller numbers of shot in the buck shot, BB, and number 2 shot sizes cause serious crippling far beyond the effective range of effective patterns.

5. Exchangeable permits. If permits were exchangeable among hunters, many hunters would ask friends and relatives to apply for quota permits so that they could hunt more than once, thereby obtaining an unfair advantage over others by monopolizing the permits. This would be contrary to the philosophy of maximum hunter opportunity and would eventually lead to irritation with the hunting rules by some hunters when they learned that they were being deprived of hunting because of the system.

6. Filling out the quota at the gate. This would result in many highly dissatisfied prospective hunters being turned away at the gate after traveling to the management area in the anticipation of getting a "standby" permit. This could result in a complete breakdown of quota concept for the hunts if the agency yielded to the complaints that would result.

No-show Hunter Survey

A mail questionnaire was sent to permit holders who did not hunt in 1979 and 1980 to find out why they did not come to hunt. Responses were straightforward and similar in both years. About 70 percent expected to hunt at the time they applied for their permit (but nearly 10 percent did not expect to). Over 70 percent of those who did not hunt had an unexpected conflict, most often personal illness. The fact that friends could not obtain permits to hunt was cited second only to personal illness as a reason for not hunting.

The most practical way to deal with the no-show problem is to offset it by increasing the number of permits issued (as was done effectively in 1978 and thereafter).

Disturbance of Hens

Due to the dense cover that most hens use for nesting and the tendency of hens to hold tight to the nest when a man approaches, the likelihood of a hunter flushing a nesting hen is low. As far as we were able to determine, none of the radio instrumented hens that produced 141 nests in the hunting portion of the study area was caused to desert by a hunter. During more than 6000 man-days of hunting in the spring study, only one hen was reportedly flushed by a hunter (it was not radio instrumented). During the Easter weekend each year, which was usually near the peak of turkey nesting activity, about 2000 campers, fishermen, and picnickers used the study area without restrictions on where they could camp or go, with or without vehicles. Their activity was concentrated in the 10 000 acres (4000 ha) of turkey woods for a density of one person per 5 acres (2 ha). The only nest being monitored that was known to have been disturbed by this concentrated human presence was one that was abandoned because of a van that was stuck in the sand for several hours within about 15 m of the nest. Several occupants of the van created a great deal of disturbance in the vicinity as they attempted to move the disabled vehicle.

We believe that the disturbance effect of spring hunting on nesting hens is negligible under the conditions on the Lykes Fisheating Creek and Lochloosa WMAs. The most important factors contributing to the low accidental flushing rate was dense nesting cover and the reluctance of hens to flush from their nests. This may not be the case in open hardwoods.

A more detailed discussion of nesting and possible impacts of spring hunting are presented in Chapter 3.

Spring Harvest Rates

Concurrent with the harvest management studies, an attempt was made to measure the proportion of gobblers harvested legally or crippled, and hens harvested illegally, during the open spring gobbler seasons on Lochloosa and Fisheating Creek study areas.

During a period of seven consecutive years on Lochloosa, 110 turkeys of both sexes were captured with drugs or cannon nets in late winter, radio instrumented, and tracked before, during, and after the 16-day spring gobbler hunting season in late March and early April. There was no check station or limit on the number of hunters using the area. It is estimated that about 1200 hunter-trips occurred per season (table 5.5).

Illegal Hen Kill Of the 44 hens being tracked on the Lochloosa WMA at the beginning of the spring gobbler season, 38 were determined

Table 5.5 Summary of hen survival during spring hunting on Fisheating Creek and Lochloosa study areas

Year	Number monitored	Number survived	Died during hunting season[a]	Open days of hunting	Man-days hunting[b]
Fisheating Creek					
1978	11	8	3	40	902
1979	15	12	3	30	1420
1980	13	11	2	35	1611
1981	27	23	4	44	2314
TOTAL	66	54 (82%)	12 (18%)	149	6247
Lochloosa					
1969	3	3	0	16	1200
1970	8	6	2	16	1200
1971	5	3	2	16	1200
1972	3	3	0	16	1200
1973	9	9	0	16	1200
1974	11	10	1	16	1200
1975	5	4	1	16	1200
TOTAL	44	38 (86%)	6 (14%)	112	8400

a. Possible hunter kills.
b. Checking station count on Fisheating Creek; estimated without checking station on Lochloosa.

to be alive and uncrippled at the close of hunting. One that did not survive was known to have been shot by a hunter. Two others were found dead and thought to have been shot (table 5.5). The causes of death of the remaining three were unknown, but their deaths may have been related to hunting. Whatever the cause of the deaths, 86 percent of the hens survived and 14 percent died. A 95 percent confidence interval calculated for the proportion of survivors is 76 to 96 percent (86 percent ± 10 percent), meaning that no less than 76 percent of the hens in the Lochloosa population survived the spring gobbler seasons of 1969 through 1975, and that survival may have been as high as 96 percent of the total hen population. Conversely, 24 percent was the highest proportion that may have been killed.

During the four hunting seasons that hen survival was monitored on Fisheating Creek, 70 hens were tracked through the hunting season or until their deaths. Fifty-four survived, four were known to have been killed illegally, eight others died during the hunting season of unknown causes that were probably associated with hunting, and four died of known causes that were not related to hunting (table 5.5). Disregarding the four hens that died of causes not associated with hunting, there was a 76 percent survival rate of hens on the area. A 95 percent confidence interval for the proportion of survivors is 66 to 86 percent (76 percent ± 10 percent).

Gobbler Harvest The confirmed annual legal harvest of gobblers during spring hunting on Lochloosa was 12 of 35 (34 percent) in the radio-tracked sample. A 95 percent confidence interval would be 18 to 50 percent (34 percent ± 16 percent). In addition to the 12 gobblers known to have been harvested, three others failed to survive the 16-day spring hunting season, raising the possible total hunting mortality to 46 percent with a 95 percent confidence interval of 29 to 62 percent. This indicates that the annual spring gobbler harvest, including cripples, was probably no higher than 62 percent of the male population. The three gobblers that were confirmed as lost cripples amounted to 9 percent of the birds being tracked, equaled 20 percent of the total not surviving the season, and was equivalent to 25 percent of the legal harvest. The 34 percent annual harvest rate of gobblers on the Lochloosa study area compares to 51 percent in an Alabama study (Gardner et al. 1972) and 18.7 percent reported in a Missouri study (Lewis and Kelly 1973).

The proportion of legal gobblers killed was not being monitored on Fisheating Creek.

Standard Kill Index

The survival rates of radio instrumented hens on Lochloosa and Fisheating Creek are not directly comparable because of the differences in hunting pressure on the two areas, a difficulty that exists in comparing harvest rates between other management units. There is a need for a standard index that takes hunting pressure into account. If a common denominator for hunting pressure is used, comparisons in levels of harvest and illegal kill on different areas can be made. One approach would be to use man-days of hunting or hunter visits as the measure of hunting pressure. When hunting pressure is not known or cannot be accurately estimated, days open to hunting could be used. The concept is similar to Mayfield's (1961) nest-days of exposure for calculating bird nesting success. In this case, we would calculate survival (or death) of turkeys experiencing various numbers of days of hunting exposure.

Index Based On Days Open To Hunting This index consists of the proportion of radio instrumented turkeys dying per hunting day. For Lochloosa, 6 of 44 hens were killed during 16 days of spring hunting (table 5.5). The kill index for the proportion of the hens dying per hunting day would be $(6/44) \div 16 = 0.0085$. To get a more easily compared number, this can be multiplied by a given number of days, such as 100, to obtain the proportion of the hens dying per 100 days open to hunting at the hunting pressure level that existed on the area. For the Lochloosa data this would be 0.0085 × 100 = 0.85 (85 percent) of the hens dying per 100 days of hunting. Or, if a season length of, say, 37 days were contemplated, the predicted loss of hens, based on the 1969–75 kill data, would be 0.0085 × 37 = 31 percent of the hen population.

Index Based On Man-days Of Hunting

Since it is known that turkey harvest is related to the number of hunters hunting, a better index would be based on hunting pressure. This would consist of the proportion of the radio instrumented turkey sample dying per day, divided by the mean number of hunters hunting per day, yielding the number of turkeys dying per hunter-day. This would be a very small fraction which, for practical use, could be multiplied by a number such as 1000 to give the number of turkeys dying per 1000 man-days of hunting pressure. For the Fisheating Creek data (table 5.5), we have 12 of 66 turkeys dying during 1562 hunter-days of pressure which would be

$$\frac{12/66}{1562} = 0.0001164 \times 1000$$

= 11.6 percent of the hens killed per 1000 man-days.

The proportion of hens that will be killed can be predicted for any hunting pressure level. During, let's say, 2500 hunter-days of gobbler-only spring hunting at Fisheating Creek, 29 percent of the hens will die (.0001164 × 2500 = 0.291). Using the real data from Fisheating Creek in 1981 we have 0.0001164 × 2314 = 26.9 percent of the hen population killed.

There are undoubtedly interactions between hunting pressure, turkey population density, kill rates, and other factors. As turkey population density decreases, for example, the kill rate per hunter day probably diminishes. However, within the limits expected on Florida wildlife management areas, these indexes could be useful. They can be refined into practical tools for comparing harvest rates among areas and predicting the consequences of increasing or decreasing hunting pressure. Harvest goals could thus be pursued in a direct way. Statistical confidence limits could be placed on the indexes, but this would be impractical with the small amount of data presently available.

These indices may not fully account for the nonhunting-related death rates of the hens. Research on death rates, employing nonhunted "control" populations, are needed to make the predictions more accurate.

Recommendations For Spring Hunting On WMAs

Specific recommendations are applicable mainly to the annual spring gobbler hunts under conditions that existed on Lykes Fisheating Creek WMA while this study was in progress. To determine the applicability of the recommendations to other management areas, it will be necessary to do similar work on those areas. The following recommendations are tentatively presented for spring gobbler hunting areas.

Morning shooting hours should begin no earlier than 10 minutes before sunrise. Light conditions are sufficient to distinguish gobblers at that time. To await actual sunrise would increase the likelihood of turkeys leaving the roosting area before shooting time, which would be annoying to hunters who have "roosted" or heard turkeys gobbling early and expect to take advantage of it. The 10-minute rule would be applicable whenever hens are not legal.

Fishing should remain closed during hunting hours if the area experiences a high demand for fishing, but it may be feasible to allow fishing after 4 P.M. by hunters only. If this is done, care should be taken to enforce the time limit and to monitor any possible drift in participation away from turkey hunting toward fishing. That would make it almost impossible to anticipate proper quotas for turkey harvest purposes. The most likely problem will be persons obtaining permits and entering the area to fish, rather than to hunt. Nonhunting visitors will become an increasing problem if fishing regulations are made liberal. There may be antagonism between hunters and fishermen. The safest course is to prohibit fishing during the spring gobbler hunts.

A provision is needed that would allow a nonresident hunter to apply for a quota permit before having to purchase a management area stamp. This has been an imposition on out-of-state hunters who have been required to buy permits by mail and thereby gamble on being selected for a hunt. Only a minor administrative decision is required to correct this.

A limitation should be placed on persons hunting without having to participate in the quota permit system. To allow persons access at will, without permits, will undermine control of the hunting pressure. It is recommended that "overage" hunters be required to apply for hunt permits as everybody else does.

Quota permits should not be transferable. If transferable, anyone who wishes could obtain several permits by merely applying for permits in the names of friends and relatives. That would prevent many deserving hunters from participating while others will hunt several times each year. An unfair system will create dissatisfaction with the hunts.

It would be desirable to have the permit application forms available when the fall hunting season opens and to accept them in the Tallahassee office postmarked after some announced date in late November. This will help ensure that persons who hunt the management areas in the fall will have an opportunity to apply in time to get a turkey hunting permit. This will help prevent unrest with the fall closure of turkey hunting.

When the "first-come, first-served" application rejection rate becomes substantial, it will be advisable to use a lottery system for selecting applicants.

Better publicity about the hunts would help spread the opportunity to hunt more widely among more citizens than does the word of mouth. One improvement in that regard would be to include special spring gobbler hunt quota permit information in routine quota hunt information releases. It seems to have been the practice in the past to mention only the fall hunting quota permit information in such releases, and this tends to confuse the public about special spring turkey hunting permits.

The rules for special hunts are relatively complicated. A stable set of hunting regulations and procedures from year to year will lead to better knowledge about, and acceptance of, the rules by hunt participants over a period of time. However, some wildlife management areas are unique in certain respects and that should be taken into account in implementing controlled spring gobbler hunts. Such rules as shooting hours, open dates, and shot size restrictions can be easily standardized.

For the time being, spring gobbler hunting is probably a better alternative than fall gobbler-only hunting for most wildlife management areas where overharvest of hens in fall is anticipated. This is because few Florida hunters presently have the skills necessary to distinguish young gobblers from hens in the fall. When hunting in the competitive atmosphere of a public area, not all hunters will let a turkey of undetermined sex go by without shooting at it. There would be more flexibility in setting turkey hunting regulations if Florida hunters were more skilled in turkey sex identification, particularly in the fall. It would be in the best interests of the Game and Fresh Water Fish Commission, the turkey resources, and the hunting public to more vigorously pursue an education program to this end.

Adjustments in the quotas may be warranted since we do not know whether the quota used at Fisheating Creek is optimal. The 75 hunters per day at Fisheating Creek was set for 10 000 acres of habitat, or about three hunters per square mile. The habitat there is so accessible during dry weather conditions that roads are not used in connection with hunting—hunters tend to disperse through the woods. In hilly (and swampy) terrain where hunters travel ridge tops and roads and where physiographic features cause hunters to concentrate, a lower quota per unit of area may be necessary. The key to a correct quota is to survey the hunt participants about their satisfaction and find out from them whether there are too many hunters on the management area. Regardless of the quota set, other rules will affect the number of hunters showing up to hunt. Unlimited overaged permits, free exchange of permits, and more than a single permit per hunter will affect the participation rates and hunting pressure. These should be standardized, and when changed the effect of the change on hunting pressure should be assessed.

How many more hunters can be accommodated on a particular wildlife management area without loss of an acceptable hunter satisfaction level? That may be difficult to determine. If surveys of hunting quality are made on the same individual hunters over a period of time, increasing dissatisfaction among them will be evident when quality goes down. But if hunting quality surveys are made on the changing population of hunters using a particular public area over a period of time the major effect being observed will be the lower average quality standards of the changing participants because those who no longer enjoy hunting on the public area will stop hunting there. This has been happening on Florida's public hunting areas and is one of the primary reasons why so many hunters have joined private hunting clubs and no longer hunt on public hunting areas. This is probably also what is causing some people to quit hunting altogether. In effect, the Commission has been catering to hunters on public hunting areas who have somewhat different standards than those who have joined private hunting clubs or hunt mainly out-of-state. It would seem useful to learn more about hunter attitudes toward hunting on Florida's public hunting areas. Surveys for that purpose should include hunters who do not hunt regularly on public areas.

Good recordkeeping of hunting pressure and harvest and

close attention to hunter satisfaction should be expected on Florida wildlife management areas. Checking station personnel should be literate and well instructed. They need to understand the regulations and the rationale behind them since it is they, and not the biologists, who will meet the hunters. It would also be helpful for wildlife officers who work on the areas to know more about the rationale behind the rules and other hunt procedures. In the early stages of implementing spring gobbler hunts, biologists or game managers should be on hand at the checking stations. High-caliber volunteers, such as wildlife students and reservists, should be used to the greatest possible extent at the checking stations during spring gobbler hunts.

It is recommended that the spring hunting system described be implemented on a trial basis on other wildlife management areas, where appropriate, and made a part of the management plan for each wildlife management area. As the concept is implemented on management areas, practical experience will be gained and less monitoring will be required.

6

Synopsis of Research and Management Needs

Harvest management studies have produced information suggesting that some turkey populations are being overharvested. The same thing may well be happening in the unmonitored hunting areas. In 37 days of spring hunting, 31 percent of the hen population on Lochloosa Wildlife Management Area would be killed illegally, according to data collected in the 1970s, and over 20 percent of the male population there would be crippled and lost. These findings point to a serious need for better turkey harvest management program in Florida. A number of suggestions for additional research have been made in earlier sections of this bulletin. Some of the more important management and research needs, including harvest management, and other subjects will be briefly discussed in the present chapter.

Gobbler-Only Fall Hunting

On much of the land now open to the public for either-sex turkey hunting, hens are being overharvested. A crucial management question is whether to continue fall turkey hunting, and if so, how and where. It is likely that fall gobbler-only hunting cannot be allowed without a substantial proportion of the hens being shot, but this is partly because current regulations, such as the shooting hours, contribute to the problem.

Our recommendation is to allow fall gobbler-only hunting on the large public hunting areas and closely monitor hunting pressure, harvest, illegal hen kill, crippling losses, and hunter skills and satisfaction. The studies should be designed to give gobbler-only fall hunting a chance to work effectively. The regulations should be adjusted as indicated by the results of the trial hunts. This work would lead to considerably more knowledge than we now have about how to conduct public hunting without overkilling the hens.

It might appear that hunting pressure will be light on land hunted by private lease and that the Commission need not concern itself with hunting pressure and overhunting problems on these areas. That will be true only as long as the leases are large and the hunting clubs are small. As lease fees increase there will be tendency for hunters to lease smaller tracts and this will result in excessive hunting pressure and probably to overharvest of wild turkeys and other game.

Tagging System

Bag limits are intended to serve the important purposes of controlling the harvest and helping apportion a limited resource among a number of users. However, an annual turkey bag limit cannot be effective unless it can be enforced, and it is common knowledge that most turkey hunters will violate the annual bag limit if they have the opportunity. There is little value in Florida's present honor system turkey bag limit.

Potential tagging systems are nearly infinite in variety and several states have workable systems at this time. An inquiry into tagging systems used in other states should be made, and the best features should be incorporated into a system for testing in Florida. There has been resistance to a tagging system in the agency, primarily because some personnel feel that the tagging system used during the 1950s did not work. That should not stand in the way of investigating potential systems now that the need is so much greater than before.

Legal Shot Sizes and Gauges

There is little question that certain shotgun loads and rifle calibers are unsuitable for taking turkeys because they either increase crippling losses or are too powerful (in the case of some high-powered deer rifles) and simply destroy rather than harvest turkeys. This needs to be investigated scientifically and appropriate regulations implemented. In the meantime, it would be prudent to prohibit the use of shot larger than number 4 and the use of the standard .22 caliber rimfire rifle and .410 shotgun for taking turkeys.

Hunting Closure in West Florida

Turkey hunting in west Florida has been curtailed by closed seasons for several years. The turkey population will not improve further under the closed season, and there is no doubt that the turkey populations in west Florida can tolerate some level of hunting.

At the present time there is no method of accurately counting turkeys. The only way to determine the efficacy of turkey hunting in western Florida is to permit hunting accompanied by adequate monitoring. The most important indicator of the feasibility of hunting will be a harvest level maintained within reasonable limits during a monitored period of three or more years of hunting.

Ingredients of Satisfying Hunting

Although the agency attempts to accommodate the hunting public to the greatest extent possible, it has little or no information about what Florida hunters need or desire in order to be satisfied with their recreational turkey hunting. Improved hunting quality should be a primary turkey management policy of the Commission.

There is little basis for management goals that specify increased turkey population densities or harvest levels without clear evidence that these will lead to higher levels of hunting enjoyment by the participants. The rationale that more turkeys will allow an increased number of hunters to enjoy turkey hunting is open to question in view of the ample supply of turkey hunters that now exists.

The public meetings and invited written comments do not provide adequate representation or sample size for making turkey harvest management decisions based on public needs. Well-planned surveys should be used to obtain accurate information about the things hunters perceive as quality hunting and their needs should be targeted in the management program whenever possible. We recommend that such surveys be initiated soon.

Habitat Improvement

While it may be possible to improve the carrying capacity of Florida turkey habitat through management, methods to do so are not known because no habitat management practice has ever been adequately tested. Studies are needed to measure the effects on turkey populations of cattle grazing, controlled burning, food plantings, artificial feeders, and various timber management practices.

A comprehensive study should be conducted on all important managed wildlife species simultaneously, including the wild turkey. Of special interest should be productivity of the resident populations, their use of managed food and cover patches, movement into and out of managed areas, habitat preferences, general movement parameters, and productivity of the populations.

Timing of the Spring Gobbler Season

A five-week-long, statewide spring season from mid-March through late April was initiated in 1983. Before that, the open hunting season had been two or three weeks long with the state divided into three zones from south to north. One question about the present season is whether mid-March is early enough to open the season in south Florida and whether the last week in April is late enough in west Florida. A study of gobbling levels by regions and by calendar dates would be useful in predicting the consequences of changes in gobbler hunting season dates hereafter.

The spring gobbler season should probably be opened no later than mid-March in south Florida to take advantage of adequate gobbling levels there.

Population Model

In suitable habitat, turkey productivity is greatly influenced by the size of the breeding population at the beginning of the nesting season. Since the turkey is polygynous, the exact number of gobblers in the population is of little importance—the number of hens determines the reproductive potential of the population. Overharvest of hens will result in a reduced breeding population, lower production, and a lower yield. The proportion of hens that may be safely harvested from a population and still maintain high production is not known at this time. Until it is, harvest management policy will be based on supposition. A practical population simulation model, or a similar approach, would help answer this question. A significant research effort should be made to determine the impacts of various levels of hen harvest.

Poult Survival

As mentioned in an earlier section of this bulletin, poult survival during the first two weeks of life may have a great influence on the fall and winter densities of turkey populations. Poult survival may be dependent on the placement, quality, and quantity of food and the arrangement and types of cover available. An in-depth study of turkey predation, with emphasis on predation on poults during the first two weeks of life, is needed. The relationships among cover types, predator levels, and predator populations and their impacts on the turkeys should be of special concern.

Census Method

Very little can be done to measure the effects of habitat improvement or to test various hypotheses about turkey management until a census method or suitable alternative is available. Development of a census method should have high priority in the future turkey research program. Turkeys are particularly suitable for a census because of the ease with which they can be attracted to bait sites and counted.

Harvest Estimates

A method is needed to measure the turkey harvest in Florida with reasonable accuracy. The information obtained from the mail survey may have administrative uses, but it is of questionable management value. Reliable harvest information is needed to help gauge the success of the management program and to monitor the broad effects of regulation changes over time and from region to region. The "scale" needs to be fine enough to permit practical estimates of harvest down to the region level, at about the 10 percent level of confidence. A county by county breakdown would be useful.

Very few historic data are available concerning turkey harvest on wildlife management areas largely because there is no present provision for standardized recordkeeping. This is partly because many management areas have too few, if any, check stations, and many areas do not have qualified check station operators. Records should be kept on the sex, age-class, dates of kill and weights of turkeys harvested. Permanent computerized records should be kept on hunting pressure, dates of open seasons, and regulations in effect. Trained wildlife management personnel should be in charge of the checking stations and data collection to ensure that these are done properly.

Law Enforcement Needs

Public compliance with turkey hunting regulations is essential. Although enforcement activities are needed, the wildlife law enforcement program should undergo the same scrutiny as to objectives, procedures and cost-to-benefit considerations as wildlife research and management; it should be closely linked to the needs of the management program.

Is statewide law enforcement emphasis presently addressing the needs of turkey management? In some cases it may not be. With the statewide turkey population decreasing, and the deer population increasing to the point of legalized doe shooting and large bag limits, emphasis should be redirected to turkey enforcement problems.

Present rules allow hunters to legally shoot turkeys in near darkness. This results in hens being shot by mistake. Even if shooting hours are changed as recommended, to 10 minutes before sunrise, public compliance is likely to be poor unless enforcement emphasis is given to the problem. Hunters will continue to roost turkeys and will attempt to shoot them before they leave the roosts, even if that violates the shooting hour rule.

The enforcement needs of the turkey management program should be enumerated and incorporated into the law enforcement program as soon as feasible.

Other Needs

The possibility exists that there are blocks of suitable turkey habitat in Florida that are not presently stocked. A statewide turkey population survey has not been done since 1975—another should be completed in the near future. If suitable unstocked habitat is found, an appropriate restocking program should be undertaken.

Since the majority of Florida's turkeys are on property that is not managed by the Commission, an extension program is needed to provide advice and assistance to landowners and lessees. Literature and basic advice about turkey management should be available for the asking. Educational literature (such as how to distinguish hens from gobblers) should be available to clubs and other organizations. An active liaison program should be maintained between the turkey project and turkey hunters and other interested groups. The nonhunting public needs to know enough about the turkey management program to know whether the species is being properly managed.

Little is known about private hunting clubs and the paid hunting industry in Florida. Such business enterprises have reached a high state of development in certain other states, and they may presently or soon constitute a significant factor in Florida wildlife conservation. Turkey hunting is particularly conducive to this type of enterprise. One of the beneficial aspects of paid hunting and leases is that they channel some of the landowner's attention toward recognizing and increasing the land's wildlife values and away from the routine preoccupation with the economic enterprises that tend to be destructive to wildlife habitat. A certain amount of assistance and management guidance from the Commission would pay great dividends in furthering the management of turkeys and wildlife in general. The first step would be to determine the extent and nature of this industry in Florida and to establish contacts with it.

In addition to the research and management needs that have been briefly discussed, there are a few routine research and monitoring jobs that should not be neglected. Disease continually threatens the state's turkey populations. It is only a matter of time until another serious turkey population decline occurs, similar to the die-off of the mid–1960s. Expertise and diagnostic capabilities should be available at all times and basic research on the general problem of wild turkey health should be continued, as it has been since 1969.

A Management and Research Philosophy

Research must be a vital part of the Florida turkey management program because simple management procedures do not presently exist. Unless research and monitoring accompany every substantial management effort, success or failure will not be known and no foundation for further progress can be established. Management without results is no more justified than is research without results.

It will be many years before enough is known about turkey management to permit practices to be prescribed by anyone who is not especially familiar with the species. Managers and researchers should have considerable hands-on experiences with turkeys and familiarity with the scientific and management literature and other information sources. It will not be possible for any wildlife agency to attract and hold, or train and hold, highly qualified biologists unless they can be a part of a definite program with adequate and stable funding and a personnel complement that is encouraged to participate in interesting and challenging research and managment programs. That applies to research and management of other wildlife species as well.

As we near the end of the twentieth century we are enjoying the fruits of science and being frustrated by the side effects of technology. It should be clear by now that no important human endeavor will ever see its research needs reach completion. Even if everything were somehow to be known about the wild turkey today, or any other wildlife species, the march of time and technology would demand additional research everyday to take advantage of new opportunities and to solve new problems that do not now exist. Where wildlife research is concerned, we are getting farther behind all the time and we have not even begun to understand the basic biology and ecology of the species we are exploiting and attempting to manage. This bulletin reflects only the very beginning of what is needed in wild turkey research in Florida.

Appendix

Experimental Regulations at Lykes Fisheating Creek Wildlife Management Area

1. A wildlife management area permit and regular hunting license must be in the possession of any person (except residents 65 years of age and over) to enter the area. A special wildlife management area quota permit issued from the Game and Fresh Water Fish Commission is required for any person (except residents 65 years of age or over) to enter the area for the purpose of hunting. These permits shall be displayed upon request of any Commission employee.
2. Four two-day hunts (Tuesday and Wednesday), five three-day hunts (Friday, Saturday, and Sunday) and six four-day hunts (Friday, Saturday, Sunday and Monday) will be held during the special season. The special quota hunt permit entitles the bearer to participate in one hunt only. There will be no hunt on Easter weekend.
3. A quota of 75 hunters has been set for each hunt. Hunters wishing to participate must submit a written application, available at any regional office of the Game and Fresh Water Fish Commission, to the Game and Fresh Water Fish Commission, Tallahassee office. The quota

will be filled on a first-come, first-served basis, as received by mail in the Tallahassee office.
4. Persons between the ages of 16 and 65 entering the area in the company of a quota hunt permit holder to camp must possess a valid recreation permit. Other recreational use is prohibited except by persons participating in Lykes Brothers organized canoe trips.
5. Guns other than shotguns are prohibited.
6. Legal shooting hours are sunrise to 4 P.M. Sunrise time will be posted at the gate.
7. Hunters, after reaching the area in which they intend to hunt, are prohibited from operating motor vehicles until 9 A.M., unless they are finished hunting.
8. The possession of any loaded gun is prohibited except during legal shooting hours.
9. Cutting of live trees is prohibited.
10. Persons under the age of 16 may not be in possession of a firearm unless in the presence of a supervising adult.
11. Fires, other than campfires, are prohibited.
12. Any camp, person or conveyance may be searched while in, entering, or leaving the area.
13. The discharge of guns is prohibited on, from, or across any public campsite.
14. Guns and camps may be taken into the area beginning at 1 P.M. on the afternoon prior to the hunt and must be removed by 6 P.M. on the last day of the hunt. All persons must leave the area on the last day of the hunt.
15. Hunters must enter and leave the area only through the Palmdale Gate. Camping permitted only at Shady Acres and Ingram Crossing campsites.
16. Hunters are required to check their kill at the Palmdale check station.
17. Littering is prohibited. Persons are required to take all refuse out of the area.
18. Persons determined by Commission personnel to be intoxicated will be required to leave the area.
19. Possession of shot shells containing shot larger than number 4 shall be prohibited.

Dates of Hunts

Hunt No. 1
Friday, Saturday, Sunday, and Monday (4 days)
Hunt No. 2
Friday, Saturday, Sunday, and Monday (4 days)
Hunt No. 3
Friday, Saturday, Sunday, and Monday (4 days)

Hunt No. 4
Friday, Saturday, and Sunday (3 days)
Hunt No. 5
Tuesday and Wednesday (2 days)
Hunt No. 6
Friday, Saturday, and Sunday (3 days)
Hunt No. 7
Tuesday and Wednesday (2 days)
Hunt No. 8
Friday, Saturday, and Sunday (3 days)
Huint No. 9
Tuesday and Wednesday (2 days)
Hunt No. 10
Friday, Saturday, and Sunday (3 days)
Hunt No. 11
Friday, Saturday, Sunday, and Monday (4 days)
Hunt No. 12
Friday, Saturday, Sunday, and Monday (4 days)
Hunt No. 13
Tuesday and Wednesday (2 days)
Hunt No. 14
Friday, Saturday, Sunday, and Monday (4 days)

Open Season

Spring Gobbler Season—February 13 through April 27. Tuesday and Wednesday for two (2) day hunts. Friday, Saturday and Sunday for three (3) day hunts. Friday, Saturday, Sunday and Monday for four (4) day hunts. No hunt on April 17–20.
　Trapping—Prohibited.
　Camping—Permitted at designated campsites during periods in which hunting is allowed. Camping permitted at other times with permission from Lykes Brothers Inc.
　Fishing—Prohibited.
　Legal to Take: Two (2) bearded turkeys per season. In addition to the regulations which follow, all general laws and regulations relating to wildlife shall apply unless specifically exempted for this wildlife management area.

Literature Cited and Publications of the Florida Turkey Project

Publications of the Florida Turkey Project are indicated by an asterisk (*).

Abbott, U. K. and R. M. Craig. 1960. Observations on hatching time in three avian species. Poult. Sci. 39:827–30.

Akey, B. L. 1981. Mortality in Florida wild turkey poults (*Meleagris gallopavo osceola*). M.S. Thesis. University of Florida, Gainesville, Florida. 78 pp.

Aldrich, J. W. and A. J. Duvall. 1955. Distribution of American gallinaceous game birds. U.S. Fish and Wildlife Serv. Circ. 34.

American Ornithologists' Union. 1982. Thirty-fourth supplement to the American Ornithologists' Union check-list of North American birds. Auk 99:1CC–16CC.

Audubon, J. J. 1831. Ornithological Biography. Vol. 1. Adam Black, Edinburgh, Scotland.

*Austin, D. H. 1965. Trapping turkeys in Florida with the cannon net. Proc. Annu. Conf. Southeast. Assoc. Game and Fish Comm. 19: 16–22.

*Austin, D. H., T. E. Peoples, and L. E. Williams, Jr. 1973. Procedures for capturing and handling live wild turkeys. Proc. Annu. Conf. Southeast. Assoc. Game and Fish Comm. 26:222–36.

Austin, D. H., and Jerry H. Peoples. 1967. Capturing hogs with alpha-chloralose. Proc. Annu. Conf. Southeast. Assoc. Game and Fish Comm. 21:201–05.

Averill, C. K. 1923. Black wing tips. Condor 25:57–59.

Bailey, R. W. 1956. Sex determination of adult wild turkeys by means of dropping configuration. J. Wildl. Manage. 20:220.

———. 1972. Use of stimulants in reducing mortality in narcotizied wild turkeys. Proc. Annu. Conf. Southeast. Assoc. Game and Fish Comm. 26:212–13.

———. 1976. Live-trapping wild turkeys in North Carolina. North Carolina Wildlife Resources Commission, Raleigh, N.C., 21 pp.

Bailey, R. W., D. Dennett, Jr., H. Gore, J. Pack, R. Simpson, and G. Wright. 1980. Basic considerations and general recommendations for trapping the wild turkey. Pages 10–23 in J. M. Sweeney, ed. Proc. fourth national wild turkey symp. National Wild Turkey Federation, Edgefield, South Carolina.

Bailey, R. W., and R. V. Doepker. 1978. Problems in capturing wild turkeys with trichloroethanol. Proc. Annu. Conf. Southeast. Assoc. of Fish and Wildlife Agencies. 31:283–84.

Bailey, R. W., and K. T. Rinell. 1965. Wild turkey population trends, productivity, and harvest. Annu. Pittman-Robertson Project Rept., W. VA. 15 pp. (mimeo).

———. 1967. Events in the turkey year. Pages 73–91 in O. H. Hewitt, ed. The wild turkey and its management. The Wildlife Society, Washington, D.C.

Bailey, R. W., H. G. Uhlig, and G. Breiding. 1951. Wild turkey management in West Virginia. Conservation Comm. of West Virginia Tech. Bull. 2. 49 pp.

Baldwin, William P. 1947. Trapping wild turkeys in South Carolina. J. Wildl. Manage. 11:24–36.

Barkalow, F. S., Jr. 1942. Inventory of wildlife resources. Pages 59–60 in Annual Report of 1939–40. Alabama Dept. Conservation, Montgomery. 92 pp.

*Barwick, L. H., D. H. Austin, and L. E. Williams, Jr. 1971. Roosting of young turkey broods during summer in Florida. Proc. Annu. Conf. Southeast. Assoc. Game and Fish Comm. 24:231–43.

*Barwick, L. H., W. M. Hetrick, and L. E. Williams, Jr. 1973. Foods of young Florida wild turkeys. Proc. Southeast. Assoc. Game and Fish Comm. 27:92–102.

Beckman, H. 1961. Pharmacology: the nature, action and use of drugs. 2nd ed. W. B. Saunders Company, Philadelphia and London. 805 pp.

Bendire, C. E. 1892. Life histories of North American birds. U.S. Nat. Mus. Special Bull. 1, Vol. 1. 446 pp.

———. 1937. Life history of North American birds of prey. U.S. Nat. Mus. Bull. No. 167. Washington, D.C.

Bent, A. C. 1932. Life histories of North American gallinaceous birds: orders Galliformes and Columbiformes. U.S. Nat. Mus. Bull. 162. 490 pp.

Bevill, W. V. 1973. Some factors influencing gobbling activity among wild turkeys. Proc. Southeast. Assoc. Game and Fish Comm. 27: 62–73.

———. 1975. Setting spring gobbler hunting seasons by timing peak gobbling. Pages 198–204 in L. K. Halls, ed. Proc. third national wild turkey symp. Texas Chapter, The Wildlife Society, Austin, Texas.

Bjarvell, A. 1967. The critical period and the interval between hatching and exodus in mallard ducklings. Behavior 28:141–48.

Blackburn, W. E., J. P. Kirk, and J. E. Kennamer. 1975. Availability and utilization of summer foods by eastern wild turkeys broods in Lee County, Alabama. Pages 86–96 in L. K. Halls, ed. Proc. third national wild turkey symp., Texas Chapter, The Wildlife Society, Austin, Texas.

Blakey, H. L. 1937. The wild turkey on the Missouri Ozark range: preliminary report, U.S.D.A. Bur. Biol. Surv. Leaflet BS-77. 32 pp. Mimeo.

Boeker, E. L. and V. E. Scott. 1969. Roost tree characteristics for Merriam's turkey. J. Wildl. Manage. 33: 121-24.

Borg, Karl. 1955. Om chloralosen och dess anva. ndning vid fangst av krakoch masfaglar, duvor etc. Viltrevy 1(1):88-121. (In Swedish; English summary.)

Bowman, B. E. and L. D. Harris. 1980. Effect of spatial heterogeneity on ground-nest depredation. J. Wildl. Manage. 44:806-13.

Brower, L. P., B. S. Alpert, and S. C. Glazier. 1970. Observational learning in the feeding behavior of blue jays (Cyanocitta cristata). American Zoologist. 10:475-76.

Brown, E. K. 1980. Home range and movements of wild turkeys—a review. Pages 251-261 in J. M. Sweeney, ed., Proc. fourth national wild turkey symp., Natl. Wild Turkey Fed., Edgefield, S.C.

Bump, G. R., W. Darow, F. G. Edminster, and W. F. Crissey. 1947. The ruffed grouse: life history, propagation and management. New York Conserv. Dept. 915 pp.

Cole, L. J. 1917. Determinate and indeterminate laying cycles in birds. Anat. Record 11:504-05.

Conway, W. G., and J. Bell. 1968. Observations on the behavior of kittlitz's sandplovers at the New York zoology park. Living Bird. 7:57-70.

Cook, R. L. 1972. A study of nesting turkeys in the Edwards Plateau of Texas. Proc. Anu. Conf. Southeast. Assoc. Game and Fish Commissioners 26:236-44.

Crider, E. D. and J. C. McDaniel. 1967. Alpha-chloralose used to capture Canada geese. J. Wildl. Manage. 31:258-64.

———. 1968. Oral drugs used to capture waterfowl. Proc. Annu. Conf. Southeast. Assoc. Game and Fish Comm. 22:156-61.

Crider, E. D., Vern D. Stotts, and Jimmie C. McDaniel. 1968. Diazepam and alpha-chloralose mixtures to capture waterfowl. Proc. Annu. Conf. Southeast. Assoc. Game and Fish Comm. 22:133-41.

Curio, E., U. Ernst, and W. Veith. 1978. The adaptive significance of avian mobbing. II. Zeitschrift fur Tierpsychologie 48:184-202.

Dalke, P. D., A. S. Leopold and D. L. Spencer. 1946. The ecology and management of the wild turkey in Missouri. Missouri Conservation Comm. Tech. Bull. No. 1. 86 pp.

Davis, J. R. (c. 1960, undated). Marking wild turkeys by toe clipping. Alabama Dept. Conservation, mimeo. 26 pp.

DeGraff, L. W. and D. E. Austin. 1975. Turkey harvest management in New York. Pages 191-97 in L. K. Halls, ed. Proc. third national wild turkey symp., Texas Chapter, The Wildlife Society, Austin, Texas.

Dill, H. H. and W. H. Thornsberry. 1950. A cannon-projected net trap for capturing waterfowl. J. Wildl. Manage. 14:132-37.

Donohoe, R. W., C. E. McKibben, and C. B. Lowry. 1968. Turkey nesting behavior. Wilson Bull. 80:103-04.

Dwight, J., Jr. 1900. The molt of the North American Tetraonidae (quails, partridges and grouse). Auk 17:34-51, 143-66.

Edmunds, M. 1974. Defence in animals. Longman Group, Essex, England. 357 pp.

Eichholz, N. F. 1974. Movements, behavior and population dynamics of relocated wild turkeys in the Georgia Piedmont. M.S. thesis. Univ. Georgia, Athens, Georgia. 119 pp.

Eisner, E. 1958. Incubation and clutch size in gulls. Anim. Behav. 6:124-25.

Ellis, C. R. J. 1961. Trapping and marking Rio Grande wild turkeys. Proc. Okla. Acad. of Sci. 41:202–12.

Evans, R. R., J. W. Goertz, and C. T. Williams. 1975. Capturing wild turkeys with tribromoethanol. J. Wildl. Manage. 39:630–34.

Everett, D. D., D. W. Speake, W. K. Maddox. 1980. Natality and mortality of a north Alabama wild turkey population. Pages 117–26 in J. M. Sweeney, ed., Proc. fourth national wild turkey symp., Natl. Wild Turkey Fed., Edgefield, S.C.

———. 1979. Wild turkey ranges in Alabama mountain habitat. Proc. Annu. Conf. Southeast. Assoc. Fish and Wildl. Agencies. 33:233–38.

Fabricius, E. 1962. Some aspects of imprinting in birds. Symp. Zool. Soc. London 8:139–48.

———. 1964. Crucial periods in the development of the following response in young nidifugous birds. Z. Tierpsychol. 21:326–37.

Fabricius, E., and H. Boyd. 1954. Experiments on the following reaction of ducklings. Report of the Wild owl Trust 6:84–89.

Fernald, M. L. 1950. Gray's manual of botany. 8th Ed. American Book Co., N.Y. 1632 pp.

Frye, O. E., Jr. 1954 Aspects of the ecology of the bobwhite quail in Charlotte County, Florida. Ph.D. diss. University of Florida, Gainesville. 362 pp.

Florida Department of Administration. 1974. Soil map of Glades County, Florida.

Gardner, D. .T., D. W. Speake, and W. J. Fleming. 1972. The effects of a spring "gobblers-only" hunting season on wild turkey reproduction population size. Proc. Annu. Conf. Southeastern Assoc. Game and Fish Commissioners. 26:244–52.

Genovese, R. F., and M. P. Browne. 1978. Sickness-induced learning in chicks. Behavioral Biol. 24:68–76.

Glazener, W. C. 1967. Management of the Rio Grande turkey. Pages 453–92 in O. H. Hewitt, ed. The wild turkey and its management. The Wildlife Society, Washington, D.C. 589 pp.

Gliden, J. W. and D. E. Austin. 1975. Natality and mortality of wild turkey poults in southwestern New York. Pages 48–54 in L. K. Halls, ed., Proc. third national wild turkey symp. Texas Chapter, The Wildlife Society, Austin, Texas.

Green, H. E. 1982. Reproductive behavior of female wild turkeys in northern lower Michigan. J. Wildl. Manage. 46:1065–71.

Hale, E. B. 1969. Domestication and the evolution of behavior. Pages 21–53 in E. S. E. Hafez, ed. The behavior of domestic animals. Williams and Wilkins, Baltimore, Maryland.

Hale, E. B., W. M. Schleidt, and M. W. Schein. 1969. The behavior of turkeys. Pages 554–92 in E. S. E. Hafez, ed. The behavior of domestic animals. Williams and Wilkins Co., Baltimore, Md.

Halls, L. K. 1975. Procceedings of the third national wild turkey symp. Texas Chapter, The Wildlife Society, Austin. 227 pp.

Hamrick, W. J. and J. R. Davis. 1971. Summer food items of juvenile wild turkeys. Proc. Annu. Conf. Southeast. Assoc. Game and Fish Comm. 25:85–89.

Hartley, P. H. T. 1950. An experimental analysis of interspecific recognition. Philology mechanisms in animal behavior. Symposia of the Society for Experimental Biology. Vol. 4. Academic Press, New York, New York.

Haucke, H. H. 1975. Winter roost characteristics of the Rio Grande turkey in south Texas. Pages 164–69 in L. K. Halls, ed. Proc. third national wild turkey symp. Texas Chapter, The Wildlife Society, Austin, Texas.

Healy, W. M. 1978. Feeding activity of wild turkey poults in relation to ground vegetation and insect abundance. Ph.D. diss. West Virginia Univ. Morgantown, West Virginia. 117 pp.

Healy, W. M., and E. J. Goetz. 1974. Imprinting and video-recording wild turkeys—new techniques. Northeast. Fish and Wildl. Conf. 31:173–182.

Healy, W. M., R. O. Kimmel, and E. J. Goetz. 1975. Behavior of human-imprinted and hen-reared wild turkey poults. Pages 97–107 in L. K. Halls, ed. Proc. third national wild turkey symp., Texas Chapter of The Wildlife Society, Austin, Texas.

Healy, W. M., and E. S. Nenno. 1980. Growth parameters and sex and age criteria for juvenile eastern wild turkeys. Pages 168–85 in J. M. Sweeney, ed., Proc. fourth Natl. Wild Turkey Symp.

Hendee, J. C. 1971. Human behavior in wildlife management: needed research. Transactions North American Wildlife and Natural Resources Conference. 36:383–96.

Hess, E. H. 1972. The natural history of imprinting. New York Acad. Sci. Ann. 193:124–36.

Hillestad, H. O. 1970. Movements, behavior, and nesting ecology of the wild turkey in east central Alabama. M.S. thesis, Auburn University, Auburn, Ala. 70 pp.

———. 1973. Movements, behavior, and nesting ecology of the wild turkey in eastern Alabama. Pages 109–23 in G. C. Sanderson and H. C. Schultz, eds. Wild turkey management: Current problems and programs. Univ. Missouri Press, Columbia, MO.

Hillestad, H. O., and D. W. Speake. 1970. Activities of wild turkey hens and poults as influenced by habitat. Proc. Annu. Conf. Southeast. Assoc. Game and Fish Comm. 24:244–51.

Hitchcock, A. S. 1950. Manual of grasses of the United States. 2nd Ed. U.S. Government Printing Office, Washington, D.C. 1051 pp.

Hoffman, D. M. 1968. Roosting sites and habits of Merriam's turkey in Colorado. J. Wildl. Manage. 32:859–66.

Hon, T., D. P. Belcher, B. Mullis, and J. R. Monroe. 1978. Nesting, brood range, and reproductive success of an insular turkey population. Proc. Annu. Conf. Southeast. Assoc. of Game and Fish Comm. 32: 137–49.

Humphrey, P. S. and K. C. Parkes. 1959. An approach to the study of molts and plumages. Auk 76:1–31.

Hurst, G. A. 1972. Insects and bobwhite quail brood habitat management. Pages 65–82 in J. A. Morrison and J. C. Lewis, eds. Proc. First Nat. bobwhite quail symp. Oklahoma State Univ., Stillwater, Oklahoma.

———. 1973. Insects and bobwhite quail brood habitat management. Proc. national bobwhite quail symp. 1:65–82.

Hurst, G. A., and B. T. Stringer, Jr. 1975. Food habits of wild turkey poults in Mississippi. Pages 76–85 in L. K. Halls, ed. Proc. third national wild turkey symp. Texas Chapter, The Wildlife Society, Austin, Texas.

———. 1978. Effects of controlled burning on wild turkey poult food habits. Proc. Southeast. Assoc. Fish and Wildl. Agencies. 32:30–37.

Hutt, F. B. 1949. Genetics of the fowl. McGraw–Hill, New York, New York. 590 pp.

Kear, J. 1965. The internal food reserves of hatchling mallard ducklings. J. Wildl. Manage. 29:523–28.

Kelly, G. 1975. Indexes for aging eastern wild turkeys. Pages 205–09 in L. K. Halls, ed. Proc. third national wild turkey symp. Texas Chapter, The Wildlife Society, Austin, Texas.

Kennamer, J. E. 1982. Take a close look at your gobbler. Turkey Call. 9:20–21.

———, ed. 1982. Present status and needs of the wild turkey in the United States. National Wild Turkey Federation, Edgefield, South Carolina. Mimeo.

Kennamer, J. E., and W. H. Lunceford, Jr. 1973. Armadillos tested as potential egg predators of wild turkeys in the Mississippi Delta. Pages 175–77 in G. C. Sanderson and H. C. Schultz, eds. Wild turkey management, Univ. of Missouri Press, Columbia, Missouri.

Knoder, C. E. 1959. An aging technique for juvenal wild turkeys based on the rate of primary feather molt and growth. Pages 159–76 in Proc. first national wild turkey symp. Memphis, Tennessee.

Knopf, R. C., B. L. Driver, and J. R. Bassett. 1973. Motivations for fishing. Transactions North American Wildl. and Natural Resources Conf. 38:191–204.

Knowlton, F. F., E. D. Micheal, and W. C. Glazner. 1964. A marking technique for field recognition of individual turkeys and deer. J. Wildl. Manage. 28:167–70.

Kothmann, H. G. and G W. Litton. 1975. Utilization of man-made roosts by turkey in west Texas. Pages 159–63 in L. K. Halls, ed. Proc. third national wild turkey symp. Texas Chapter, The Wildlife Soc., Austin, Texas.

Kozelka, A. W. 1929. Integumental grafting in the domestic fowl. Transplants of combs, spurs and feathers in the study of sex bimorphism. J. Hered. 20:3–14.

Labisky, R. F. 1968. Ecology of pheasant populations in Illinois. Ph.D. thesis, Univ. Wisconsin, Madison. 511 pp.

Laessle, A. M. 1942. The plant communities of the Welaka area. Univ. Florida Press, Biol. Sci. Series IV:1–143.

Latham, R. M. 1956. Complete book of the wild turkey. Stackpole, Harrisburg, Pennsylvania. 265 pp.

Leopold, A. S. 1943. The molts of young wild and domestic turkeys. Condor 42:133–45.

———. 1944. The nature of heritable wildness in turkeys. Condor 46:133–97.

Lewis, J. B. 1975. Evaluation of spring turkey seasons in Missouri. Pages 176–83 in L. K. Halls, ed. Proc. third national wild turkey symp. Texas Chapter, The Wildlife Society, Austin, Texas.

Lewis, J. B., and G. Kelly. 1973. Mortality associated with the spring hunting of gobblers. Pages 295–99 in G. C. Sanderson and H. C. Schultz, eds. Wild turkey manage.: Current problems and programs. Univ. of Missouri Press, Columbia, Missouri.

Lewis, J. C. 1967. Physical characteristics and physiology. Pages 45–72 in O. H. Hewitt, ed. The wild turkey and its management. The Wildlife Soc., Washington, D.C.

Ligon, J. S. 1946. History and management of Merriam's wild turkey. New Mexico Game and Fish Comm., Albuquerque. 84 pp.

Litton, G. W. and H. G. Kothmann. 1975. Utilization of man-made roosts by turkey in west Texas. Pages 159–63 in L. K. Halls, ed. Proc.

third national wild turkey symp. Texas Chapter, The Wildlife Soc., Austin, Texas.

Logan, T. H. 1973. Seasonal behavior of Rio Grande wild turkeys in western Oklahoma. Proc. Annu. Conf. Southeast. Game and Fish Comm. 27:74–91.

Lorenz, K. Z. 1937. The companion in the bird's world. Auk 54:245–73.

Lucus, A. M. and P. R. Stettenheim. 1972. Avian anatomy: Integument. U.S. Dept. Agriculture Handbook 362. 750 pp.

Lyon, D. L. 1962. Comparative growth and plumage development in Coturnix and bobwhite. Wilson Bull. 74:5–27.

Madson, J. B. 1975. The crowd goes turkey hunting. Pages 222–27 in L. K. Halls, ed. Proc. third national wild turkey symp. Texas Chapter, The Wildl. Soc., Austin, Texas.

Marsden, S. J. and J. H. Martin. 1949. Turkey Management. Interstate Publishing Co., Danville, Ill. 774 pp.

Martin, D. D. and B. S. McGinnes. 1975. Insect availability and use by turkeys in forest clearings. Pages 70–75 in L. K. Halls, ed. Proc. Third National Wild Turkey Symp. Texas Chapter, The Wildlife Society, Austin, Texas.

Martin, L. L. 1967. Comparison of methoxymol, alpha-chloralose, and two barbituates for capturing doves. Proc. Annu. Conf. Southeast. Assoc. Game and Fish Comm. 21:193–200.

Martin, L. M. and T. Z. Atkeson. 1954. Swimming by wild turkey poults. Wilson Bull. 66:271.

Mayfield, H. 1961. Nesting success calculated from exposure. Wilson Bull. 73:255–61.

Mazzeo, R. 1953. Homing of the manx shearwater. Auk 70:200–01.

McCabe R. A. and A. S. Hawkins. 1946. The Hungarian partridge in Wisconsin. Amer. Midl. Nat. 36:1–75.

McDowell, R. D. 1956. Productivity of the wild turkey in Virginia. Ph.D. Thesis, Virginia Polytechnic Institute, Blacksburg, Va.

McIlhenny, E. A. 1914. The Wild Turkey and its hunting. Doubleday, Page and Co., Garden City, New York. 245 pp.

Mewaldt, L. R., and J. R. King. 1978. Latitudinal variation of postnuptial molt in Pacific coast white-crowned sparrows. Auk 95:168–74.

More, T. A. 1973. Attitudes of Massachusetts hunters. Trans. N. Am. Wildl. and Natural Resources Conf. 38:230–34.

Mosby, H. S., and D. E. Cantner. 1956. The use of avertin in capturing wild turkeys and as an oral-basal anaesthetic for other wild animals. Southwest. Veterinarian 9:132–36.

Mosby, H. S., and C. O. Handley. 1943. The wild turkey in Virginia: Its status, life history and management. Comm. Game and Inland Fisheries, Richmond, Virginia. 281 pp.

Murry, R. E. 1965. Tranquilizing techniques for capturing deer. Proc. Annu. Conf. Southeast. Assoc. Game and Fish Comm. 19:4–15.

Murry, R. E., and D. Dennett. 1963. A preliminary report on the use of tranquilizing compounds in handling wildlife. Proc. Annu. Conf. Southeast. Assoc. Game and Fish Comm. 17:134–39.

Murton, R. K. 1962. Narcotics v. wood-pigeons. Agriculture 69:336–39.

Murton, R. K., A. J. Isaacson, and N. J. Westwood. 1963. The use of baits treated with a-chloralose to catch wood-pigeons. Annals of Applied Biol. 52:271–93.

———. 1965. Capturing columbids at the nest with stupefying baits. J. Wildl. Manage. 29:647–49.

National Oceanic and Atmospheric Administration. 1978. Climates of the states. Gale Research Co., Detroit, Mich. 601 pp.

Nenno, E. S., and W. M. Healy. 1979. Effects of radio packages on behavior of wild turkey hens. J. Wildl. Manage. 43:760–65.

Nenno, E. S., and J. S. Lindzey. 1979. Wild turkey poult feeding activity in old field, agriculture clearing, and forest communities. Trans. Northeast. Fish and Wildl. Conf. 36:97–109.

Newman, C. C. and E. Griffin. 1950. Deer and turkey habitats and populations of Florida. Florida Game and Fresh Water Fish Comm. Tech. Bull. No. 1. 29 pp.

Nixon, C. M. 1962. Wild turkey aging. Game Res. in Ohio 1:107–17.

Norris, R. T. 1958. Comparative biosystematics and life history of the nuthatches Sitta tygmaea and Sitta tusilla. Univ. Calif. Publ. Zool. 56:119–300.

Oring, L. W. 1982. Avian mating systems. Pages 1–92 in D. S. Farner, J. R. King, and K. C. Parkes, eds. Avian biology. Academic Press, New York, N.Y.

Owen, C. N. 1976. Food habits of wild turkey poults (*Meleagris gallopavo silvestris*) in pine stands and in fields in east central Mississippi: and the effects of mowing hay field edges on arthropod populations in relation to poult food production. Masters thesis. Mississippi State University, Mississippi State, Mississippi. 162 pp.

Pattee, O. H. and S. L. Beasom. 1977. Rio Grande turkey hens with leg spurs. Auk 94:159.

Petrides, G. A. 1942. Age determination in American gallinaceous birds. Trans. North American Wildl. Conf. 7:308–28.

———. 1945. First-winter plumages in the Galliformes. Auk 62:223–27.

Pomeroy, D. E. and M. H. Woodford. 1976. Drug immobilization of marabou storks. J. Wildl. Manage. 40:177–79.

Potter, D. R., J. C. Hendee, and R. N. Clark. 1973. Hunting satisfaction: game, guns, and nature? Trans. North American Wildl. and Natural Resources Conf. 38:220–29.

*Powell, J. A. 1965. The Florida wild turkey. Florida Game and Fresh Water Fish Comm., Tech. Bull. No. 8. 28 pp.

Raitt, R. J. and R. D. Ohmart. 1966. Annual cycle of reproduction and molt in gambel quail of the Rio Grande Valley, Southern New Mexico. Condor 68:541–61.

Ramsay, A. O. 1951. Familial recognition in domestic birds. Auk 68:1–16.

Reagan, J. M. and K. D. Morgan. 1980. Reproductive potential of Rio Grande turkey hen in the Edwards Plateau of Texas. Pages 136–44 in J. M. Sweeney, ed. Proc. of the Fourth National Wild Turkey Symposium, Nat'l. Wild Turkey Fed., Edgefield, S.C.

Salzen, E. A., and C. C. Meyer. 1968. Reversibility in imprinting. J. Comp. Physiol. and Psychol. 66:269–75.

SAS Institute, Inc. 1982. SAS user's guide: statistics. SAS Institute, Inc. Gary, NC, 584 pp.

Schein, M. W. 1963. On the irreversibility of imprinting. Z. Tierz. 20:462–67.

Schemnitz, S. D. 1956. Wild turkey food habits in Florida. J. Wildl. Manage. 20:132–37.

Schorger, A. W. 1957. The beard of the wild turkey. Auk 74:441–46.

———. 1966. The wild turkey: its history and domestication. Univ. Oklahoma Press, Norman, Oklahoma. 624 pp.

Schumacher, R. W. 1977. Movements of eastern wild turkey released in a cottonwood plantation. M.S. thesis, Mississippi State University, Mississippi State. 98 pp.

Scott, W. E. D. 1890. Description of a new subspecies of wild turkey. Auk 7:376–77.

Sherman, A. R. 1910. At the sign of the northern flicker. Wilson Bull. 22:135–71.

Skutch, A. F. 1976. Parent birds and their young. Univ. Texas Press, Austin, Texas. 503 pp.

Small, J. K. 1933. Manual of the Southeastern Flora. Univ. of North Carolina Press, Chapel Hill, North Carolina. 1554 pp.

Smart, J. E. 1965. Development and maturation of primary feathers of redhead ducklings. J. Wildl. Manage. 29:533–36.

Smith, D. M. 1975. Behavior factors influencing variability of roost counts for Rio Grande turkeys. Pages 170–75 in L. K. Halls, ed. Proc. third national wild turkey symp. Texas Chapter, The Wildlife Society, Austin, Texas.

———. 1977. The social organization of Rio Grande turkeys in a declining population. Ph.D. diss. Utah State University, Logan, Utah. 98 pp.

Smith, N. G. 1967. Capturing seabirds with avertin. J. Wildl. Manage. 31:479–83.

Speake, D. W. 1980. Predation on wild turkeys in Alabama. Pages 86–101 in J. M. Sweeney, ed. Proc. fourth national wild turkey symp., Natl. Wild Turkey Fed., Edgefield, South Carolina.

Speake, D. W., L. H. Barwick, H. O. Hillestad, and W. Stickney. 1969. Some characteristics of an expanding turkey population. Proc. Annu. Conf. Southeast. Assoc. Game and Fish Comm. 23:46–58.

Stockton, K. L. and V. S. Asmundson. 1950. Daily rhythm of egg production in turkeys. Poultry Sci. 29:477–79.

Stoddard, H. L. 1931. The bob-white quail. Scribner's Sons. New York, New York.

Sylvester, W. R. and P. W. Lane. 1946. Trapping wild turkeys on the Kentucky Woodlands Refuge. J. Wild. Manage. 10:333–42.

Taber, W. 1955. Notes on behavior of the wild turkey. Wilson Bull. 67:213.

Thomas, J. W., R. G. Marburger, and C. V. Hoozer. 1973. Rio Grande turkey migrations as related to harvest regulations in Texas. Pages 301–08 in G. C. Sanderson and Helen C. Schultz, ed. Wild turkey management. Proc. second national wild turkey symp.

Thomas, J. W., J. C. Pack, W. Healy, J. D. Gill, and H. R. Sanderson. 1973. Territoriality among hunters. Trans. North American Wildl. and Natural Resources Conf. 38:274–80.

Tinbergen, N., M. Impekoven and D. Franck. 1967. An experiment on spacing-out as a defense against predation behavior. 28:307–21.

U.S. Department of Agriculture. 1980. General map of ecological communities, State of Florida. Soil Conserv. Serv., Fort Worth, TX.

U.S. Department of Agriculture and Florida Agricultural Experiment Station. 1982. Special soil survey report maps and interpretation, Alachua County, Florida. Interim report, in press.

Vince, M. A. 1969. Embryonic communication respiration and the synchronization of hatching. Pages 233–60 in R. A. Hinde, ed. Bird vocalizations. Cambridge Univ. Press, New York, N.Y.

Watts, C. R. 1969. The social organization of wild turkeys on the Welder

Wildlife Refuge, Texas. Ph.D. diss. Utah State University, Logan. 60 pp.

Webb, W. L. 1968. Public use of forest wildlife: quantity and quality considerations. J. Forest. 66:106–10.

Weidmann, U. 1956. Observations and experiments on egg–laying in the Black–headed Gull (*Larus ridibundus* L.). Brit. J. An. Behav. 4:150–61.

Welty, J. C. 1982. The life of birds. Saunders College Publishing, Philadelphia, Pennsylvania. 754 pp.

Wetmore, A. 1931. The avifauna of the Pleistocene in Florida. Smiths. Misc. Colls. 82:33–35.

Wheeler, R. J., Jr. 1948. The wild turkey in Alabama. Alabama Dept. of Conservation, Montgomery, Alabama. 92 pp.

Williams, L. E., Jr. 1961. Notes on wing molt in the yearling wild turkey. J. Wildl. Manage. 25:439–40.

*———. 1964. A recurrent color aberrancy in the wild turkey. J. Wildl. Manage. 28:148–52.

*———. 1966. Capturing wild turkeys with alpha-chloralose. J. Wildl. Manage. 30:50–56.

*———. 1966. Wild turkeys with supernumary leg spurs. Auk 84: 113–14.

*———. 1967. Erythrism in the wild turkey. Wilson Bull. 79:239–40.

*———. 1967. Preliminary report on methoxymol to capture turkeys. Proceedings of the Annual Conference of the Southeastern Association of Game and Fish Commissioners 21:189–93.

*———. 1970. A pale mutant wild turkey in juvenal plumage. Quarterly J. Fla. Acad. Sci. 32:236–38.

*———, 1981. The book of the wild turkey. Winchester Press, Tulsa, Oklahoma. 181 pp.

*———, 1984 The voice and vocabulary of the wild turkey. Real Turkeys Publishers, Gainesville, Florida. 85 pp.

*Williams, L. E., Jr., and D. H. Austin. 1969. Leg spurs on female wild turkeys. Auk 86:561–62.

*———. 1970. Complete post-juvenal (pre–basic) primary molt in Florida turkeys. J. Wildl. Manage. 34:231–33.

*Williams, L. E., Jr., D. H. Austin, N. F. Eicholz, T. E. Peoples, and R. W. Phillips. 1968. A study of nesting turkeys in southern Florida. Proc. Annu. Conf. Southeast. Assoc. Game and Fish Comm. 22:16–30.

*Williams, L. E., Jr., D. H. Austin, T. E. Peoples, and R. W. Phillips. 1971. Laying data and nesting behavior of wild turkeys. Proc. Annu. Conf. Southeast. Assoc. Game and Fish Comm. 25:90–106.

*———. 1973. Capturing turkeys with oral drugs. Pages 219–27 in G. C. Sanderson and H. C. Schultz, eds. Wild turkey management: Current problems and programs. Univ. of Missouri Press, Columbia, Missouri.

*Williams, L. E., Jr., D. H. Austin, and T. E. Peoples. 1974. Movement of wild turkey hens in relation to their nests. Proc. Annu. Conf. Southeast. Assoc. Game and Fish Comm. 28:602–22.

*———. 1976. The breeding potential of the wild turkey hen. Proc. Southeast. Assoc. Game and Fish Comm. 30:371–76.

*———. 1978. Turkey harvest patterns on a heavily hunted area. Proceedings Southeast. Assoc. Fish and Wildl. Agencies. 32:303–08.

*———. 1980. Turkey nesting success on a Florida study area. Pages 102–07 in J. M. Sweeney, ed. Proc. fourth national wild turkey symp., Natl. Wild Turkey Fed., Edgefield, South Carolina.

*Williams, L. E., Jr., and R. D. McGuire. 1971. On prenuptial molt in the wild turkey. J. Wildl. Manage. 35:394–95.

Wright, A. H. 1915. Early records of the wild turkey. IV. Auk 32:207–24.

Wright, G. A. and D. W. Speake. 1975. Compatibility of the eastern wild turkey with recreational activities at land between the lakes, Kentucky. Proc. Annu. Conf. Southeast. Assoc. Game and Fish Comm. 29:578–84.

Zar, J. H. 1974. Biostatistical analysis. Prentice-Hall, Inc., Englewood Cliffs, N.J., 620 pp.

Index

Note: The detailed table of contents and the list of tables and figures should also be consulted.

Age determination: by molt and plumage, 52–53, 64–66; by beard, 78; by spurs, 78; by tarsus color, 83
Albinism, 85–88
Alpha-chloralose, 29
Anesthesia. *See* Drugs
Armadillo, as nest predator, 125
Aversive taste of drugs, 34–36

Baiting, 10–11; best time for, 21–22; for drug capturing, 30
Baits for trapping, 10–11
Banding, 40
Beard: first appearance of, 64; absence in male, 68, 91; as age indicator, 78–79; color of, 78–79, 87–88; in hen, 88–89
Behavior: laying, 96–102; incubating, 105–12; hatching, 112–14; defensive, 126–29; roosting, 129–36; of broods, 148–50; of predators, 155; when being hunted, 179–83
Blinds, observation, 11–12
Bobcat, as predator, 125

Box: to hold turkey, 14–19; for shipping, 20
Brood patch, absent in turkey, 53

Camouflage, of nest, 98
Cannon net, 20–27; cannon angle, 22; folding when setting, 22; staking edges, 22; tie-down lines, 23; charges, 23, 27; care of equipment, 23–26; equipment required, 26–27
Capturing, 9–40
Caruncles, age of development, 61
Cattle, on study areas, 6, 8
Caution effect, 177–78
Census method, need for, 211
Climate of study areas, 1–2, 6–7
Clutch, size of, 103–5. *See also* Behavior; Nesting
Coloration: of hatchlings, 54–55; of feather generations, 66; of mutants, 85–88
Crow, common, as nest predator, 125

Determinant laying, 102
Disease: research not reported, xxi; research needs, 213
Disturbance: of nesting hens, 105, 199; interaction with habitat, 184
Dosage, oral drugs, 31–32
Drop nets, 10
Droppings, sex determination by, 77–78
Drugs: used for capturing, 27–40; effect on reproduction, 36–38
Dummy nets, 21–22
Dyes, for marking poults, 41–43

Egg: dropping, 100; breakage, in nest, 107; retrieval to nest, 107; turning, 107; hatchability, 114
Egg tooth, 54
Erythrism, 86–87

Fighting, affects in-growing feathers, 75
Fisheating Creek study area, 1–6
Flight: to and from nest, 127; age at first, 136–37
Foods, 137–45
Forest openings, 167
Fox, gray, as predator, 125

Gobbling: season of, 190, 192–93, 210; erratic during hunting season, 193

Habitat: nesting, 117–21; improvement of, 210
Handling turkeys, 12–20, 33–36
Harvest: patterns on a hunted area, 169–87; of restocked turkeys, 172; proportions by age class, 172–73, 186; of hens, 173–75; proportions by sex, 173–75, 186; illegal, 176, 185–87, 199–200, 202; affected by hunting rules, 177–78; rates measured, 199–203; recommendation concerning hens, 210–11; inaccurate estimates of, 211–12. See also Hunting; Kill
Hatching: period of, 112–14; synchrony, 116–17. See also Behavior
Hog, feral: in study areas, 6, 8; not a nest predator, 125

Holding live turkeys: in hand, 13–14; boxes for, 14–19; burlap sacks for, 19; immobilizing drugs for, 20
Home range, 143, 158, 172
Homing tendency, 158–59
Human imprinted flock, observations on, 160–65. See also Imprinting
Hunters: skills of, 175–77; attitudes of, 188; densities of, 192; weapons used by, 194; views on hunting, 195–98, 205–6, 209–10
Hunting: open season on study area, 9; study of, 168–206; regulations, 187–92, 203–6, 207–9

Illegal harvest, 199–200
Immobilizing captured turkeys, 20
Imprinting: period of, 114–16; role in wariness, 155. See also Human imprinted flock
Incubation: gradual onset of, 102; defined, 105–6; period of, 111–12. See also Behavior

Kill, index of, 201–3. See also Harvest

Law enforcement needs, 212
Laying, time of, 100–101. See also Behavior
Leg color, 79–85. See also Tarsometatarsus
Lochloosa study area, 6–9
Longevity, 160

Management: of habitat, 166; of harvest, 168–206. See also Hunting
Mating system, 95. See also Nesting
Mayfield method of calculating nesting success, 95, 123–25
Meleagris tridens, 91
Methoxymol, 29
Metrazol, as antidote, 32
Molt, 50–77; nomenclature, 57; atypical, 58; regional differences, 66, 70, 74–77; timing of annual, 68–69, 75–77; sexual differences, 73–74
Movement: between roosts,

133–35; in relation to food supplies, 143, 145; of broods, 145–48; maximum noted, 160; in relation to habitat quality, 165–66; while being hunted, 179–84

Nail color, 84
Narcosis. See Drugs
Nest: monitoring attendance of, 94; general, 96–128; attendance of, 100–103, 107–11; disturbance of, 105; departure from, 116; attendance of infertile eggs, 117; predation on, 123–26; abandonment of, 127–28. See also Behavior; Nesting
Nesting, 96–128; season of, 121–23; success of, 123–26. See also Behavior; Nest
Net: drop, 10; mist, 40. See also Cannon net

Openings. See Forest openings
Opossum, as nest predator, 125
Oral drugs. See Drugs
Overdosage, oral drugs, 28, 32, 38
Overhunting, 187. See also Harvest

Patagial marker, 40
Plumage: nomenclature, 51; at time of hatching, 53–54; color of, 61, 66, 85–88; gobbler type in hen, 92. See also Molt
Poult: capturing by hand, 38–40; survival and predation, 151–54; studies recommended, 211. See also Behavior
Powder down, absent, 53
Predation: of nests, 123–26; of young poults, 151–54
Private property, management needs on, 213

Quota limitations, 205

Raccoon, as nest predator, 125
Radio-tracking, 43–49, 93–94
Rain: effect on drug capturing, 32; hazard to poults, 157–58
Recesses from nest, 107–11
Recording equipment, audio, 94
Renesting, 105, 124–25
Restocking, 10; Florida program completed, xix; possible present need, 213
Roosting: cover types, 131; age at first use of trees, 132; on ground when hunted, 183. See also Behavior

Sacks, burlap, for holding turkeys, 19
Sex identification: by droppings, 77; by beard, 78; by spurs, 78; by head color, 79. See also Molt
Sex recognition by hunters, 176–77
Skunk, spotted and striped, as nest predators, 125
Smoke-gray plumage color, 85–86
Soils of study areas, 1, 6
Spurs: as age indicators, 78; color of, 84–85; of hens, 88; multiple, 89–91; absence on males, 91–92
Stimulants, as antidotes, 32

Tarsometatarsus: scales, 79, 83–85; color, 79–85; of hatchling poults, 83; of domestic stock, 84; without pigmentation, 84
Toe-clipping, 41
Tranquilizers. See Drugs
Tribromoethanol, 29
Trichloroethanol, toxic properties, 29

Vocalizations: of hatchlings, 113; in brood defense, 148–49

Wariness, of man, 154–56
Wing streamers, 40

www.ingramcontent.com/pod-product-compliance
Lightning Source LLC
Chambersburg PA
CBHW081805300426
44116CB00014B/2248